Exploring Jesus in the Bible

Exploring Jesus in the Bible

Jesus' Names Lenten Season Reflections
Jesus Centered Stories Reflections
Miscellaneous Social Issues Reflections

Rev. Dr. Adenike Yesufu

EXPLORING JESUS IN THE BIBLE
JESUS' NAMES LENTEN SEASON REFLECTIONS
JESUS CENTERED STORIES REFLECTIONS
MISCELLANEOUS SOCIAL ISSUES REFLECTIONS

NKJV
The New King James Version is an English translation of the Bible first published in 1982 by Thomas Nelson. The New Testament was published in 1979, the Psalms in 1980, and the full Bible in 1982. It took seven years to complete.

iUniverse books may be ordered through booksellers or by contacting:

iUniverse
1663 Liberty Drive
Bloomington, IN 47403
www.iuniverse.com
1-800-Authors (1-800-288-4677)

ISBN: 978-1-5320-8458-4 (sc)
ISBN: 978-1-5320-8459-1 (e)

Print information available on the last page.

iUniverse rev. date: 11/08/2019

Acknowledgement

Normally for Lent I always pick up various Readings that have been written by others, some with specific themes and some with general thoughts. I have done this for years. I have enjoyed reading them. Last year 2018 Lent came and I was reflecting on what to focus on during the Season. I have always been what you will call a "Fan" of Jesus and an avid reader of the Bible. I have always been fascinated by the different names of **Jesus** in the Bible. I use them in my personal prayers. Suddenly it occurred to me that I could write Lenten Reflections on Jesus' Names. So, I started writing a Forty Days Lenten Reflections with a focus on some selected names of Jesus' that I consider relevant to the Lenten Season. I wrote each day and I forwarded them via What's App to Family members and Friends. Many liked them. Many looked forward to receiving them. Many wondered if and how I would keep it up for the 40 days. It meant not sleeping at night, writing each night to send them out each morning so that they have them to reflect on Each Day of Lent. Thank God for the empowerment of the Holy Spirit. I was able to make it through the Forty days.

The Reflections were well received. It was my brother Pastor Bola Gbenga Banjo who first suggested that I have them published, so that people can have them to read annually. He said that the unusual focus on Jesus' names as Lenten Reflections makes it all captivating and inspiring for most people. Some other people also expressed the same thoughts. Many also told me they forwarded the Reflections to other friends and family members throughout the forty days. That was when I decided it would be a good idea to have them published so as to expand the Readership. Hence the Book starts with Jesus' Names Lenten Reflections.

However, while compiling the Lenten Reflections for publication, I decided to kill many birds with one stone. Many years ago, I was a Contributor to **The Messenger** of The Anglican Journal of Canada with Kelly Fowler and later Margaret Marshall as Editors under the title "Peace Thoughts". I was also a Feature Writer on Religious Issues on **Nigeriaworld.com**. My Reflections were Jesus centered, some were religious perspectives of social issues. I was also a Contributor for **Nigeria's Vanguard Newspapers Women's Page** under the Women Editor Helen Ovbiagele who kindly provided space for my Reflections on Women's Issues. I enjoyed writing those reflections as they come to me. Some of them I have presented to audiences. Thank God many of my Reflections have always been well received. Hence, I decided to include some of them in this Book, which is divided into Four Sections categorizing the Reflections as I think they enhance their commonality in the various Sections. The Word of God is forever new. So, there you have in your hand a Collection of Spirit Inspired Reflections for your Inspirational and Reading pleasure. It is a book with quantum, copious and lavish Scriptural references which you can read and reread throughout the year. These reflections have kept me centered in my thoughts, as they help me stay focused so that I may be in Perfect Peace as my heart continues to stay on Jesus (**Isaiah 23:6**). I take full Responsibility for the Reflections in this Book. They are mine as inspired I believe by the Holy Spirit, written in such a fashion for fluent flow and easy reading. May God bless the time that you invest in reading this book. Amen.

Appreciation

I want to sincerely and deeply acknowledge my nephew Elvis Kunle Iginla's generosity to this project. Thank you very much Kunle. Continued Blessings of God to you and yours. Amen

Dear Family and Friends, Peace and Blessings of the Lord be unto you All. This is to Thank God for the Lenten Season/Passion Week Journey, to thank the Holy Spirit for the inspiration to write the Reflections using the Names of Jesus each day. It is also to thank ALL of you who walked with us on the journey, those who read the Reflections, those who responded and gave feedbacks, those who thought it was a worthwhile effort and encouraged us, those who prayed for us. As iron sharpens iron, I was sharpened by all of you. Thank God for the opportunity. I am sure it was a remarkable experience for all of us, the Readers and the Writer. For many of you who think that the Reflections should be published, suffice it to say Thank God that it has become a reality. That is why you have the book in your hands. May the Lord's face continue to shine upon each and every one of us. Amen

Foreword

Lent is an important Season of Reflection in the Christian year. What a great idea to center those Reflections on the variety of different names of Jesus used in Scripture. It is my hope and prayer that these Reflections will be deeply meaningful to everyone who reads them. May you be richly blessed as they guide you in your mediations this Lenten Season, and may you be filled with the love and faith that inspired them.

David Williams, Ph.D.
President, Taylor Seminary
Professor of Theology and Ethics
Director, E P Wahl Centre
Edmonton, Alberta
Canada

SECTION ONE

Jesus Names Lenten Season Reflections

This section is a Forty days Lenten Reflections that include Reflections for the Holy week up till Easter Sunday that focus on the ***Names,*** which the Scriptures have used for our Lord Jesus Christ. Right thoughts and right knowledge of Jesus is at the root of our religion. Throughout the Reflections we will give you precisely where the names are used in the Bible. Most people know that Jesus is Lord, Savior and Redeemer. In these Lenten Reflections we will learn that Jesus is also Prophet, Priest and King in addition to many other tittles that we will learn about Him. Why the focus on Jesus Names as Lenten Reflection? This is to help all of us attain a higher knowledge and a deeper understanding of who Jesus is, hoping that we will all be moved to a renewed love for Him and a closer union with Him. Amen.

Contents

Day One: Ash Wednesday: Jesus as Alpha and Omega.

Revelation 1:8 "I am the Alpha and the Omega, the Beginning and the End says the Lord who is and who was and who is to come, the Almighty". **Revelation 1: 1** describes the Book as the Revelation of Jesus which God gave to John. Alpha and Omega are Greek alphabets equivalent of A and Z which I learnt in my Greek class in the University. Alpha indicates His Pre-eminence and Supremacy in all things. John says in the beginning was the Word and the Word was God. Christ was in God fulfilling all things. Amen. **Isaiah 44:6** puts it like this: "Thus says the Lord, the King of Israel and his Redeemer, the Lord of hosts: I am the First and I am the Last". God has the first word and the last word in history. In other words, since everything comes from God, nothing will outlast God. It also adds "Besides Me there is no God!". The implication is that God has no competitors. The reference to Jesus being at the beginning with God is found in **John 1:1** which says "In the beginning was the Word and the word was with God and the Word was God. He was in the beginning with God". Jesus borrows the first part of this name in His well-known "I AM" statements. The confidence we have is if Christ is with us at the beginning of anything, He will definitely be with us till the end. He is certainly worthy of our praises as we kick off these Reflections. Amen.

Day Two: Jesus as Author and Finisher of our Faith.

Hebrews12:2. "Looking unto Jesus the Author and Finisher of our faith" Do we ever ask how Noah came to prepare an ark for the saving of his house when there was no rain nor water in sight? **Hebrews 1:7** says he did it by faith. Verse 1 says "Faith is the substance of things hoped for, the evidence of things not seen". How is Christ the Author of our faith? Faith has two meanings. It is applied to the religion that we practice or follow. Jesus is the Initiator and the Foundation of our religion. That is the reason we are called Followers of Christ, Christians. Secondly, Christ through the Holy Spirit works faith in us, which is the ability to believe in God, the ability to believe in His Word, and the ability to believe in His power. It is this ability that helps us to go through the daily streams of life knowing fully well as **Ephesians 2:8** reminds us that "By grace we are saved through faith and not by ourselves. It is the gift of God". Jesus Himself is the Initiator of our being saved. He is the one who knocks on the Door of our hearts to receive Him and when we do, He is the One who walks with us along till the end of the journey. It is just so good to trust in Jesus. What Jesus says He will do, He does. We are therefore strengthened to know that The Author of our faith is always there to help our unbelief, to prepare our hearts and give us that precious faith which is like gold tried in fire to keep us going even when we do not see the end. Jesus finishes it all for us especially as He has said "It is finished" on the Cross. Amen.

Day Three: Jesus as All and In All.

Colossians 3:11: describes Christ as "All and In All". All means everything. Jesus is Everything in All things. Jesus is All in creation, He was there at the beginning of creation. **John 1:3** says all things were made through Him and without Him nothing was made. Jesus is All in providence, the cattle on a thousand hills belong to His Father all the gold and silver are all His. He is therefore able to supply all our needs according to His riches in Glory. Jesus is All in salvation, He is responsible for our salvation by His shed blood. Jesus is All in redemption, He is the essence of our being redeemed. He took it upon Himself to redeem us for His Father. Jesus is All in the fullness of God, All in the grace of God, and All in the glory of God. He is a reflection of All these in God. Jesus is also In All. He is in all places, In all our paths, In all our laying down, In all our rising up. He is in all events making all things work together for the good of all of us. His eyes are everywhere seeing all. He is also everywhere, the Ever Present One. If we ascend up in heaven, He is there. If we make our bed in hell, He is also there. (**Psalm139:8**). He is in the depth of the sea. He is at the top of the mountains. He is in the snow. He is in the rain. He is in the sun.

He is in the moon. He is in all the gathering of all His people. He is in our living. He is in our dying. He is in our hearts. What comforting thoughts. With all these we can All gladly proclaim Jesus Lamb of God as our All in All, the All Sufficient One. Amen.

Day Four: Jesus as Advocate.

1John 2:1 says "And if anyone sin, we have an Advocate with the Father, Jesus Christ the Righteous". An advocate is the One who pleads for another in a court of Justice. Why do we need an Advocate? Verse 8 reads "If we say we have no sin the truth is not in us". Jesus is the propitiation for all our sins. Sins of commission, doing things we should not do. Sins of omission not doing things that we should do. Sins in thought, sins in words, sins in deeds. We are all guilty. The good thing is when the Accuser of the Brethren goes before God to tell Him of our sins like he accused Job of being a hypocrite. (**Job.1:11**) Jesus is always there as our Advocate to plead for us. His Precious Blood covers our sins. Since Lent is a time of Penitence, what a better time to ask our Advocate Jesus like David did in **Psalm 51** to Have Mercy upon us according to His loving kindness. We are assured of forgiveness. Amen.

Day Five: Jesus as Ancient of Days.

Daniel 7:9: says "I watched till the thrones were put in place and the Ancient of Days was seated, His garment was white as snow and the hair on His head was like pure wool". **Verse 22**. "The Ancient of Days came and a Judgment was made in favor of the Saints of the Most High". If like me you have always wondered about who Daniel saw in his vision, the Person who gave that judgment in favor of the Saints that they were able to possess the kingdom. 2 Corinthians 5:10 provides the answer. It says "for we must all appear before the Judgment Seat of Christ that each of us may receive the things done in the body according to what he or she has done whether good or bad. Wow! Jesus our Advocate is the Ancient of Days clothed in white garment. He is The Judge seated on throne who will give judgment in favor of the saints. Wow!!! What a great comfort that the One who knows us very well, the One who has been interceding for us before God, the one who has been making a case for us against the Accuser of the brethren, (**Revelation 12:10**) is now the One before whom we will appear for our rewards at the end of time. This is definitely uncommon in the Justice System of the world. But of course, we are talking about the Kingdom of God. Take some time to reflect on what your reaction will be when you see the Lord face to face: awe, wonder, comfort, fear. I leave you with that thought.

Day Six. Jesus as Blessed and only Potentate, the King of Kings, the Lord of Lords.

1Timothy 6:15: "That you keep this commandment until our Lord Jesus Christ's appearing which He will manifest in His own time, He who is the Blessed and Only Potentate, The King of kings and Lord of lords". **Revelation19:16** adds. "And He has on His robe and on His thigh a name written King of Kings and Lord of lords". Potentate, King, Lord all mean the same thing; a ruler, someone in authority, someone who has dominion over, someone with sovereign power. Who alone has all these attributes? The One whom the Father has placed all things under Him, made all things subject to Him, our Lord Jesus Christ. Jesus then talked about His kingdom, about those His Father had given Him, about those who are part of His Kingdom. Who are these? Jesus acquired this prevalence over all by His death on the Cross. He died for all that all might become His. The question then is: Are you one of those who have accepted His reign over your life, His ruler ship, His sovereignty in your existence, His dominion over your heart? We all accept these and become members of His kingdom by choice. We know that there are some who would like to accept but are not able to for many reasons. We pray for them. However, Kings have responsibilities. Subjects too have responsibilities. This period of Lent let us consider responsibilities. Do you believe that Jesus is meeting His responsibilities in your life? Is Jesus Potentate over you? Is Jesus your King? Is Jesus your Lord? Only you can tell. Has Jesus been meeting your expectations of Him? Has he proved Himself faithful and reliable in your life? Unlike the rulers of this world who lord it over their people, Jesus banner over us is Love. Can you boast of His love for you? What about your responsibilities as His subject? Have you been meeting these? Jesus law is simple If you love me you will keep my commandments. Obedience is what He expects of us. How are you doing on that? Only you can tell. Let this be a time of self-introspection. Amen.

Day Seven: Jesus as the Bright and Morning Star.

Revelation 22:16. Jesus says of Himself "I am the Bright and Morning Star". In **John 9:5** He also says of Himself "I am the Light of the World". These two powerful imageries represent Jesus ultimate illumination in pervasive darkness. We all know how fearful and at times scary, the nighttime is. We also all know how welcoming and beautiful the morning is after a tedious almost frightening night. Jesus came into the world in a prevailing darkness. The Star foretells His coming. The Star guided the shepherds and the wise men to where He lay. The Star, The Light is the fulfillment of a promise to the world. The Star represents the dawn of a new day. **Hebrews 1:3** calls the Star the Brightness of the Father's glory. **Numbers 24:17** says a Star shall come out of Jacob. **Isaiah 9:2** declares that the people walking in darkness have seen a great Light. Jesus said that by His coming those who sat in darkness have seen a great Light. The Star guides us into the way of Peace. The Light leads us into repentance. The Light awakens us from the deep slumber in the dark recesses of our soul. Those who do not walk in darkness will have the Light of Life the Bible says. Follow the Light and you shall be saved. When the darkness of life assails us and deepens at times as it does, may the Star of the Morning, the Light of the World continue to shine His glory into our every dark situation. Amen.

Day Eight: Jesus as Bread of Life.

John 6:35: Jesus said to them, "I am the Bread of Life. He who comes to me shall never hunger" John chapter six is one of my Bible's favorite chapters in the Bible because of it's main theme "Bread" which I like especially the freshly baked ones. uhm!. In this chapter, Jesus talked extensively about bread, starting from when He asked His Apostles where they would buy bread for the large gathering that have come to hear Him. There was no bread available, but a young boy offered his meager lunch of five loaves (which are actually slices in today's world) and two pieces of fishes. When given to Jesus He did not focus on the smallness of the quantity. Instead He prayed and thanked His Father for that little provision. With God little is much the Bible tells us. In the end, five loaves were multiplied to feed 5000 people, with a lot of remnant. Later Jesus took a jab at some people who were following Him asking them if they had come for more "bread". He then compared His bread with the manna that was provided in the wilderness. He finished His discourse by calling Himself "Bread of Life", "Living Bread", "Bread which has come from heaven", and then presenting His Flesh, His Body as bread. So, Jesus as Bread. What does that mean? Globally bread is staple food, a principal item of sustenance. People eat bread with anything which makes it a complete meal. Jesus offered bread as a concrete physical food and as a spiritual food. We need fresh supplies every day. The consumption of yesterday will not suffice for today. Jesus also offers Himself as the Divine Bread, the All satisfying food for our body and our soul. He adds that if we eat His Bread we shall live forever. Jesus in His death became the Everlasting Bread for us. How do we access this Bread? We must believe in Him. We must accept Him. We must appropriate Him. We must consume Him. Just as our physical body requires frequent supply of food we must continually feed on Christ, by reading His Word, in prayers, in communion with Him, in devotion and adoration of Him. May we all by the grace of God continue to desire this Bread more and more and more, to our benefit. Amen.

Day Nine: Jesus as The Christ.

In several places in the Bible, Christ appears alongside Jesus, and at times He is called the Christ. When I was young in school in our Bible Studies' class I used to think that Christ is Jesus surname. I later learnt in my Greek and Theology classes that Christos (Christ) is not a name but a title which means the Anointed One, the Chosen One, the Messiah. But then I started to relate the title to the Jewish people who have spent their historical lives waiting for the Messiah. But when He came, they did not recognize Him neither did they accept Him. In several places in the Bible, at different times, by different people, Jesus was specifically addressed as Jesus Christ or Jesus the Christ. When Jesus asked His disciples, who do they say He is. Peter's response was emphatic "You are the Christ" (**Mark 8:29**). In **John 7** some people who marveled at Jesus knowledge, said "This is the Christ". In **John 4** the Samaritan woman was so impressed with the fact that Jesus knew everything about her that she pronounced to others "Could this be the Christ?". In **Mark 15:32** when Jesus was on the Cross some people mocked Him and said, "Let the Christ, the King of Israel descend from the cross that we may see and believe." In **Colossians 3:27** Paul called Jesus "Christ in you the hope of glory". Even the demons that Jesus cast out in **Luke 4:41** said of Him, "You are the Christ, Son of God". John's last verse of the Bible **Revelation 22:21** says "The grace of our Lord Jesus Christ be with you all. Amen". Jesus is Christ for very many reasons. We cannot address them all in this short space. But in our Reflection today we have heard the various affirmation of Jesus as the Christ and as the Messiah. Like Jesus would say "Flesh and Blood" did not reveal that to them. They all came to that awareness by the power of the Holy Spirit. The whole exercise started with Jesus wanting to know what His disciples thought of Him. Suppose Jesus would ask each and every one of us today who do we think He is, what would we say? Let us all prayerfully reflect on the answer to that question. What does Jesus mean to us? Let us all tell it to Jesus Himself. He will surely appreciate that. Amen.

Day Ten: Jesus as Man of War.

Exodus 15:3 says "the Lord is a Man of war. The Lord is His name". War the antithesis of peace. Every Easter we are reminded of Jesus victory over death, over Hades and over Satan. The Songwriter says, "The Strife is over the battle won". Yet the battle continues. Which battle is being referred to? It is the war started by Satan's rebellion against God. When he said in **Isaiah 14:13** "I will ascend into heavens. I will exalt my throne above the stars of God. I will be like the most high". We are talking about the war in heaven when Angel Michael fought the dragon and the dragon and his angels fought. But as **Revelation 12** says they did not prevail, nor was there a place found for them in heaven any longer. So, the great dragon, that old serpent of old called the Devil, Satan who deceives the whole world was cast to the earth and his angels were cast out with him. When Satan lost his battle with God, he began to direct his attack at God's creation. Satan remains a powerful adversary. Satan has been and is still waging war against God, against Jesus his Son, against the Church of God, against the Body of Christ and against the people of God. This war is alive and well. Jesus knows this. In **John12:13** He calls Satan "the ruler of this world". **1Peter 5:8.** says "Be sober, be vigilant, because your adversary the devil walks about like a roaring lion seeking whom he may devour". Satan has continued his all-out war. I am sure we are all aware of the various ways that the devil attacks against lives, health, family, finances, work etc. We also know that we cannot undermine his position. Even though we have been told to put on the whole armor, we know that we are all insufficient by ourselves to fight this war. Hence in this fight of faith, in this fighting the good fight, as the songwriter says, in this wrestling with powers and principalities, in this putting the body in subjection and resisting various temptations, in these various rules of engagement, we are constantly reminded that the Battle belongs to the Lord. We need a Man of War at the front to lead us, at the helm to be in charge, at the back to guide us, to instruct us, to show us the way as long we are willing to follow. Above all, we need to continue to pray David's prayer in **Psalm 144**, that Jesus, the Man of War our Commander should continue "to train our hands for war and our fingers for battle". With the Man of War and the Cross of Jesus going on before, Victory is assured. Amen.

Day Eleven: Jesus as the Cornerstone.

Isaiah 28:16: "Therefore thus says the Lord God: Behold I lay in Zion a stone for a Foundation, a tried stone, a precious cornerstone, a sure foundation whoever believes will not act hastily" Builders will tell us that the cornerstone is the first and most important stone that unites all the parts of the building. The term cornerstone is also used to denote any principal person in the society such as rulers and leaders. Jesus was chosen by God to be the sure Foundation, the Precious Stone, the Divine Cornerstone of His Building, His Temple where He lives with the Power of His Spirit. This Stone is an epitome of strength and durability, which is able to stand all that would be laid on Him. Jesus is a tried Stone that was tempted yet prevailed. Jesus is a Strong Stone that we can lay our hopes on. Unfortunately, this Stone was rejected. Jesus in **Mathew 21:42** talked about the stone which the builders rejected that have become the cornerstone. **John 1: 11** talks about Jesus who came to His own and His own did not receive Him. The second part of the narrative according to Paul in **Ephesians 2:19** is that all of us who believe in this Cornerstone are no longer strangers and foreigners but fellow citizens with the saints and members of the Household of God that have been built on the foundation of Apostles and Prophets with Jesus Christ Himself as the Cornerstone. This means we have been carefully joined together to become part of this Holy Temple of God, His dwelling place where He lives. Wow!!! What a privilege. As we all know in the process of building not all stones bought and gathered are used. Some are thrown away. These are the ones who have rejected the Cornerstone. The Bible calls them blind. For those of us who have become fused into this Building of God, this Everlasting Temple of the Almighty, how much do we admire this Cornerstone. How much are we at One with Him. How much confidence do we place on this Eminent Cornerstone and Foundation? **1 Peter 2:5** says those who believe in this Cornerstone will never be put to shame. Amen.

Day Twelve: Jesus as Counselor.

Isaiah 9:6 says "Unto us a child is born, unto us a Son is given. He would be called Counselor". A counselor is a person people turn to for advice and direction in solving personal problems. As a Certified Canadian Counselor, I can tell you that counselors do not seek out counselees. Those who need counsel seek out counselors and go to them. In **Luke 9:56** Jesus indicated His counseling paradigm. He said that He has not come to destroy lives but to save them. The Bible tells us about some people who have sought Jesus for counsel. In **Matthew 19:16** a rich young ruler came to Jesus to ask what he could do to have eternal life. Jesus told him about keeping the commandments of God, giving to the poor and following Jesus. In **John 4** a Samaritan woman met Jesus at the well. Jesus talked to her about her having had five husbands and currently living with a man she is not married to. Talk of serial monogamy. In **John 5** a woman caught in the act of adultery about to be stoned ran to Jesus for protection. Jesus rescued her from her assailants but told her to go and sin no more. In **Mathew 5-7** Jesus even did Group counseling. Many people came to Him. He sat on a mountain top and addressed them on very many issues of life. I counsel you all to go through those three chapters at least once a year. There is a lot to learn there. Children also came to Jesus to hear words of love. Jesus rebuked adults who tried to prevent them from access to Him. In counseling we talk about the qualities of a counselor. Jesus met them all. To mention a few, Jesus is empathetic. Jesus is not judgmental. Jesus shows genuine love for all people. Jesus is always available when people need Him. Jesus demonstrates wisdom, knowledge and understanding of the issues at hand. Above all in His Compassionate Self, Jesus now sends out an open invitation to all. In **Mathew 11:28** Jesus said "Come to me all of you who labor, who are weary and are heavy laden, who are burdened and I will give you rest. For I am gentle and in me you will find rest for your souls". Wow!!! What a Wonderful Counselor! Jesus is ready, willing and able to help. Seek Him out and be blessed. Amen.

Day Thirteen: Jesus as Comforter.

After 40 days in the wilderness, Jesus being filled with the Holy Spirit, on a particular Sabbath day went to the Synagogue for worship. He read from **Isaiah 61:2**: "The Spirit of the Lord is upon me". One of the things He told the audience that He had been anointed to do was "to heal, the broken hearted", to be a Comforter to them. Jesus on His Sermon on the Mount, **Mathew 5-7** proclaimed that those who mourn are blessed because they shall be comforted. Jesus fulfilled His call to be a Comforter in many ways. The most notable was His visit to Mary and Martha when their brother Lazarus died. In **John 14:18** When Jesus was leaving the earth, He told His disciples that He will not leave them comfortless. He said He would ask the Father to send them Another Comforter to fill the gap that He would create. Jesus a Man of Sorrow was very mindful of the emotional turmoil that would befall His disciples when He is gone. Jesus the Comforter is in us, around us and with us. Paul in **Romans12**: urges all of us to rejoice with those who rejoice and to mourn with those who mourn. The good thing about life is that most cultures support rejoicing with those who rejoice and mourning with those who mourn. **2 Corinthians 2:3** says "Blessed be the God and Father of our Lord Jesus Christ the Father of all mercies and God of all comfort who comforts us in all our tribulations that we may be able to comfort those who are in any trouble with the comfort which we ourselves are comforted by God". Not only does God comfort us through His Son Jesus, God wants us to follow in the footsteps of Jesus by offering comfort to others who need it in the same fashion that we too have been comforted. Amen.

Day Fourteen: Jesus as Deliverer.

Isaiah 61:2: Jesus says, "The Lord has sent me to proclaim liberty to the captives and to open the prison to those who are bound". Another assignment of Jesus as indicated by Him is to deliver people from all types of bondages. Part of Jesus healing activities is to deliver people from demon possession. A deliverer also delivers people from the bondage of slavery. In the Old Testament it was said many times that when the Children of Israel would be held captives by some foreign powers and they would cry to the Lord, the Lord would raise a deliverer to set them free. God at a time appointed Moses to deliver the people of Israel from slavery in Egypt. King David in **Psalm 18** calls the Lord his Rock, his Fortress and his Deliverer in whom he will trust. In **Luke 11** after Jesus had delivered a man from demons, there was a discussion about the legitimacy of Jesus to deliver people from demons. Some said it is because He is a demon himself that is why He has the powers to cast out demons. Jesus then asked them a poignant question "If Satan is divided against himself how will his kingdom stand"? Jesus eventually affirms to the people that He does what He does by the power of God against Satan the adversary. In **Mathew 10:1** we are told that when Jesus has selected his twelve apostles, He gave them power to deliver the people from demonic forces. To prove the authenticity of the power that has been bestowed upon Him, Jesus imparted the same power to His disciples. **Luke 10:19** tells us that Jesus sent out the Chosen 70 with power to trample over all the power of the enemy. Jesus the Deliverer then is still the Deliverer today. His power still avails. When troubles strike, call on Jesus The Deliverer in whom we trust and He will come to our rescue. Amen.

Day Fifteen: Jesus as The Door.

John 10:9: Jesus says "I AM the Door. If anyone enters by me, he/she will be saved". Doors are for exits and entrances. Jesus is the entrance to salvation and exit from darkness into light. Doors are for protection and security. Doors are locked to keep out unwanted guests, thieves, home invaders and predators. But open to welcome friends and family. Jesus as the Door keeps out the enemy, the devil roaming around looking for whom to devour. Doors are for decorations: different types with its own appeal and attractiveness; carved doors, metal doors, painted doors, glass doors. Think of Jesus as symbol of beauty, Rose of Sharon, His Holiness, His Majesty, His Loveliness beyond description. Jesus attach a promise to this statement. Anyone who enters through this Door will be saved into redemption, shall find nourishment for both body and soul, provision and the strength to go on. Closed doors always look ominous. But Jesus as Door is always open with welcoming arms. Let us therefore go through it with joy in our hearts. Amen.

Day Sixteen: Jesus as Friend.

John 15:13 Jesus says, "Greater love has no man than this, than to lay down one's life for his friends". Jesus died for ALL. But He chooses His Friends. Jesus said, "You did not choose Me but I choose you". When Jesus has chosen people, He says to them "Come Follow me". When they respond they become His Followers, but they are not just called to follow they are also called to be His Servants. So, they serve in various ways with the various gifts that have been bestowed on them. Becoming a friend of Jesus is a process. Jesus then says "You are my friend if you do what I command you". Jesus is talking of obedience. It is at this stage that Jesus upgrades those whom He has called, those who are following and those who are serving. Jesus says to them "No longer do I call you Servant, but I have called you Friend". It is a great privilege to be Jesus' Friend. But becoming His friend is a position or a status that we have to earn. Today let us reflect on how we are doing, where we are in the process and what we need to do to become Jesus friend. There is an expanded version of this reflection somewhere else in this book. Enjoy.

Day Seventeen: Jesus as Fortress.

Psalm 18:2 David says "The Lord is my Rock, my Fortress. He is also my Refuge. In Him will I trust". The Oxford dictionary defines a fortress as a place that is protected against any form of attack, a place of exceptional security, a stronghold, a symbol of protection". Countries build fortress, for protection against enemy countries. **Proverbs 10:15** says the rich man's wealth is his Fortress. People build fortress to keep themselves safe. They build high towers with massive stones. They add iron bars and concrete to make them impregnable. But as we all know fortresses can be leveled down. They can be destroyed. Fortresses, towns, and cities have been mowed down during wars. King David has built fortresses and he has seen them pulled down by enemies and he too had demolished other people's fortresses. He has seen the futility of having fortresses made by human hands. For him then the only option is to acknowledge and relate to God as the Lord, the Rock, the Fortress. Are we assailed and we need to escape to the Fortress? Let us start by praying to the Lord who grants protection against all attacks, who is a place of Refuge, our Strength who is always around to keep us safe and secure from all storms of life. Amen.

Day Eighteen: Jesus as Living Water.

John 7: 37: Jesus stood and cried out saying "If anyone thirsts let him come to me and drink". Water is life. Water is powerful. Water is needed for all. Jesus had various engagements with water. Starting with His own baptism with water, His first miracle of turning water into wine, calming the stormy seas, going fishing with His disciples, washing His disciples feet with water, having personal need for water as He experienced thirst, asking a strange woman to give Him water to drink, having a discourse about water with this Samaritan woman at the well, offering the woman Living water and finally on the Cross asking for water saying "I thirst". Jesus knows a lot about water. Hence in **John 4**

Jesus told the Samaritan woman that whosoever drinks the water that He has to give will never thirst again. This woman who did NOT give Jesus water when He asked for it now said, "Give me this Living water so that I may not thirst again". It is significant that an encounter that started with Jesus asking for water ended with Him offering and giving water. Jesus set his physical need aside and attended to the woman's request. Today we ask, Are you thirsty? Ask the Fountain of Living Water for water. Be rest assured that He will grant it unto you as He has promised. He even adds that if we believe in Him, out of our hearts will flow rivers of living waters. This means that we will too be a fountain where others will come to have a drink. Amen.

Day Nineteen: Jesus as Husband.

Isaiah 54:5 says "Your Maker is your Husband. The Lord of Hosts is His name". We have looked at Jesus as Friend. A friend is someone who knows, likes, favors, supports and belongs to another. In **Psalm 68:5** God is also described as "the Husband and Defender of the widows". However, Isaiah describes God as the Husband of all people. **Genesis 1:27** says God created man in His own image, in the image of God He created Him, male and female He created them. This is essentially saying that God created both men and women, male and female which means that if He is the Creator of both He is also the Husband of both. Uh! This has an interesting implication for men because in normal traditions, husband is gendered and skewed to the male. Who is a husband? It is not just someone who has married a wife and consummated the relationship. A husband is also someone who continually fulfills his responsibilities. **Isaiah 54** lengthily describes the duties of God as a Husband. Today in our reflection, let us all consider Jesus as a Husband. It does not matter whether you are male or female. He is the Husband of all. However, Jesus is also described as a Husband to the Church, the Body of Christ. **Revelation 19:7**. Says let us be glad and rejoice and give Him glory for the marriage of the Lamb has come and His wife has made herself ready. As the faithful wife of Jesus, the Husband of the Church are you prepared and ready for the Marriage of the Lamb? Hopefully we all are. We should all be. Amen. Again there is an expanded version of this Reflection in another part of this Book. Enjoy.

Day Twenty: Jesus as High Priest.

Hebrews 4:14 says "Seeing that we have a great High Priest who has passed through the heavens Jesus the Son of God, let us hold fast our confession, we have a great High Priest who has gone to heaven we must cling to Him and never stop trusting Him". **Hebrews 3:1** also says that we are partakers of the heavenly calling of the Apostle and High Priest of our confession Christ Jesus who was faithful to Him (God) who appointed Him just as Moses was faithful too. **Hebrews 5:1** defines the responsibilities of a High Priest. It says it is a man chosen among men to represent other human beings in their dealings with God. He presents their gifts to God and offers their sacrifices for sins. Aaron the older brother of Moses was the first High Priest called by God. A priest is an ordained minister having authority to perform certain rites and administer certain sacraments. A High Priest is the Chief of Priests who is able to perform some rites that other priests cannot perform. The Bible says no one can become a High Priest simply because he wants such an honor. He has to be called by God for this work. (**Hebrews 5:4-6**). The responsibilities of the High Priest are multifaceted. Jesus as High Priest makes intercession for the people. Jesus offers Himself as the final sacrifice on the Cross. Jesus blesses the people with prayers. Jesus as High Priest understands our weaknesses for He faced the same temptation that we do. How do we respond to Jesus as the great High Priest? We must put our needs before Him. The encouraging side of Jesus priesthood is that He remains Priest forever. Hence as **Hebrews 3:16** says we must always come boldly to the throne of grace taking our prayers to our High Priest that we may obtain mercy and find help in time of need. Amen.

Day Twenty-one: Jesus as The Holy One.

Isaiah 6 reveals a glimpse of the Holiness of God. Isaiah saw The Lord sitting on a throne, high and lifted up, resplendent surrounded by angels who sang "Holy Holy Holy is the Lord of Hosts, the whole earth is full of His glory." Holy means pure, sacred, divine, majestic, engulfed in light, no darkness. God the Most Holy One, is the quintessence of holiness. In **Mathew17:1** the Apostles saw Jesus transfigured before them. His face shone like the sun, and His clothes became as white as the light. Isaiah was spurred to deep reverence so were the Apostles. In **Leviticus 11:48** God calls us to holiness. "I am the Lord your God, you shall be holy for I am holy". Is this a tall order? I think not. As God's children we should make an effort to reflect his character and conduct. In **Ephesians 1:4** God wants us to be holy and blameless before Him. We are saved through His Son Jesus. Just as Jesus is the image of the Invisible God, His Father, we are called to be like Jesus and ultimately like God. However, we are all aware that attaining this level of perfection is impossible while in human flesh. But **Psalm 24** simplifies it for us. It asks who can stand in the Holy place of God? The response is "He who has clean hands and a pure heart". Fairly simple, I think. The thought I think behind that is one who is making the effort, doing good and having pure thoughts. **1Peter 2:9** says that we God's people are "a chosen generation, a holy nation, God's own special people". The implication is that since we are created by a Holy God, and created in His image, this means that right from the beginning we have some essence of His holiness, being chosen by Him to receive this portion. So today let us reflect on what should be our reaction to the Holiness of God? What are the steps that we can take in our journey and efforts towards our sanctification? What about can simply offering Him our worship? Amen.

Day Twenty-two: Jesus as Image of the Invisible God.

Colossians 1:15 tells us that God is a Spirit, a Force, a Power that brought the world into being. This in essence means that God is invisible.

Throughout the ages people have had problem relating to this Invisible God. Even Moses at a time desired to see God's face. God said in **Exodus 33:20,** "You cannot see My face, for no man shall see me and live". How do we love, trust and have faith in and relate to the Unseen God? We human beings are physical people. We believe in what we can see, in what we can touch. It is what the anti-God people use as a point of argument against us. "How do you know that God exist. Have you seen Him?" But for those of us who believe, it is a question of faith. Faith is belief in what you cannot see. Thankfully Jesus came and said, "When you have seen me you have seen the Father". What a bold statement to make. From then on, many people find it easy to relate to the Invisible God. God became real in Jesus. He became human. He lived, He moved, He spoke, He ate, He was hungry, He was thirsty, He touched, He was touched, He even cried. Jesus then introduced God to us as Our Father and taught us things that we need to know about God. Relating to the Invisible God became much easier. Jesus said, "I speak for my Father, the things that my Father does I do too". Presto! What a relief! Jesus Imago Dei, God's living likeness, in Jesus "dwells all the fullness of the Godhead bodily" (**Colossians 2:9**). We no more have to wonder. **1Timothy 1:17** tells us "Unto the King Eternal, Immortal, Invisible the Only Wise God, be all honor and glory forever and ever". Amen.

Day Twenty-three: Jesus The Lamb of God.

John 1: 29 John the Baptist saw Jesus coming towards him and said "Behold the Lamb of God who takes away the sins of the world". **1 Corinthians 5:7** calls Jesus The **Passover Lamb**. Lamb is a symbol of patience, gentleness, meekness. Jesus in His meekness and humility resembles a Lamb. **Isaiah 53:7** says Jesus is brought as a Lamb to be slaughtered......and He did not open His mouth. There was no resistance. He willingly submitted Himself for that sacrifice. In the Jewish tradition lamb is used for Passover sacrifice with individuals bringing their own lamb. But Jesus was chosen and provided by God as sacrifice for the remission of the sins of humanity. Jesus was not chosen by anybody certainly not even by Himself but by God. **Revelation5:12** says "Worthy is the Lamb that was slain". This means that this sacrificial lamb carefully selected met certain criteria to be deemed worthy. Equally, being meek and gentle as a Lamb is quite important to Jesus that in His Sermon on the Mount in **Mathew 5:7** Jesus said "Blessed are the meek for they shall inherit the earth". **Revelation 19:9** also says "Blessed are those who are called, invited to the Marriage Supper of the Lamb". One can assume that only the meek and the humble will be invited to that event. May we be deemed worthy for that invitation to the Marriage Supper of the Lamb. Amen.

Day Twenty-four: Jesus as The Lion of Judah.

John in **Revelation 5:5** calls Jesus the Lion of Judah. Judah is the fifth son of Jacob by Leah the unloved wife who was displaced by her sister Rachael. In Genesis when Judah blessed his sons, he calls Judah the Lion. The tribe of Judah had adopted the Lion as its biblical symbol. Jesus' descendancy is traced to David and ultimately to Judah. Hence Jesus titles of The Root of David and The Lion of Judah. However, most people like me find it intriguing that Jesus would be both a Lamb and a Lion. Two completely opposite personalities rolled and blended into One. The Lamb meek and gentle, the Lion with a strong personality. Lions are hunters, aggressive large cats with the dignity and presence of nobility, the king of the jungle. Jesus the one carrying a whip, the One who turned the tables in the temple is the same Jesus who demonstrates compassion and gentleness towards children and women. This perfect blend that exists in Jesus; the "Lamb and the Lion" is one of the reasons why we should be in awe of Him. Amen.

Day Twenty-five: Jesus as The Vine.

In **John 15** Jesus used a garden scenario to depict the picture of the relationship we have with Him. Verse 1 Jesus says, "I am the true Vine".

Verse 4 "Abide in Me and I in you. As the branch cannot bear fruit of itself unless it abides in the Vine, neither can you unless you abide in Me". Verse 5 says "I am the Vine and you are the branches. He who abides in Me and I in him/her bears much fruit; for without Me you can do nothing". Verse 6 says "If anyone does not abide in Me he/she is cast out as a branch and is withered". Verse 7 says "If you abide in Me and My words abide in you, you will ask what you desire and it shall be done for you". The branch of any tree gets nourishment from the main branch, if it is severed it dies. For example, when winter comes the apple tree withers and all the leaves fall off. But as long as the branch remains part of the tree, which root is still in the ground when Spring comes it begins to flourish again. The same way it is with us. A Christian life is a living union with Christ. We are joined to Him, as long as we remain in Him, as long as we abide in Him, we have life, we have energy. This life and energy flowing into us is the Holy Spirit. In several places in the Bible we read about "being in Christ, being in Jesus and being in the Lord". As long as we remain grafted to Jesus, nourishment flows into us. As long as we remain connected to Jesus, we will bear fruit. For us it is bearing the Fruit of the Spirit; a reflection of God's character: as found in **Galatians 5:22** love, joy, peace, patience, kindness, goodness, faithfulness, humility and self-control. Lord Jesus the Vine as we continue to make the effort to abide in you, help us to bear much fruit. Amen.

Day Twenty-six: Jesus as The Good Shepherd.

In **John 10** Jesus calls Himself the Good Shepherd. He uses the pastoral image to define His relationship with us and outlines the responsibilities of the Shepherd as well as that of the sheep. The Good Shepherd knows His sheep. Jesus knows us by name. The Good Shepherd provides abundant life for His sheep. Jesus provision for us is immeasurable. The Good Shepherd protects and fiercely defends His sheep. Jesus guards us so that nothing else can snatch us from Him. The Good Shepherd gives His life for His sheep. Jesus lays down His life for our redemption and salvation. Now to the Sheep. The sheep knows the Shepherd. Do we know enough about our Shepherd to trust and follow when He calls? Do we recognize His voice so as not to respond to all the strange voices and cacophonies out there? Do we trust our Shepherd enough to submit totally to Him? Thank God that we have a Good Shepherd that was clarified for us by David in **Psalm 23** "The Lord is my Shepherd I shall not want…He restores my soul, … He leads me in the paths of righteousness. For His name sake". Amen.

Day Twenty-seven: Jesus as The Prince of Peace.

Peace is tranquility, harmony, equanimity. **Isaiah 9:6** predicted "Prince of Peace" as one of the names of Jesus. In **Luke 2:14** Jesus birth was linked to the era of "Peace on earth" by the Angels. In **Mathew 5:9** Jesus taught peace. "Blessed are the peacemakers for they shall be called children of God". In **Mark 4:39** Jesus stills the storm with the words "Peace be still". Before His death in **John 14:27** Jesus prayed for His disciples "My Peace I leave with you. My peace I give to you not as the world gives". After Resurrection Jesus appeared to His disciples in a room and said to them "Peace be with you". Jesus entire life was an engagement with peace. **Ephesians 2:14** says "Christ is our peace". **Colossians 3:15** says we should allow the Peace of God to rule our hearts. **Philippians 4:7** prays that the peace of God which passes all understanding will guard our minds and hearts. **Romans 5:1** says we have peace through Christ Jesus. **Romans 14:19** asks us to pursue the things which make for peace. Peace is at the Centre of all things. Peace is a gift. It is also a Fruit of the Spirit needed for our journey of sanctification. May God give us His peace that passes all understanding. (**Philippians 4:7**) Amen.

Day Twenty-eight: Jesus as Only Begotten Son.

John 3:16 declares for God so loved the world that He gave His Only Begotten Son that whosoever believes in Him should not perish but have everlasting life. **1John 4:9** says In this the love of God was manifest towards us that God sent His only Son into the world that we might live through Him. Jesus the Only Begotten Son of God is affirmed in the Nicene Creed which is a Profession of Faith widely used in the Christian Liturgy and read at every service. It was adopted in the city of Nicaea (present day Turkey) in 325 AD. Only Begotten Son highlights Jesus as uniquely God's Son sharing the same divine nature of God as well as the human nature of His mother Mary. Jesus miraculous and unique conception is at the center of this tittle. **John 1:14** says Jesus the Word became flesh and dwelt among us. Jesus being of one substance with the Father. As believers we are also Sons and Daughters of God by adoption through Christ Jesus. (**Ephesians 1:5**). Hence, we receive grace and peace through Jesus Christ and so all our worship is for Jesus because no one comes to the Father except by the Son, Jesus Christ. Amen.

Day Twenty-nine: Jesus as Prophet.

In **Mark 6:3-4** Jesus was teaching in the synagogue demonstrating great wisdom. Many were astonished at the depth of His knowledge that they asked, "Is this not the Carpenter, the Son of Mary?" Jesus response, "A Prophet is honored everywhere except in His own hometown and among His relatives and His own family". At another time in **Luke 13:33** Jesus was in Galilee and was told that Herod was after Him to kill Him. Jesus again referred to Himself as a Prophet and said that it is prudent for Him to get out of the city. It would not do for a Prophet of God to be killed anywhere else except in Jerusalem. In **Mathew 22:11** at Jesus Triumphant Entry into Jerusalem the people referred to Jesus as the Prophet from Nazareth of Galilee. Who is a Prophet? It is One who makes known divine truth and conveys divine messages to the people. In **Deuteronomy 18:18** Moses a Prophet of God told the people of Israel that God said He would raise up for the people another prophet and God would put His words in His mouth. And He will speak to them all that God would command Him to say. Many years later among the people of Israel Jesus came on the scene as an oracle of

God, speaking God's Word, revealing God, and communicating the truth about God to the people. Since He was twelve years old Jesus would sit with much older people, speaking with authority, saying that He speaks what He hears His Father says. He would cite the Scriptures to the extent that people wondered where He learnt all these things from. A Prophet also foretells of things to come. Jesus spent a lot of time predicting His death, what would happen to Him, who would betray Him, who would deny Him. Jesus has the mantle and the Ministry of the Prophet. As a point of interest, forgetting the other controversy about Jesus, Islam recognizes and affirms Jesus as a Prophet of God. Muslims are required to honor Him as a Prophet as contained in the Holy Quran, the Scriptures of Islam. May Jesus Prophet of All people grant us illumination. Amen.

Day Thirty: Jesus as The Physician.

In **Mathew 9:12** The Pharisees complained about Jesus eating at table with sinners and tax collectors. Jesus responded that those who are well have no need of physician but those who are sick. In **Luke 4:23** Jesus was preaching in the Temple, the people were so amazed at His wisdom and asked "Is this not Joseph's son". Again Jesus refers to Himself as the Physician saying He knows what the people will say "Physician heal thyself". Healing was the hallmark of Jesus ministry. Jesus healing was dramatic and diverse. Jesus healed all sorts of people men, women, children, the young, the old and lots in between. Jesus cured a variety of diseases blindness, paralytic, bent back, epilepsy, leprosy, dumbness, demon possession, flow of blood, and even raised the dead. Jesus methods were unique to Him. He healed mostly out of compassion. In many cases He made the first move without the people even asking Him. In some cases, those who needed healing called out to Him. At other times some walked to Him and asked if He was willing to heal them. Jesus would lovingly respond that He was willing and He would heal them. Jesus healed by proxy. He would just say the word and the people would be healed. At times Jesus forgave sins before healing. At other times He demanded faith. Jesus at times had to throw out skeptics and doubters from the room to heal. Jesus used unusual items to heal, sputum, clay. Jesus healed anytime of the day, morning, noon, evening, and even on Sabbath day. Jesus even healed at a critical moment of His own life. At the time of His arrest Jesus stylishly restored Malchus' ear that had been sliced off in anger by Peter. (**Luke 22: 49-51**). Do you need any type of healing today? Physical, emotional, psychological, etc. Remember the "The Sun of Righteousness is here NOW with healing in His wings". **(Malachi 4:2)** Be healed in His name. Amen

Day Thirty-one: Jesus as Life.

In **John 14:6** Jesus says, "I Am the Life". Life is a state of living or being alive. Jesus in **John 10:10** also says that He has come so we may have life and have it more abundantly. This means an enhanced quality of life in Jesus. The opportunity to live like He did for humanity and outside of ourselves. The opportunity to relate to God our Heavenly Father as He has shown us. Life in itself is transient. **James 4:14** tells us that life is like vapor that appears for a little time and then vanishes. But **1John 5:12** says He who has the Son has life. Vs11 says God has given us "eternal life" and this life is in His Son. So not only do we have some quality of life on earth because Jesus is Life. Jesus gives us eternal life which is not some meaningless endless life. But the continuance of blessed communion with God and His Son. **Colossians 3:4** says when Christ appears who is our Life, we who have faith in Him will also appear with Him in Glory. Jesus our Life giver is worthy of the attention, the commitment and devotion so that even if we die, we shall live. We shall still have life in Him. Amen.

Day Thirty-two: Jesus as Love.

1John4 says God is Love and he/she who abides in Love abides in God and God in him/her. He who does not love does not know God for God is Love. Love is a very complex multidimensional concept to reflect on, starting from the social, rational, secular, emotional, relational, spiritual, religious dimensions. However, they all remain intertwined and interconnected and we cannot fragmentize them. There is a blend somewhere. Love is an attribute of God. Love is emotional. God is emotional. Love is passion, God has passion. God created the world and the people in passion. Love is the highest attribute of God from which we His beings have derived our sense and perception of self, of God and of others. The love that God has for His beings underlies what He has done and what He is doing and what He expects of us all. The reality and power of love cannot be ignored. It is also a religious virtue of various dimensions. It is not just expressed as a Christian virtue, it is a human virtue promoted by all religions and even secular societies. Love is fundamental in all our relationships. It is the motive for all moral laws and actions. It is the stimulus for our entire living and relationships. Jesus said: We must love God. We must love Others. We must love Self. Love is truth. Love is real. Love is adoring. Love is understanding. Love is engulfing in all ways. Above all love is wholesome. God is love. Jesus is Love. Holy Spirit is Love. May we all be endued and imbibed with Love in a redeeming, fulfilling and complete way. May we find ourselves in His Love. Amen.

Day Thirty-three: Jesus as The Truth.

John 14:6 Jesus says I AM the Truth. Truth is what aligns with the fact. It is reality. Truth is also subjective. Everyone constructs his/her truth. But there is also Absolute Truth. Jesus is saying to us, in terms of God the Father I AM the Truth. I know Him and I represent Him to you. In terms of God the Son I Am He because the Father says so. "This is my beloved Son". In terms of God the Spirit, it is affirmed by "The Spirit of God is upon Me". Jesus is the Truth of all Mysteries: Those things which we cannot understand but which will be revealed in time. The Truth of all Prophecies: All that which have been said by the Prophets of old and which have come to pass concerning He who was yet to come. But has come and will come again. We pledge allegiance to the Truth of All. Amen.

Day Thirty-four: Jesus as Teacher.

John 3:2 Nicodemus a Jewish ruler came to Jesus in the night and said "Rabbi we know that you are a Teacher sent from God, for no man can do these things that you do unless God is with Him. Moses and Aaron and his sons as priests were also teachers of Israel in the laws of God. Moses taught the people and also instructed them to teach what they have learnt to their children. To teach means to instruct, to impart, to give or convey knowledge or information to someone about a concept or subject. In the New Testament Jesus taught on the Mount and in the synagogue. Teaching is also an important part of the Commission which Jesus gave to His Apostles. In **Mathew 28:20** Jesus says Go make disciples of all nations teaching them to observe all things that I have commanded you. Teachers are mentioned as among the spiritual gifts of Apostles, Prophets, Evangelists, Pastors and Teachers. **Ephesians 4:1.** Jesus the Great Teacher taught not just by words but by deeds. Jesus offers profound statement to the astonishment of the people. He said some things that are easy to understand and some difficult to comprehend. Teachers are required for teaching the people unto salvation. **Romans 10:14** asks How can the people know if they are not taught. Teaching is generational for passing instructions down from generation to generation. Teachers have a great responsibility **James 3:1** says they shall receive a stricter judgement. A case of unto whom much is given much will be required. In it all Jesus was taught of the Lord by the Power of the Holy Spirit. In **John 6:45** Jesus said we shall all be taught of the Lord as said by the Prophet. **Isaiah 54:13** says all our children shall be taught by the Lord and great shall be their peace. As a professional teacher, both of the Word and in secular context, my continued prayer for those of us called to be Teachers and those yet to be called to always surrendered to the power of the Holy Spirit, the Ultimate Teacher. Amen.

Day Thirty-five: Jesus as Gift.

John 3:16 For God so loved the world that He gave His beloved Son (as a Gift). Paul in **2Corinthians 9:15** says Thank God for His indescribable

Gift. God is a Giver. He gives bounteous gifts to mankind, the sun, the moon, daily benefits too numerous to mention. **James 1:17** says every good and every perfect gift comes the Father of Lights. God's most perfect gift is Jesus. This gift was freely given out of pure love. Jesus as a Gift to every believer is ours to keep. All that Jesus is, All His great and glorious attributes are ours. Thanks be to God for His indescribable Gift. Jesus, I receive you again as a Gift to me. I also receive a gift from you. Let me use your gifts for your glory. Amen.

Day Thirty-six: Jesus as Wisdom of God.

1Corinthians 1:30 says Jesus became for us Wisdom from God. Wisdom is having knowledge and applying that knowledge in what is true and right. It is demonstrating sound judgement in deciding and acting. **Proverbs 2:6** tells us that the Lord gives wisdom from His mouth**. James 3:17** now describes what Wisdom from God looks like. He says it is pure, peaceable, gentle, full of mercy, without partiality and hypocrisy. **Proverbs 13** says He who walks with wise men will be wise. **James 5** also says if anyone lacks wisdom we should ask and God who gives liberally will give it to us. Wisdom does not happen instantaneously. It is incremental. **Luke 2:52** says Jesus "grew in knowledge, wisdom and understanding". **John 1:16** says that we have of the fulness of God in Christ Jesus, grace for grace, measure for measure. Jesus is the Wisdom by whom God communicates with us. May God grant us the those righteous qualities that define Wisdom. Amen.

Day Thirty-seven: Jesus as Lord.

The word Lord means owner, ruler, master, one who has power over. In the English tradition it denotes a nobleman, the highest ranking Official of State hence they have Lord Chancellor, Lord Chamberlain, Lord Mayor. The term in spiritual context was ascribed to Jesus in many ways denoting ownership and supremacy. Hence Jesus is Lord of the Sabbath, (the One who owns the sabbath), Lord of the Harvest, (the one who controls the great harvest field of the world, the vineyards and all those who work in there), Lord of hosts (the One in charge of all the entities of the heavens, the angels, authorities and powers), Lord of the dead (the souls of the departed are with Him), Lord of the living (the multitude still on earth are also His), Lord of the whole earth (in charge of the universe that He co-created, all things and all people with the Father who says "Let us make man in our own image").(**Genesis 1:26)** Lord God (First of all created beings). Lord from heaven (the One who has descended from above), Lord of all (the One who has dominion over all worlds, the entire systems, all things, all persons, all events that are put under His feet). In addition. Jesus has the Lord's Day, (the first day of the week in the Christian calendar), the Lord's Supper, (the meal belonging to Jesus established by Him), the Lord's Prayer (formulated by Jesus in honor of His Heavenly Father whom He shares with all believers). While on earth some of Jesus disciples acknowledged His Lordship. Peter called Him Lord, the One who has all authority. Thomas called Him Lord, after His resurrection. Paul recognized Jesus as Lord, at his conversion. Martha called Jesus Lord, when He raised her brother from the dead. Finally. why do many Christians claim Jesus as their Lord? Jesus with His death redeemed us, bought us back like goods from the pawn shop, and so we belong to Him. Jesus has a claim over our lives**. 1 Peter 1:18** says we were not redeemed by the perishable things but with the Precious Blood of Jesus. That is why we shall continue to proclaim that JESUS IS LORD. Amen.

Day Thirty-eight: Jesus as Root.

The root is that part of the tree that grows downwards and deeper into the ground to hold the plant in place, to absorb the water and the nutrients that supply the food that plants need for survival. Even when the tree is cut down as long as the root remains in the ground the tree would continue to thrive and flourish. The Root of the family is also the one from which the clan emerges and develop, the Patriarch or the

Matriarch. Jesus is called the Root of Jesse, the Root of David, the Root out of dry land. Jesus human descendancy is traced to David and of course Jesse his father.

David was one of the greatest kings of Israel, reigned for 40 years with spectacular achievements. Fought and won wars to ensure the survival of his kingdom. His son Solomon took over. Although with initial success, the kingdom became divided and it's supremacy challenged by other powers. The tree of David for a thousand years looks dry and withered. But **Isaiah 14:29** has warned "let not the enemy rejoice because the King is dead, even though the rod that struck is dead, out of the serpent's root will come a viper whose offspring will be more fiery". A thousand years later Jesus shows up with more power, more glory, the conquering Lion, the Man of War whose might is greater than His progenitor. A lesson for all of us. Never disregard anyone or anything because they do not look promising. Jesus is not only the Root out of David's dry land, Jesus is for us the Root that continues to nourish us as Christians. May we all continue to flourish from the nourishment that comes from our Root the Lord. Amen.

Day Thirty-nine: Jesus as Word of God.

John1:1 says "In the beginning was the Word and the Word was with God and the Word was God". Verse 14 adds "And the Word became flesh and dwelt among us". Words are the vehicle for revealing our thoughts and intentions of the mind to others. Words are a lot more expressive than nonverbal communication which is quite prone to misinterpretation. Jesus as the Word consists of the Revelation of God to man. **Hebrews 1** says God has spoken at various times through the Prophets but in the Last Days God chose to speak to us through His Son, the Word. The Word of God is a Master Communicator, the Bible says the people marvel whenever He spoke. May the Word continue to enlighten and illuminate us, Amen.

Day Forty: Sunday of the Passion, Palm Sunday.

The Triumphant Entry into Jerusalem. Jesus for the last three years had been doing all that He proclaimed He was anointed to do at the beginning of His Ministry. Healing, Teaching, Preaching, even Raising the dead. His time was up. And He knew it. So He decided to go into Jerusalem for His last Passover celebration in style, on a donkey. He sent for one and He got it. The people placed him on the donkey and there was excitement in the air. They removed their shawls, and other clothing items and paved the roads with them. Instantaneously without anyone organizing them. There was an exuberant crowd following, praising, singing, waiving leaves and palm leaves in honor of Jesus who surprisingly did Not stop them. Many came out to see Him, many joined in the celebration. The highlight of the day was when the Pharisees came to Jesus told Him to stop His followers from making all that uncalled-for noise. Jesus classic response was "if I stop these people from singing praises to me the stones on the ground would immediately rise up and replace them and the praise, worship and adoration would continue". Wow!!! I will Not want the inanimate objects, the stones to replace me. David said, "Let everything that has breadth praise the Lord". (**Psalm 150:60**). Palm Sunday is the beginning of the countdown to Good Friday when He died and Easter when He Resurrected. The week is traditionally called Passion Week or Holy Week. We shall follow the events of the week. Meanwhile let us join the crowd in hailing Jesus, giving Him all glory and honor. Amen.

Passion/Holy Week Reflections

Monday. Jesus as Sacrifice.

Ephesians 5:2 says "And walk in love, as Christ also has loved us, and hath given himself for us an offering and a sacrifice to God for a sweet-smelling savor". Sacrifice is something offered and given up for something else. Jesus entire life was a sacrifice. Jesus willingly offered

Himself as a Sacrifice for our reconciliation with the Father. Ever wondered what Jesus did the last week of His life. He spent most of it in the Temple. However, on this first day of the week of Passion Jesus again revealed to His disciples what would happen soon. He started to prepare them for what is to come, what this sacrifice would look like. In **Luke 18**, Jesus said "Behold we are going up to Jerusalem and all things that are written by the Prophets concerning the Son of Man will be accomplished. For He will be delivered to the Gentiles and will be mocked and insulted and spit upon. They will scourge Him and kill Him and the third day He will rise again". The Bible says, "but they understood none of these things". Where they in stubborn denial or all what Jesus was saying was simply incomprehensible. Dying and resurrecting again. I would be confused too. The thought of losing their Beloved Master! Tough pill to swallow. But Jesus was focused and ready to offer Himself as the Ultimate Sacrifice for you and I. Thank you Jesus. Amen.

Tuesday. Jesus as Savior.

1 Timothy 4:10 says we trust in the Living God who is Savior of ALL especially of those who believe. In the Old Testament in **Deuteronomy 20:4** kings were deemed as saviors because they fought against the people's enemies to save them. Saving the people included granting assistance, helping and protection. However, in the New Testament the term is applied solely to Jesus as the Ultimate Savior of humankind not because He went to physical war for the people but because He laid His life down to reconcile us to His Father. We all need a Savior for we have All sinned and come short of the glory of God. **1John 2:2** says Jesus died for the sins of the whole world. **Isaiah 53:6** predicts that the iniquity of all fall upon Him. **Mathew1:21** says Mary will bear a Son and He will be called Jesus for He will **save** His people from their sins. **John 4:12** adds that "there is no Salvation in any other, for there is no other name given among men by which we shall be saved". On this Second day of the Week of Passion as we walk along with Jesus towards the fulfillment of God's plan of Salvation let us continue to remember that Salvation has emanated from the Love of God who has ordained His Son Jesus to execute it for All. Let us thank God that it is available for all and it is realized in Forgiveness, Sanctification (righteousness), and the Glorification of all believers. In **Psalm 106** David asks God to visit him with His Salvation but we have a better deal because we are beneficiaries of God's Plan of Salvation. Thanks be to God. Amen.

Wednesday. Jesus as Redeemer.

Isaiah 59:20 says "The Redeemer will come to Zion and to those whose sins have been forgiven. Redeem means to buy back, to rescue. Jesus pattern of Salvation is a process. It is a continuum. It starts with repentance and forgiveness of sins and goes through this unique act of Redemption. Jesus redemption design is that having accepted Salvation, He rescues believers from all forms of bondage, from slavery to sin, and from the power of Satan. With original sins forgiven we are saved from eternal condemnation and rescued from many other sins that easily beset us. Part of the redemption process is to make us pure and clean like Christ. To become like Christ, we must be in Christ. This is a powerful deal for believers. Who else could do this for us except the One who has the Power to save through death on the Cross and the ability to purchase us back by His precious Blood of Jesus our Redeemer. **Psalm 107:2** says "Let the Redeemed of the Lord say so whom He has redeemed from the hand of the enemy". Halleluiah. Amen.

Maundy Thursday. Jesus as Servant Leader.

Maundy Thursday was quite a busy day for Jesus. All the Gospels have an account of how Jesus gathered His friends with Him for the Last Supper. He gave them bread. He gave them wine and He said "Take, eat and drink. Do this in remembrance of me". Jesus instituted this everlasting memorial, the Last Supper, the Eucharist which has continued to be a significant part of our spiritual growth in the Lord. After Supper, Jesus washed the feet of His disciples. He then said to them in **John 13:14** "Now that I your Lord and Teacher have washed your feet, you should wash one another's feet". Jesus modelled for us how to "**lead and serve**" at the same time. After that Jesus prayed His most remarkable lengthy Intercessory Prayers for His disciples, that include you and I. He says in **John 17:20** "I do not pray for these alone but for all those who will believe in me through their message ". You and I were on Jesus mind even in His last moments. What a blessed assurance. Jesus later went to the Garden to pray where Judas Iscariot one of His disciples who had eaten with Him and had his feet washed would betray Him. Jesus showed great love to Judas and taught us how to love those who would persecute us. At the time of His arrest on that same day, Jesus performed one more miracle, He put back Malchus ear that was sliced off by Peter, His foremost disciple who would also deny Him before the end of the day. Jesus would later restore Peter. What a day! As we go through this day let us reflect on the significance and relevance of each of these events in our lives. May we be attentive to what we are supposed to learn. Amen.

Good Friday. Jesus as Ransom.

1Timothy 2:6 The Man Christ Jesus gave Himself a Ransom for all. **John 19**: says They took Jesus. He carried His Cross to Golgotha. There they crucified Him. Jesus said, "I thirst". When He had taken the wine, He said "It is finished". With that He bowed His head and gave up His Spirit. This is the day we solemnly remember Jesus Death. In spite of the gruesome reality of it all this is the day we celebrate Life. Jesus died that we might live. Christ's perfect life was given as Ransom, a Substitute for ours. This is the Day we rededicate our lives to Jesus because He gave

All of Himself for us. Thank you, Jesus for your sacrifice and your gift of eternal life. Amen.

Holy Saturday. Jesus our Righteousness.

1Corinthians 1:30 says We are in Christ Jesus who became for us Wisdom from God and Righteousness. Righteousness is upright conduct. It is a state of being right and just. Righteousness of Christ is **imputed** to us when we become saved. By Jesus death on the Cross and His shed Blood and by His perfect righteousness we are made righteous through faith in Him. We are deemed to be righteous. We are counted as righteous. We are treated as righteous. The Penitent thief on the Cross beside Jesus recognized the ability and power of Jesus to save even at the moment of His death. In **Luke 23:42** he said, "Lord remember me when you come into your Kingdom". Jesus acknowledged his faith and assured him that he would be with Him in Paradise. His sins were forgiven and he was deemed righteous for entry into the Kingdom. May God continue to be favorable to us through the expression of our faith in Christ His Son, that God's righteousness may be attributed to us and be made manifest in us. Amen.

Easter Sunday. Jesus as Resurrection.

Alleluia!!!!! Christ is risen. In **John 11:25** Jesus says "I am the Resurrection and the Life. He who believes in Me though he/she may die, he/she may live. And whoever lives and believes in Me shall NEVER die. Do you believe this?". Jesus said this not at or about His own resurrection but at His raising of Lazarus from the dead preparing the people for His own resurrection. Jesus had raised others from the dead like Jairus daughter but in Lazarus case he had been dead and buried. When Jesus said, "I am the Resurrection and the Life". He not only established a connection between Resurrection and Life, He addressed the reality of "physical/spiritual death" and the reality of "physical/spiritual life".

When Lazarus was raised, he was immediately restored to life. When Jesus resurrected, His post resurrection appearances confirmed His being raised to life. Of course, today there are still doubters regarding Jesus resurrection. But Jesus as Resurrection tells us that if we believe in Him, we will NOT live a "spiritually dead" life because "He lives". Also, if and when we are confronted with the reality of "physical death" we will not be lost in "eternal death" because He is Alive and we have the hope of "eternal life" in Him? Amen. Do you believe this?

SECTION TWO

Jesus Centered Reflections

The Section contains Reflections that are Jesus focused, Jesus centered with fresh perspectives as regards some of the stories of Jesus as contained in the Bible. In the Church Calendar, the Pentecost Season comes right after Easter. This Section contains some Reflections relevant to the Pentecost Season. The Advent Season comes right after Pentecost. This Section also contains some Reflections that are relevant to the Advent Season. Enjoy.

Contents

Reflection on Lent and the Subject of Sin: 1 John 1:8

Ash Wednesday usually marks the beginning of the Lenten season when in some traditions, adherents are marked with ashes as an ancient sign of penitence. Some Christians ignore the Lenten season saying that there is nothing in the Bible that says we should observe lent and fast. For many Lent is a period of 40 days in which Christians live a life of prayer, fasting, penitence, self-denial and sacrifice in commemoration of Jesus Christ's fasting in the desert before the commencement of His public ministry and in preparation for Christ's resurrection on Easter Sunday. As a period of reflection, I allow my thoughts to dwell on the subject of Sin. Generally, sin is seen as a violation of God's moral code. Sin is also a rebellion against, or resistance to the direction of some supreme deity. It is also seen as the hatred of that which is good and the deliberate choosing of that which is evil. Any thought, word, or act considered immoral, harmful, or alienating might be termed "sinful". Sin is also an action that is prohibited or considered wrong.

In Christianity, sin is a deliberate violation of the law of God, an abomination and an act of lawlessness (**1 John 3:4**) that separates us from God. There are not only sinful acts but also sin in thoughts and words. In Eastern Christianity, sin is viewed in terms of its effects on relationships, both among people and between people and God. In the Russian variant of Eastern Christianity, sin sometimes is regarded as any mistake made by people in their lives. From this point of view every person is sinful because every person makes mistakes during his/her life. When a person accuses others of sins, they always must remember that they are also sinners and so they must have mercy for others remembering that God is also merciful to them and to all of humanity.

Sin is not a concept that exists only in Christianity. All the other religions also affirm the existence of sin in different ways. Judaism teaches that any thought, word, or deed that breaks God's law by commission which is doing what should not be done and by omission which is not doing what should be done is sin. Islam sees sin "khati'a" as anything that goes against the will of Allah. The Quran teaches that the human soul is prone to evil, unless Allah bestows His mercy.

https://en.wikipedia.org/wiki/Islamic_views_on_sin

Buddhism has no concept of sin, but it promotes the Four Noble Truths and some ethical Ten Precepts, rules to live by, Do not kill, Do not steal. Do not lie, Do not misuse sex etc. Buddhism also recognizes a natural principle of "Karma" whereby widespread suffering is the inevitable consequence of greed and hatred of others. Buddhism therefore seeks to end suffering by replacing greed with selflessness, hatred with compassion and delusion with wisdom. https://en.wikipedia.org/wiki/Karma_in_Buddhism

Within Shinto there is no doctrine of sin, but the concept of good and evil. Evil is divided into the most vicious crimes "amatsu tsumi" and common misdemeanors or delinquency "kunitsu tsumi".

The Baha'i Faith defines sin as disobedience to God and His laws and is the result of the soul's attachment to material and worldly things. Zoroastrianism says the conflict in the human soul is between good and evil, the struggle to choose between Ahura Mazda the supreme God of Good and Angra Mainya, the god of evil and darkness who opposes God.

https://www.google.com/search?q=zoroastrianism+ahura+mazda+angra+mainyu&rlz=Although sin has its roots in religion there is a social response to sin. At times moral, religious and legal codes are intertwined for example killing is illegal, it is also a sin. However socially, many dismiss the concept of sin as a notion that belongs to the Stone Age, a bygone era. Many say sin is subjective and relative. Who defines sin anyway? Many add that humanity is better off not talking about sin. It is a way of enslaving people, a fear mongering tactic, they add. Hence socially sin has become a politically incorrect topic to engage in and the concept is gradually eroding away. However, some accept the reality of sin but deny or ignore their own sins. Many others especially in the media and the political world see sin as providing opportunity for entertainment. Sin is the core subject of many shows, movies, and even the news. Some even parade their sins, their own moral failure as a way of establishing a sense of belongingness and connectedness to a society that has gone depraved. Some others gleefully and publicly confess their own sins before the cameras to appease an equally sinful, prying yet forgiving society. Hollywood portrays sin in its most exotic form in the movie "Sin City".

https://www.google.com/search?q=movie+sin+city&rlz= Michelangelo gives us a classic depiction of sin in his painting in the Sistine Chapel in the Vatican fresco with the expulsion of Adam and Eve from the Garden of Eden. http://www.italianrenaissance.org/a-closer-look-michelangelos-painting-of-the-sistine-chapel-ceiling/Great thinkers like Richard Henry Dana an American lawyer and politician a champion of the downtrodden, wondered in frustration "O sin what has thou done to this fair earth".

https://www.goodreads.com/author/quotes/192314.Richard Henry Dana Jr Thomas Fuller an English church man and an historian says, "he that falls into sin is a man, he that grieves at it is a saint, he that boasts of it is a devil". https://www.brainyquote.com/authors/thomas-fuller-quotes

However, in religious/spiritual context sin has also become a difficult concept to deal with. Many do not want to be burdened by any guilt-arousing talk from the pulpit. Life is hard enough, they say. A friend of mine says her own sins she can deal with but not the sin of Adam. I agree with her. Many people say they only want to be encouraged by the truth of God's love. Rightfully so! Getting people to fill the pews has become a very competitive enterprise. Religious leaders therefore have a hard time preaching sin. Nobody wants to scare away an already fragile congregation. I have sympathy for them, after all **Deuteronomy 24:16** says that everyman shall be put to death for his own sin. Who can preach that? In any case there is a more exciting ongoing topic of wealth and lively competition among the preachers of Prosperity Theology.

It does not matter the ongoing discussions about sin, unfortunately sin is still a reality no matter how much we try to run away from it. Common ideas surrounding sin include consequences to sin either in this life or in afterlife, punishment for sins, from other people, or from God or from the Universe in general. There is also the question of whether an act must be intentional to be sinful and that one's conscience should produce guilt for a conscious act to be sin. There are also schemes for determining the seriousness and punishment of sin like stoning people to death which Jesus did not support in the case of the adulteress and His classic challenge: "Let him who is without sin cast the first stone".

The classical Biblical dimension to sin is found in **1 John 1:8**, "If we say we have no sin, we deceive ourselves and the truth is not in us". However, there is the possibility of forgiveness of sins, often through communication with a deity or intermediary. In Christianity it is often referred to as salvation. The consoling part of sin is that God says even if our sins are red as crimson they shall be made as white as snow (**Isaiah 1:18**). Many Christians rest on the promise found in **Romans 8 1** which states that believers in Christ are no longer under condemnation. However, some forget Paul's poignant question to the Romans: "Yes where sin abounds grace abounds much more, should we then continue to sin so that grace may abound?". Paul's response is an emphatic Certainly Not. There is also the question of intentional and deliberate sin? How then do we deal with the subject of sin in all these discourses? The good news is that there is room for repentance. **1John 1:9** says If we confess our sins, God is faithful and just to forgive us our sins, and to cleanse us from all unrighteousness. Christianity offers forgiveness for past sins through Christ in a process called Salvation. But what about our everyday sins? Some denominations go for formal confession which is scriptural: confess your sins to one another (**James**

5:16). Some routinely offer the prayers of Penance or Confession, during worship service.

The bible is quite realistic about sin. Its accounts are not filled with super saints whose perfection we must admire. Instead it represents the lives of real people and makes full disclosure of their failings. **2 Samuel 11** shows us a classic sinner's response to sin. King David's sins of adultery and murder were not hidden from God. David initially tried to cover up his sins but when confronted, he owned them, confessed them and asked to be forgiven acknowledging that he had sinned against a Holy and Righteous God who alone is able to forgive (**Mark 2:7). Proverbs 28:31** says "he who conceals his sins does not prosper, but whoever confesses and renounces them finds mercy". As for me, I am thankful and continue to relish the fact that I belong to the Anglican denomination that provides me with the opportunity to routinely confess my sins during worship service. Like David in **Psalm 32:5** I will continue to acknowledge my sins to God because He is able to forgive them. I am also grateful that each year the Lenten season provides me the opportunity to reflect deeply on the Subject of Sin. My private prayers to God will continue to be King David's prayer in **Psalm 19:13** "Keep me from presumptuous sins let them not have dominion over me". Amen

Reflection on the Significance of Palm Sunday and Passion Week

Palm Sunday, a glorious day, a day that is usually described as the Day of Jesus Triumphal Entry into Jerusalem. Before the day Jesus had sent two of His disciples to go ahead to a nearby town where they would find a colt, which is a young donkey that no one has ever ridden. He told them to untie the donkey and bring it to Him. He added that if anyone would ask what they want to do with the colt, they should say that He the Lord has need of it. Note that Jesus said nothing about what He was going to do with the colt. Everything happened as Jesus had informed the disciples on the errand. On return, **Mathew 21:7**: says that the people brought the donkey to Jesus. The people spread their clothes on the donkey. Then the people sat Jesus on the donkey. The people spread their clothes on the road that Jesus would pass. Others plucked the palm tree branches and laid them on the road that Jesus would pass. Many people, the multitude, as the Bible calls them, started going before Jesus and many more were coming behind him. All of them were in joyous mood and exuberance shouting and praising Jesus saying "Hosanna to the Son of David. Blessed is He who comes in the name of the Lord. Hosanna in the highest". Note the role of the people in all these. The people were all involved in the activities of the day. It is what we call Collective Behavior in Sociology. The people were very excited about Jesus. They were hailing Him. They all wanted to be part of this significant celebration.

At this point, I could not help wondering why the people were so excited about Jesus coming in to Jerusalem?" Remember, before this event, Jesus had been performing various miracles, healing the people, teaching the people, preaching to the people and feeding the people. This meant that many, if not all of them had been touched by Jesus in one way or the other. He has fed some, He has healed some, and He has taught some. Every one of them had a personal reason to be there. Some may even have just heard of Him and were curious and wanted to see for themselves. Another reason could be that the people had come to some great awareness and revelation that Jesus was not just a Teacher, a Healer, and a Provider of food. But that Jesus was the Messiah that they have been waiting for, the Redeemer from God who would deliver them from the oppression of the Romans. The remarkable thing about it all was that these people's response and reaction to Jesus arrival was spontaneous. Nobody told them what to do. There was no leader mobilizing this Mass Movement. There was no Grass root organized rally to welcome Jesus. The activities and involvement ALL just happened.

The people felt a stirring within them, an urge to give something to Jesus out of the abundance of their hearts and their gratefulness for who He is and what He has done for them. This spontaneous reaction is the most notable thing reported in the bible: Men pulling off their clothes, women spreading their shawls, on the road, younger people climbing the trees to see more of what was happening, more people tearing off more palm trees branches and children picking handful of spring flowers in Jesus path, more people running down the road just to join the crowd. Wow!!! What a sight!!!! How remarkable!!!

My second question is "Suppose Jesus suddenly shows up physically in a congregation on Palm Sunday walking down the aisle and we know for sure that the person walking down the aisle is Jesus the Christ, what would you and I do? What would be our reactions collectively and individually to Him showing up in our space? I know, some would dismiss it as a ruse, a trick, a fake. Some would be skeptical and will pay no attention. Yet some would not be too surprised because Jesus has warned that He will show up like a thief in the night, and so they would indeed welcome Him. This definitely was not Jesus' first visit to Jerusalem for the Passover. I am sure Jesus has been attending this annual event quietly participating in the celebration. Remember He was a Jew and the Passover is a significant religious event of the Jewish people. On the previous occasions, it did not seem that Jesus had drawn any attention to Himself. But on this particular Passover celebration, Jesus chose to make this Grand Entry having all these people showing up in this flamboyant display of affection. Jesus was watching it all, I am sure in quiet bemusement, taking it all in, and I think quite pleased with what He saw. But note: Jesus did NOT stop the people. It is as if Jesus expects it, He desires it, and He approves of it. Remarkable isn't!!!!

In another account in **Luke 19:39-40** the Bible says that when the Pharisees saw all the excitement of the people, they were all surprised and irritated. they decided that they were not just going to stand around and do nothing. So they went near to Jesus and told Him to tell all His followers to stop all these commotion. Ah!!! Jesus gave them an astounding and astonishing response. He said that if He stopped all the people from worshipping and praising Him, all the stones on the ground would immediately rise up and replace the people, and the Pharisees would still hear the loud worship and adoration going on. Wow!!!! David in **Psalm 150:6** says "Let everything that has breadth praise the Lord".

On Palm Sunday while celebrating Jesus Triumphal Entry to Jerusalem, we are reminded that it is the beginning of the Passion Week, at times called the Holy Week, when the reason for Jesus coming to earth became fulfilled. It was during the Passion Week that Jesus was arrested, tried, dragged to the Criminal Justice System, before the Roman Judges. False charges were brought against Him by the prosecutor. He was accused of all sorts of things, including calling Himself the Messiah. Jesus was required to defend Himself. He did not have the privilege of a Defense Lawyer. He was found guilty, sentenced to death, nailed to the cross, where He died on Good Friday.

It was during the Passion Week that Jesus had the Last Supper with His disciples, and initiated what we call the Eucharist or Communion which is a significant ritual and practice that all Christians are required to participate in. It was during the Passion Week that Jesus went to the Garden of Gethsemane to pray and sweats of blood flowed from his body. It was during the Passion Week that Jesus was beaten with the whip and received 39 lashes on His body. It was during the Passion Week that the question of "who killed Jesus" came up. Jesus Himself answered the question; He said that nobody had any control over his life not even the rulers of Rome. He said that He willingly gave up His life for mankind, to achieve salvation for all, for you and for me.

It was during the Passion Week that Jesus forgave one of the thieves on the cross, crucified alongside with Him that we may know that there is Salvation even at the last moment. It was during the Passion Week that Jesus said, "It is finished", when after all the suffering, He hung his head and expired, the indication of a "fait accompli" meaning that He has accomplished all that He came to do. Passion Week was very emotional for Jesus, for His disciples, for His family, and for all around

Him. Passion Week also has a lot of meaning for us. It is the time for us to allow ourselves some thoughts about the Passion of our Lord Jesus Himself. It is a time of sober Reflection, a time of Triumph, and a time of Hope. At the end of Passion Week we celebrate the Resurrection of Jesus. Everything that Jesus did during the Passion Week was sealed and made secure by His VICTORY in Resurrection. The Resurrection establishes Jesus supremacy over death.

Finally, the Passion Week is a time to be reminded of what must be at the end of time. Eschatology it is called. **Revelation 7:9-10** says "After these I looked and saw a great multitude which no one can count, people of all nations, tribes, tongues, different languages standing before the Lamb, Jesus, clothed with White robes with Palm branches in their hands crying out with a loud voice saying "Salvation belongs to our God who sits on the throne and to the Lamb". Verse 13 reads "Then one of the elders answered saying to me who are these arrayed in white robes and where did they come from?" Verse 14 adds: "So he said to me these are the ones who have come out of tribulation and washed their robes and made them White in the Blood of the Lamb". Passion week is a Dress Rehearsal of what we will be doing at the end of time, all dressed up in white, with palms in our hands, singing praises to our God. May we be counted among the multitudes and multitudes and multitudes clothed in White, with Palms in hands forever singing praises to the Lamb who died on the Cross. Amen

Reflection on the True Meaning of Easter and the Resurrection

Thankfully the Lenten season is over and we have been greeted with the Death and Resurrection of Jesus. Alleluia!!!! Christ is Risen. He is Risen indeed. The Scriptures tell us that on the third day following Jesus' crucifixion, there was a great earthquake. The stone was rolled back from the door of the tomb. Some of the women, Mary, Mary Magdalene and Salome devoted followers of Jesus came to the place with spices to anoint the body of the crucified Christ but when they got there they did not find the body of the Lord Jesus. They were startled to find the tomb empty. Note that they were all women. I always wonder where the men were. An angel appeared and sat on the stone by the door of the tomb and said simply, "Why are you looking for the living among the dead? He is not here but is risen." (**Luke 24:3–6.).** "I know that you seek Jesus. He is not here; for He is risen" (**Matthew 28:5–6**). Profound statement.

The greatest good news that mortal ear has ever heard is that Jesus Christ has risen from the dead, as He had promised. The risen Lord later appeared to Mary, and then to the two disciples on the road to Emmaus, to Peter, to the Apostles; and "after that," as Paul reported, "he was seen of above five hundred brethren at once" And last of all he was seen of Paul also" (**1 Corinthians 15:6, 8**). The apostle Paul presents the Easter message quite clearly in First **Corinthians 15:3-4** when he writes: "Christ died for our sins according to the Scriptures, and that He was buried, and that He was raised on the third day according to the Scriptures". So the evidence is strong that that Jesus died and rose from the dead. For every Christian, the resurrection is not only real, but relevant. It is the truth that lies at the very foundation of the Gospel. Other doctrines of the Christian faith may be important, but the resurrection is essential. The fact of our Lord's resurrection is based on the testimonies of many credible witnesses. The long and short of it is that Jesus Rose.

What then is the True meaning of Easter? Why is Easter significant? Easter is the evidence of God's love. **I John 4:16** tells us that God is **love.** The entire Bible is a testament to God's love. But the events of that first Easter weekend long ago exhibit clearly God's love for humanity. **John 3:16** says For God so loved the world, that He gave His only begotten Son, that whoever believes in Him shall not perish, but have eternal life". **1 John 4:9-10** puts it this way. "By this the love of God was manifested in us, that God has sent His only begotten Son into the world so that we might live through Him. In this is love, not that we loved God, but that He loved us and sent His Son to be the offering, payment for our sins."

Now that we know the reality and the truth that Jesus rose and came out of the grave, we must answer the questions: What does this really mean for us collectively, and individually. The Almighty Creator of the universe gave His Son as a sacrifice for your sin and mine. Jesus did the hard part. He died on the cross for us. So, what is in it for us? What do we benefit from it all? **Romans 10:9** says, "If you confess with your mouth the Lord Jesus and believe in your heart that God has raised Him from the dead, you will be **saved**. "Everyone lives with the consequences of sin. At times we all experience brokenness, shame and guilt because of sin but **Romans 8:1** tells us this quite plainly: "Therefore there is now no condemnation for those who are in Christ Jesus". The Resurrection assures us that Jesus can transform our lives every day. We not only are forgiven, but we are filled with the mighty power of God who raised Jesus from the dead.

Jesus also promises us that He will be by our side through whatever life may bring our way. **Matthew 28:20** "I am with you **always**, even to the end of the age." Is there anything more comforting than to know that the Lord of the universe is by our side through thick and thin? Facing any challenge, known and unknown, is no longer a cause for anxiety, rather confidence, when we know that the Lord who loves us is with us. also spoke these words of encouragement to his followers, both in His day and ours: In these present trying times of moral laxity, economic uncertainty, natural disasters, and many other causes of difficulty, Jesus says that He is present in our lives at all times and that He will be a source of peace and power that will enable us to be victorious over the hardships of life. Amen.

Reflection on the Holy Spirit at Pentecost: Acts 2 1-4

On the Seventh Sunday after Easter the Church celebrates the Pentecost. What is Pentecost? It is the Christian festival celebrating the descent of the Holy Spirit on the disciples of Jesus after His ascension. Personally, I have always been drawn to the celebration and implication of Pentecost, which is about the Holy Spirit. It is always inspiring to celebrate the Holy Spirit. Pentecost reminds me of the workings of the Holy Spirit in our lives. Who/What is the Holy Spirit? Many Christians know and understand who the Father is, God the Creator. They know who His Son is, Jesus Christ who died for our sins to reconcile us with the Father. But they do not quite know or understand who the Holy Spirit is.

Some call Him the Mystical Force, some call Him Power. For some it is something that gives you goose pumps and makes you go uh uh uh. Some people call Him "the active force of the Almighty Jehovah" Some say He is the invisible power or kinetic energy of God. Some say he is not a Person, but just a personification of God's Power. In the Christian denomination we hear that the Holy Spirit is the Third Person of the Trinity. Some people wonder about that. Putting aside all the confusing theology that surround the concept of the Trinity, all it means is that the Holy Spirit is the Spirit of God. It is this same Spirit that created the whole word. It is the same Spirit that raised Jesus from the dead. The Holy Spirit is at times called the Holy Ghost. The Holy Spirit is the Power and Essence of God. He is the Invisible Presence of our Living God. We may not see Him, but He is ever there. For some of us the Holy Spirit is a Loving Divine Person. When you begin to see the Holy Spirit as person it's only then you can have the maximum benefit of His power and really experience Him. Holy Spirit is a Person because the Bible says He is.

Romans 8:27 tells us He has a mind, He bears witness, convicts, hears, speaks, guides, glorifies, helps, intercedes, searches, teaches, distributes, and He can be fellowshipped with. He has emotions. He can be grieved. He does not like it when you lie to Him. Jesus even warned that the sin against the Holy Spirit is the most grievous. The Holy Spirit has been manifested in every dispensation of the Gospel since the beginning. People always say that the Holy Spirit is not known in the Old Testament but **Genesis 1:2** says The Spirit of God was hovering over the face of the waters. The Old Testament records number of incidents when the coming of the Holy Spirit was made evident by a supernatural spiritual experience. **Numbers 11:25** says Then the Lord came down in the cloud and took of the Spirit that was upon Moses him and placed the same spirit upon the seventy elders and it happened when the spirit rested upon them that they prophesied. The Holy Spirit grants prophesy.

Jesus predicted the coming of the Holy Spirit. In **Acts 1:8** He said, "But you shall receive power when the Holy Spirit has come upon you". Power to do what? Primarily to become witnesses for Jesus. In **John 14:18** Jesus promised to send the Holy Spirit. He said, "I will not leave you as orphans; I will come to you". Pentecost was the full coming of the Holy Spirit on all the people. In **John 16:12-15** Jesus said I have many things to say but you cannot bear them now. When He the Spirit of truth has come, He will guide you into all truths for He will not speak of His own authority, but whatever He hears He will speak, and He will tell you all things to come.

How was the Holy Spirit Received? **Acts 2:1-4** describes the event. "When the day of Pentecost had fully come, they were all with one accord in one place and suddenly there came a sound from heaven as of a rushing mighty wind and it filled the whole house where they were sitting. Then there appeared to them divided tongues as of fire and one sat upon each of them and they were all filled with the Holy Spirit and began to speak with other tongues as the Spirit gave them utterance". In fact, in **John 20:22** we learnt that the Holy Spirit was first received by the Apostles when the doors were shut and Jesus came and stood in their midst and said to them, "Peace be with you" and He breathed on them and said to them "Receive the Holy Spirit". In **Acts 4:8** we read about Peter being filled with the Holy Spirit again after the Pentecost. **Acts 4:31** talks about the Holy Spirit coming again and how when they were all filled with the Holy Spirit, they spoke the Word of God with boldness. Hence the coming and presence of the Holy Spirit is not a onetime event. It is a continuous process. The "in filling" of the Holy Spirit is also continuous.

What does the Holy Spirit do in our lives? **In John 14:26** He is called the Helper, who will teach us all things. In **John 16:13** Jesus calls Him the Spirit of Truth who will guide us into all truths. **Isaiah 30:21** predicted that the Holy Spirit will be our guide. It says, "your ears shall hear a word behind you saying, this is the way walk in it". The Implication is that we shall all be led by the Spirit of God, in our major and minor decisions and we will be directed in our paths and in our ways by the Holy Spirit. **Romans 8:26** indicates that the Holy Spirit will help us to pray. The Holy Spirit articulates those things that burden us in prayers to God, bringing our needs to God even when we cannot express them. What a great help. The Spirit's intercession can be trusted because He intercedes according to God's will. The workings of the Holy Spirit in us are diverse, intense and extensive.

1 Cor 3:16-17 tells us that we are the temple of God and that the Spirit of God dwells in us. How do we then manifest this great privilege when the Holy Spirit is in us? **Roman 8:1-27** is one chapter in the Bible that talks most about the Holy Spirit. It tells us all the things that the Holy Spirit does for us. About twelve things are mentioned. It is a powerful chapter and we should all read it later, but I will just give an overview of what is contained in the chapter. The Holy Spirit (1) frees us from the law of sin, (2) frees us from death (spiritual), (3) fulfills righteousness in us,(4) indwells in us, makes His abode in us (5) gives life, to the body that is dead in sin, (6) quickens the mortal body, to make it alive, (7) mortifies the deeds of the body which are sins, renders impotent all the sins that beset us (8) leads us as sons and daughters of God showing us the way, guiding us through paths unknown, (9) adopts us into God 's family, not only that, as adopted children we have all the rights and privileges as the biological Son of God Jesus Christ so we are joint heirs with the Son. (10) He bears witness that we are the sons and daughters of God that is confirms to our mind the understanding that we are children of God. (11) The Spirit helps our infirmities, physical, moral, and mental inadequacies, flaws, weaknesses, helps us to shake them off, (12) He makes intercession for us. He knows we do not know how to pray, not that we cannot put words together, but we can ask amiss. He therefore helps us to pray according to God's desire and will for us.

However, in **Mathew 12:31** Jesus warned that sin against the Holy Spirit is the most grievous sin. He said: "Every sin and blasphemy will be forgiven but the blasphemy against the Spirit will not be forgiven". David knows and understands the power and workings of the Holy Spirit hence in **Psalm 51:11** he prays "do not take your Holy Spirit from me". This has set me thinking. Can the Holy Spirit withdraw from us? Can we become devoid of the Presence of the Holy Spirit? Can the Holy Spirit be taken from us? After King Saul's disobedience of God's instructions, the Bible tells us in **1Samuel 16:14** that the Spirit of the Lord departed from Saul. The manifestation of which is that he was being troubled by an evil spirit. David must have seen what happens when people are removed from the presence of the Holy Spirit. David understands that without the workings of the Holy Spirit people become dysfunctional. In fact, David was instrumental in restoring some equilibrium to Saul through his music whenever Saul was troubled.

Jesus promised that the Holy Spirit would take His place within us and will abide with us forever. The Holy Spirit will make us strong. Without the Holy Spirit the world is too strong for us. Remember the Holy Spirit did not come only once. He came more than once. Whenever you think you need the Holy Spirit to help in any of the numerous ways mentioned, just ask Him to come. Amen. And do not forget to always pray St Augustine's powerful and helpful Prayer.

Breathe on me Holy Spirit, that my thoughts may be Holy,
Act in me Holy Spirit, that my works may be Holy
Inspire my heart Holy Spirit that I may love only that which is Holy.
Strengthen us Holy Spirit that may defend all that is Holy
Guard me always Holy Spirit that I may remain Holy. Amen.

http://rediscover.archspm.org/prayer-2/st-augustine-holy-spirit-prayer/

Do not Quench nor Grieve the Holy Spirit: 1Thessalonians 5:19

According to the Church Calendar the celebration of Pentecost spans for a season. It is not just celebrated on One Sunday. As I was reflecting on the Pentecost Season, I was reminded of Paul warning **1Thessalonians 5:19** which says: “Do not quench the Spirit”. I have always wondered if the Spirit of God is quenchable. Can we humans extinguish such a phenomenal power? Apostle Paul thinks we can. On reflection, I also think we can and we do, but inadvertently. How do we quench the Holy Spirit of God? In today’s world, there is the erosion of the absolute dependence on the Spirit of God for guidance, for power and for intervention in some situations. The workings of the Holy Spirit are being replaced by human skills, abilities, capabilities and scientific knowledge. Not that these are awful. After all **Daniel 12:4** tells us that in the last days knowledge shall increase. It is the over dependence on human learnedness that may be the problem. It seems that we have returned to the era which in **Judges 21:25** is described as “when men did that which was right in their own eyes”. This is the era when the voice of the Holy Spirit is being silenced. It is the era when the Holy Spirit as base of spiritual authority is being abandoned. It is the era when every revealed truth is being replaced by rationalization, liberal reasoning and political correctness. It is the era when there is an intentional desire and moves to restrict the freedom of God’s presence in all our enterprises. It is also the era when there is a rigid separation of the secular from the spiritual with no meeting point for both.

The Holy Spirit can be quenched in many ways. One of the functions of the Holy Spirit is to reveal the truth. The Holy Spirit is quenched when we close our minds to the truth of God, as revealed by Him in His word. The Holy Spirit is quenched when all things sacred are being distorted, and the truth about God is being exchanged for a lie. The Holy Spirit is quenched when the creature rather than the Creator is worshipped and served (**Romans 1:25**). The Holy Spirit is quenched when the will of God made known and revealed through the prophetic Word of God and the prophets of God is being undermined. The sacred fire of the Spirit is quenched when we expressly refuse to walk in God's way and in God's path. We quench the Spirit when we do not speak the words that God lays upon our hearts. We quench the Spirit when we do not give Him the opportunity to use us to reach those around us, to touch, to heal, to deliver and to bless others through us. We quench the Spirit when we refuse to allow God to manifest Himself in ways of His own choosing. We quench the Holy Spirit when we live disconnected from God's power, and we do not heed that which we have been told and learnt. We quench the Spirit when we do not respond to His promptings both subtle and overt. We quench the Spirit of God whenever and wherever God's leading is stifled. The Spirit of God is quenched when we over assert ourselves and we do not allow Him to take pre-eminence in all that we do. The Spirit of God is quenched when He is not given full rein in our lives and we do not allow God's will to prevail. After all Jesus taught us to pray that the Lord's will be done in our lives.

Paul again in **Ephesians 4:30** warns "Do not grieve the Holy Spirit of God". Grieve means to cause pain, or to hurt. There are many things that we can do to hurt or cause pain. The Holy Spirit is grieved when we yield to worldly motives rather than godly motives. The Holy Spirit is grieved when we rigidly hold on to our own agenda instead of yielding to God's agenda and explicit direction. The Holy Spirit is grieved when we become self-indulgent, which the Bible describes as becoming the "lover of self". The Holy Spirit is grieved when we are controlled by prejudiced and vengeful spirit. The Spirit of God is grieved by procrastination. If we continue to put off till tomorrow the good that we can and ought to do today, the Holy Spirit is grieved. The Holy Spirit is grieved when we lay off temporarily or permanently the spiritual or scriptural directives for selfish reasons. In many issues in our interactions, the Holy Spirit is grieved when we make choices that can hurt or cause pain to another. The sum total is that the indwelling Holy Spirit is affected by our negative attitudes and behavior.

Quenching and grieving the Spirit is not a single act but a combination of events which when prolonged, could result in the permanent drowning of the Spirit's voice and the replacement with our own voice and our own passions. However, the scary part is that not only can we quench the workings of the Spirit in ourselves, we can also quench it in others and others too can also quench it in us. While people are required to be submissive to their leaders, manipulative and domineering leaders can quench the Spirit by imposing their will on those under them. Self-willed people can bully others into submission, asserting control and power over them and thus quenching the Spirit in them.

The Spirit of God is quenched in people when their potential and abilities to respond to the Spirit of God is limited and restrained by others. The Spirit of God is quenched when people are brainwashed into losing all sense of reasoning. Some individuals can quench the Spirit, in the lives of many others when they use their position and authority to ensure that their wills, patterns and choices always prevail. The Spirit of God can be quenched in people when they are manipulated by others to fear man rather than to fear God and when they are goaded to heed man's directive rather than God's thereby displeasing God.

The Spirit of God is freely given. It is available for all. It cannot be purchased like Simeon wanted to in the Bible. David's most significant prayer found in **Psalm 25:4** says "Lord show me your way, teach me your path". With all these in mind, Paul's alert messages need to be kept in view. Individuals need to make the decisions not be the one to pour **cold** water on the workings of the Holy Spirit. In all collective, those in position of power need to create an environment where the Spirit and power of God can thrive and be demonstrated not through emotionalism but in the true presence and manifestation of God's

Spirit. **2Corinthians 3:17** says where the Spirit of God is there is liberty. Supreme and conscious efforts need to be made to keep the Holy Spirit alive in us and in others. My personal response to all these is "Lord, help me to keep your Spirit alive within me and in others". Amen.

Spirit of God at Jesus Baptism: Acts 19: 1-2

Once I was reading about the Baptism of Jesus, in **Mathew 3:17**. Two things were manifestly present at Jesus baptism, Water and the "Spirit of God" descending like a dove on Him and a voice which said, "This is my beloved Son". In **Acts 19: 1-2** while Paul was in Corinth, Paul passed through the interior regions and came to Ephesus where he found some disciples. He asked them, "Did you receive the Holy Spirit when you became believers". They replied, "No we have not even heard that there is a Holy Spirit". They said that they have not even heard that there is a Holy Spirit.

Interesting, I thought. The sign of becoming a believer those days was when one is baptized, just like at Jesus Baptism water is present when it is splashed on the person being baptized or when the person is immersed in water. Also, the Spirit of God is present in the prayers that are said for the baptized. Jesus later confirmed this when in **Mathew 28:19** He said to baptize people "in the name of the Father and of the Son and of the Holy Spirit'. This has always been the practice of the Church. Most people are baptized "in the name of the Father, and of the Son and of the Holy Spirit", even those who choose to go along with Apostle Peter in **Acts 2:38** which says "Repent and be baptized, every one of you, in the name of Jesus Christ for the forgiveness of your sins. And you will receive the gift of the Holy Spirit". Either way there is mention of the Spirit of God.

I therefore find it very strange that after baptism these believers when asked by Paul if they have received the Holy Spirit, said that they did not even know that there was a Holy Spirit. Three things came to my mind. I thought maybe they were NOT well prepared by their religious leaders, their priests/pastors for baptism. Or maybe they were not mindful of the process of baptism. OR they definitely did not pay attention to the prayers being offered to them during baptism. Let me tell you, these believers at Ephesus are NOT the only ignorant ones in the Christian world. There are many people who do not understand the importance of Baptism in their lives and there are many priests/pastors who do not help them understand the significance and importance of baptism, and the role of the Spirit of God in the whole process. For most it is simply a ritual to follow to confirm that they have become Christians.

Jesus went through Baptism. He knew the importance of baptism. He knew the significance of the ritual. He succumbed to the ritual. He benefited from it. He did not act High and Mighty before John who was lower in spiritual rank to him. Jesus did not undermine Baptism, most of all His own. When John said that Jesus should not come to Him for baptism, Jesus told him to go ahead and do what he has been called upon to do.

For now, let me ask you, reading this reflection the same question that Paul asked the people of Ephesus. "Have you received the Holy Spirit?" **Acts 19:2.** This Paul's question is still very valid for all of us today. What is your answer to that question? I cannot answer it for you. Do you know for sure that you have received the Holy Spirit? Only you can answer that question. Or are you not sure that you have received the Holy Spirit? Or are you one of those who will say I do not even know that there is the Holy Spirit. Never Mind, Jesus is not a Task Master like some people. He is Love. He is a God of renewed opportunities. Jesus promised that the Holy Spirit, will be a personal presence within us. He says the Holy Spirit will fill us with the fullness of God, the fruit of the Spirit. He says The Holy Spirit will help us to live our lives victoriously and radiantly which will make men may see our good works and glorify our Father which is in heaven. It does not matter what your answer is to

Paul's question. Let us All of at this stage be reminded of the implication of the Presence of the Spirit of God at our baptism. May we continue to live in the reality of that presence. Amen.

Reflection on The Reign of Christ Sunday: Jesus the King: Revelation 19:16

In the Church calendar, the last Sunday in the month of November is usually designated The Reign of Christ Sunday. It marks the end of the Pentecost season and the beginning of the Advent season. It is also a day when we are reminded that Jesus Christ the Son of God who humbled himself by becoming human and dying on the cross is King of Kings and Lord of Lords for all eternity. Most Christians have always understood that Jesus has many offices, Saviour, Redeemer, Prophet, Priest, Intercessor etc. However, many do not often hear of Him and relate to Him as King, the One who rules, the lawgiver.

So, who reigns? Kings and queens as we all know. My Webster Dictionary describes a king as the male ruler of a nation usually with absolute power, the one who governs. There are four necessary things that a king has, (1) a territory, the land, the space to rule, however large or small. (2) Officials to help him rule and carry out his orders. (3) People or subjects living within the territory governed, who learn to do the king's will. (4) A system of laws, rules, and a basic structure of government. Jesus has all four. The bible in several places affirms Jesus as The King. Starting with when He was born and the three wise men who came to honor Him, called him the King of the Jews (**Mathew 2:2**). When Jesus was older, Nathaniel called Him the King of Israel (**John 1: 49**). Later Jesus was brought before Pilate, for trial because they said He called Himself a King (**John 18: 37**). Apostle Paul calls Jesus King, Eternal, Immortal, Invisible who alone is wise (**1Timothy 1:17).** Jesus is called the King of Kings the Lord of Lords in the Book of Revelation (**Revelation 19:16**). David says The Lord is King forever and ever in **Ps 10:16**.

Jesus several times talks of His kingdom, to affirm to the people that He is indeed a King and that He has a kingdom. When Jesus started to preach, He told the people to repent because the Kingdom of heaven is at hand (**Matthew 4: 17**). When Jesus disciples asked Him to teach them how to pray, He taught them the Lord's Prayer, which starts with Our Father and includes "thy Kingdom come." (**Mathew 6:10**). When Jesus has appointed His disciples, he sent them out to preach, that the Kingdom of heaven is at hand (**Mathew 10:7**). Jesus also talks about those who qualify to enter into the kingdom of heaven. He says unless we are converted and become like little children, we will by no means enter the kingdom of heaven (**Mathew 18:30**). He even adds that those who are poor in Spirit will inherit the Kingdom of heaven (**Mathew 5:3**). Jesus also indicated that His Kingdom is not of this world**. (John 18:36**). Meaning that the authority for His kingdom derives from heaven, where His Father reigns.

From All these we can deduce that Jesus is King and that Jesus has a kingdom. What does this have to do with you and me? What does that mean for us? How does this affect us? If we all agree that Jesus is King, and if we claim to be His followers, it means that we are His subjects and members of His Kingdom. **1Cor. 15:27** says that God has put all things under His feet. This means that Jesus has rulership over all things that God had created; all things are subjected to Him, all things, including you and me. If Jesus is the Sovereign ruler of all things, the implication is that those of us have agreed to follow Him have also accepted Him as the Ruler of our lives. It is the reason we call ourselves Christians. It is the reason we observe the rites, the rituals and practices of our faith, taking communion, praying, singing and even dancing as David danced in the Bible. It is the reason we go to the House of the Lord to fellowship with Him and with one another.

Rulers have responsibilities, so do followers. Jesus does what is required of Him as a King. Jesus governs. He rules in love and in fairness. Jesus protects and looks after His subjects. Jesus also provides. His provision is for all people, even those who do not accept Him as

King. But Jesus also said that we should seek first the kingdom of heaven and its righteousness and everything else, will be given unto us meaning that when we make it our task to observe the dynamics of that kingdom all things needed for our sustenance will be provided for us (**Mathew 6:33**). Above all Jesus rule is all-inclusive. He does not leave out anyone. After all His death on the Cross, is for the reconciliation of the entire humanity with the Father.

What are our responsibilities as subjects of Jesus the King and members of His kingdom? To start with, by accepting Christ as King we invite Him to take up residency in our hearts and in our lives. We ask Him to have dominion over every aspect of our being, our thoughts, our feelings, our actions, our emotions. We provide a space for Jesus to rule. I know this may be a tough pill to swallow for people living in a culture that specifies **freedom** to do whatever they please. Violation of their rights they might even call it How do we demonstrate our acceptance of His rulership over us?

The Kingdom of heaven is in churches opening their doors and serving community meals to numerous people that they do not even know. The Kingdom of heaven is taking time to write to women in prison and visiting them to share God's love. The Kingdom of heaven is in our homes where we carry out our day-to-day activities according to God's purpose. The Kingdom of heaven is in our workplace, in our neighborhood, in our communities where people express the love of God to one another, forgive one another, bear one another's burdens, work together to build just and peaceful communities. The Kingdom of heaven is wherever people are of humble heart, where people open up to their Creator and are responsive to His love to them. The Kingdom of heaven is when we allow God's loving rule to be in operation at all times. In short, the kingdom of heaven is in all that we do, in our work and in our play. May we always strive to be, true and faithful so we can truthfully say that we are children of the King

However, as we all know, there are many who still struggle with their faith. There are many who are yet to accept the sovereignty of Jesus to become part of His kingdom. There are many who do not even know Him. Jesus calls them the **sheep outside the fold**. In addition, of course there are many who have rejected Jesus and continue to reject Him. There are also many who oppose Him in many ways, in their attitudes, in their behavior, in the way they treat people, in their sense of morality, in labelling what is wrong as right, and in going after their own will. Many who deny the fact that Jesus is king, because they do not want Him to reign over them. Many reject His rulership because they do not want to obey His laws. They think of Jesus rulership in terms of oppressive political rulers who dominate and rule their people with iron hands. They forget that the rule and banner of Jesus over His subjects is Love, which He continually conveys to all.

At the beginning of each new season of Advent, let us all of us who have chosen to be followers of our Lord Jesus Christ make a renewed commitment to accept again, Jesus sovereign rule over our lives. Let us re-affirm Him as our Reigning King. Let us re-confirm our desire to live fully in His divine will. Let us re-dedicate ourselves to His Lordship. Above all, let us ask our Lord Jesus to give us the power, the ability to submit totally and absolutely to His dominion over us. Let us also remember our friends, family members, and many others who need to accept Jesus Christ as King. Let us ask Jesus to draw them to Himself and when He does, let us pray that they all respond to Him so that they may be counted among those who will reign with him in eternity, in His Father's Kingdom. Amen.

Reflection on Jesus the Light: John 8:12

In my Advent reflection my mind went to **John 1:4** where he describes Jesus as the Light of Men, and in verse 7 John the Baptist as the witness of Jesus as the Light. Light!!! A very powerful imagery! What do we know about light? Of course, there are two types of light, the physical light that we can all perceive and the spiritual light. When we are born into this world, we come into physical light. By it, we learn to appreciate God's handiwork in the things we see. Think of being awakened to the early morning while in flight. Think of a glorious sunrise or sunset that you have seen. Think of the significant **Aurora** called Northern and Southern Lights. Glorious image! Think of the sudden light in the darkness, a candle in a room to dispel the darkness. Think of the perpetual light in the Temple, at the Altar of God. The Advent is a Season of light. Think of the Christmas season and the pageantry of lights adorning all places.

We also recognize the functions of light. Physical light is necessary for physical life. Light promotes growth and life. The earth would certainly change very rapidly if there were no longer any sunlight. Plants always gravitate towards light. We know that if we want our plants to grow and flourish, they need light. Light helps us see things. Light guides us as we travel. Light warms and comforts. The Bible talks about Bright clouds, the Burning bush, and a Pillar of fire, all signs of God's presence. David in **Psalm 27:1** affirms God as Light: "The Lord is my Light and my Salvation." Light is beautiful. Light is mysterious.

John's reference to Jesus is about spiritual Light. He presented Jesus as the light that came to dispel the darkness of this world. Jesus came when there was political darkness when rulers were oppressive. There was also spiritual darkness, when people did whatever they liked, they worshipped the created things rather than the Creator, and they set up graven images in preference to the unseen Almighty God. Jesus came to reveal God to man. He came as the Light that illuminates, the Light that clarifies, the Light that reveals the truth, the Light that brightens, the Light that enlightens. Jesus would be the Light to deliver many from spiritual darkness. The world then became divided between those who responded to the Light and those who resisted. Those who did not believe in what the Light had to say remained in the darkness. Those who believed migrated to the Light. **1 Peter 2:9** says that those of us who believe are a chosen people, a royal priesthood, a holy nation, God's special possession, that we may declare the praises of him who called us, out of darkness into His marvelous light. In short, the Light forced a distinction and a dividing line between the believer and the unbeliever, between the saved and the unsaved.

To affirm John's reference of Him as the Light, Jesus in His own words in **John 8:12** says "I am the Light of the World." He did not say that He is Light only to the Jews neither did He claim to be the Light of only the Gentiles but of the whole world. This is a huge claim, a credible and an authentic claim. When Jesus made that claim, He was affirming what John said in **John 1:10** that the world was made through the Light, that we are in this world because of Him and through Him. In short, He is the exclusive source of spiritual light available to humanity. Jesus then adds to that claim by saying "Whoever follows me will never walk in darkness but have the light of life." That is where you and I come in. Jesus the true Light gives illumination to every human being coming into the world. Just as the Light shatters the confusion of the earth in the beginning, Jesus shatters the confusion in people's lives.

Those who believe in Jesus as the Light, those who recognize Him as the Light, and those who acknowledge and accept Him as the Light are placed in a separate category. Out of the seven billion people in this world, over three billion have accepted Jesus as the Light. That is an impressive number, the largest religious group in the world, a viable ecclesia to belong to, and a good point of reference. Those of us who are in this category have come to know Him and experience Him as the true Light in our lives. Through the living Christ within us, with us and through us we continue to experience the blessedness of the Light. Jesus the Light is our source, the beginning of our existence. We are comforted by the fact that we are wrought in the Light. Hence, we often think of Jesus as our Light. We are also witnesses of the Light in various ways. As children of the light, we are committed to the truth of God. We pray for the enlightenment of Christ as we continue to follow the Light. We revel in the Light. We embrace the Light. We enjoy the Light. We acknowledge the Light. We testify to the Light at every opportunity that we have. We call Jesus "Light from Light". Our greatest celebration, the Easter Vigil, opens by lighting a Paschal candle from new fire and acclaiming the Light of Christ. Traditionally, most churches never leave the altars without a fire burning in the form of candles or as a hanging light to indicate the Presence of God in His Temple. In fact, **Leviticus 6: 13** says that the fire must be kept burning on the altar continuously; it must not go out.

The Light has been shining in the world for the past 2000 years. When Jesus was born, there was an attempt to snuff out the Light, when all the baby boys were ordered to be killed by the reigning political power. The Light escaped that. Even after Jesus left this earth, there were several attempts again to put out the Light by the persecution and killing of His disciples. Nonetheless, the Light has continued to shine steadily until today. However, unfortunately the darkness that Jesus came to dispel still exists in some nooks and corners of the world. The reality in the world today is that there is still darkness of various dimensions and proportions, wars, political upheavals, violence, social injustice, poverty, aggression, all forms of discrimination and prejudice.

Isaiah 60:1 tells us to "Arise and shine for our Light has come." How do we rise and shine? True children of the Light must take the Light of God in them to the nooks and corners, to the highways and byways. We have received the Light. We are children of the Light. We are in the light. What do we do with the Light? In **Matthew 5:16** Jesus commands us to be productive lights. He says, "Let your light so shine before men, that they may see your good works, and glorify your Father which is in heaven." We are not required to hide our light under the bushel. We should see ourselves as witnesses for the Light, giving testimony after testimony to anybody who would listen. We must not allow our light to flicker. As God has loved us and called us in to His Light, we too must reach out to others sitting in the darkness and in the shadow of death. We must not count anybody out of the Light nor write them off. All are worthy. Above all, we must try to continue to live by the example of Jesus the True Light.

However, let us always remember that no matter how dark it may seem in some places, darkness cannot overcome the Light. In **Isaiah 60:19** God promised us that The LORD shall be our Light forever, so we must not be afraid or wary to venture out with our light. God wants to give us oil in our lamps so we can continue to glow in the darkness. In this Advent Season and beyond, let us ask Jesus the True Light to guide us, to nudge us at every opportunity that we may always be able, willing, and ready to present His Light to all around us in both big and small ways. Amen.

Reflection on Jesus Intercessory Prayer: John 17

In **John 17**, we see Jesus performing a very special function as an Intercessor, a Person of Prayer. **John 17** contains the most extensive and profound prayer of Jesus. I love this Prayer. I read it from time to time. Every time I read this prayer, I always come up with something that I missed before. I then decided to pen my thoughts about Jesus most significant prayer. Going through the prayer three significant things can be highlighted. Firstly, Jesus prayed to His Father. As is usual with Jesus this prayer starts with a direct call to God. The first word of the prayer is "Father", followed by Jesus many requests. Jesus' whole life has been centered on revealing to humanity who His Father is. At every point and in most situations, Jesus would refer to His relationship with His Father. Jesus would acknowledge God, His Father as the source of His being. Jesus derived His essence from God His Father and so He would always acknowledge His dependence on His Father. This was vital to Him as it has sustained Him throughout His sojourn on earth. Many times, Jesus would also teach about His Father.

When the apostles asked him to teach them to pray, Jesus taught them a Prayer that starts with "Our Father". When he raised Lazarus from the dead, He asked His Father to prove Himself for the sake of the people around so that they would know that His Father had sent Him. It is therefore not surprising that Jesus last discourse on earth would be a prayer, a deep communication with His Father, and a befitting farewell to the world that would draw a final attention to His Father. In this prayer Jesus affirmed His Father to be the Only True God. He prayed that the people may know God as such, and also know Him, Jesus as His Son whom He has sent. In this final treatise, Jesus also talked about the Glory of God of which He was a partaker. He asked His Father to glorify Him, His Son. Just as He the Son would glorify His Father. Jesus established a mutuality in that relationship. Jesus also talked about the glory which He had with God before the world was made.

Like a Good and Faithful Son, Jesus now told His Father that He has finished the work on earth that His Father had given Him to do. Jesus drew attention to His obedience to God, His Father. He also affirms His subordination in this Father/Son relationship; the Father who gives the work to do and the Son who does the work. The question then is, why would Jesus go to this great extent towards the end of His life to focus elaborately on His relationship with His Father. I believe that Jesus wanted to openly acknowledge one more time the Supremacy of God the Father.

Most times, prayers are private and secret communication between God and us. But this time Jesus said His prayers openly loud and clear for all to hear. **John 17:1** says that Jesus "lifted up His eyes to heaven", and in an overt gesture, in an open affirmation and reference to God His Father, Jesus said "The hour has come". For Jesus it was imperative that His disciples do not forget about God the Father, whom He had been talking and teaching a lot about. It was important that they forever remember what His Father meant to Him, and what His Father would mean to all who would come to the Father through Him. Remember His primary mission on earth was to reconcile humanity with His Father, to close the gulf that had been created by the disobedience of Adam and Eve. Jesus offered Himself to be the sacrificial Lamb to effect this reconciliation, through His Death, His Resurrection and His Ascension which essentially is about Jesus returning to His Father after completing the task that He came for.

Jesus then prayed for His disciples. After talking a lot about Himself and His Father, Jesus in verse 6 swung focus to the men that God His Father had given Him. Jesus said "I have manifested Your name to the Men whom you have given me out of the world. They were yours, You gave them to me and they have kept your Word". What a significant thing to say about His men. Who were Jesus men? His Disciples, of course. In this segment of the prayer Jesus acknowledges that He could not have done the work of His Father all by Himself. So, He chose some men to be part of the job, part of the agenda, and part of the program. Of course, Jesus could have chosen to ignore this fact in this Intercessory Prayer. But Jesus always doing the right thing and setting Himself up as a model for all of us, acknowledged His men and their contribution to His enterprise. A lesson for us. Many times, we forget people who have helped us along the way and act as if it has all been our effort. Jesus remembered His men and brought them in prayer before His Father.

As we know in this our world, people always ascribe ultimate power to themselves, especially in their position of authority. They see themselves as the beginning and the end of it all. Jesus was humble enough to acknowledge the role that His men had played in His Mission. Of course, He would soon be returning to His father. Who would He leave behind to continue the work that He started? His men. Many men of power in this world do not think of succession. Jesus knew that there is a continuing aspect of the job that He had come to do for His Father. Phase one was completed. Phase two was imminent. If His men were to continue with the work that he is leaving them to do, they need the empowerment of His Father that He had benefitted from and had sustained Him. He prayed for them. Jesus brought them to throne of His Father. That is what intercessors do. They pray for others.

But before Jesus prayed for them, He knew that He had to affirm them before His Father. Jesus knew that He had to tell His Father that His men were worthy of the responsibility that He was leaving them with, that His men could be depended and counted upon to continue the work He had chosen them for. Jesus citation for His men is in verse 8: "I have given to them the words which you have given me. They have received them and they have come to know surely that I came from you and they have believed that you sent me." Wow!!!!!!, What a recommendation!! A great summary of what His men represents. This is Jesus Himself writing a befitting citation of His men to justify the requests He was going to make of His Father for them. Jesus said that they have received the teaching that He gave them. They have allowed the teaching to settle in them. They have not only acknowledged the teaching that He gave them; they have acknowledged Him Jesus as God's Messenger. How significant!!!

Of course, as humans we always suspect and reject people when we are not sure on whose behalf they are speaking. But to Jesus delight, His men never doubted Him; they left all to follow Him. They unconditionally accepted Him as the Messenger of God. They emphatically embraced and accepted His message, about Himself, and His Father who had sent Him. Jesus was not making a glib claim on behalf of His men. He knew them. He taught them. He had spent time with them, watched and studied them carefully. It was from this intentional focus that He was able to make that Expert Report and Affirmation to God His Father about His men.

How many of us called to do God's work will get that type of recommendation from the One we are supposed to be working for? In the world today, we know that many who claimed to have been called have rejected the Messenger. Many called have made a turn around saying "I do not believe in this, I do not believe in that". Some have even questioned the Bible as the inherent word of God. Some would rather dilute the message of the Messenger to be politically correct. I am not sure that Jesus Men knew that their Master was watching them that closely, that He would be writing a report, making a recommendation on their behalf at the end of His sojourn on earth. I think it is important that in whatever we have been called upon to do for Jesus and His Father, to know that Jesus is watching. Hind sight is 20/20. Now that we know Jesus would be writing a report on all of us to His father, I think it is needful to be mindful. Unto whom much is given much more is expected. So we better be doing some self-evaluation and self-introspection as we continue in this journey before The Master sends out His report on us to His Father.

In our secular jobs we all worry about promotion, so we make efforts. But in God's work we usually take things for granted. I think if there is anything to learn from Jesus Prayer about His men, it is that there is an Evaluation at the end of a period. Jesus is watching and taking note. Jesus men earned an Honorable Mention, and so Jesus asked God His Father to do some things on their behalf. In Verse 11 Jesus asked God His Father to keep them, to protect them, and keep them alive. In verse 15 Jesus expanded His prayer to "Keep them from evil". Wow!!! Evil abound, evil strikes at unexpected times and places, Jesus prayed that His men may be safe and secure from all aggressions. Then in verse 17 Jesus asked God to "Sanctify His men by His truth". This is a powerful request from Jesus for His faithful men. Talk of reward for a job well done, a prayer from the Master Intercessor Himself. Jesus' affirmation of His men should be tremendously encouraging to all of us the present-day disciples.

Jesus then prayed for All Believers. In **verse 20-21** Jesus now expanded His prayer to all believers, you and me. He said, "I do not pray for these my men alone, but also for those who will believe in Me through their word". Amazing!!!!! Jesus looks down centuries later saw all the people who will come to believe in Him through the work that His men will do. Today, over three billion people are Christians, Believers in Jesus. You and I are part of the 3 billion who have come to accept Christ as our Saviour. Jesus knew that from His Twelve men, billions would hear about Him and will continue to give their hearts to Him. So, Jesus has already embraced us. He has already accepted us. He already prayed for us. Amen.

In verse 23 Jesus then added the most significant prayer that continues to resonate well with people and continues to give Hope. Jesus then said, "that they will know that I have loved them as you have loved ME". When you hear over and over again that Jesus loves you, this is where it comes from. Jesus loves us. Paul in **Ephesians 3:19** prays that we may experience *th*e "Love of Christ", though it is too great to understand fully. What is this Love of Christ that we need to know, believe, understand and experience? "Love of Christ" refers to Jesus love for humanity which was shown through His death upon the cross. **Corinthians 5:14-15** tells how the love of Christ changes our lives, when we come to believe it. His love in us allows us to see ourselves in new perspectives, no matter who we are, and no matter where we are coming from. The Love of Christ in us also helps us to show love to others, impacting people with it everywhere we go.

Jesus then prays that all of us may be ONE. He asked God to keep us together, that there may not be division among us, that we may be as ONE just as He and His Father are One. Jesus is talking of internal cohesion, that we will be in unity, that we will all be working together in unison, and that we will all be made PERFECT in that Oneness with God, Oneness with Jesus and His Father, and Oneness in our relationship with one another in God. The love the Father has for Jesus is the same love Jesus has for us believers, indeed for the whole world. It is in this love that we become living proof of God's gracious character. It is also in this love that we invite people to join and share in this union with God and His Son Jesus.

What can we learn from Jesus Intercessory Prayer? The Presence of Jesus dwells permanently in those who have accepted Him as their Savior. He will not leave us alone neither forsake us but will be in us forever. Jesus wants Unity for all His followers, for all Christians: that we may all be One. Unity!! Not that we may think and act or dress alike, but that we have Unity in Purpose, the mark of the Christian community. Every request which our Lord made on our behalf requires a personal input from all of us. We must be mindful of our own responsibilities in Jesus prayers. Jesus prayer is constant submission to His Father. Our own prayer too must be consistent submission to Jesus Father and Our Father. May we constantly be reminded of the Presence and revelation of Jesus Father in us. May we merit the love, the confidence that Jesus has in us as He continues to be our Intercessor before His Father. Amen.

Knowing God the Father through Jesus: Mathew 6:9

Jesus in His Intercessory Prayer emphasized His relationship with His Father. When His apostles asked him to teach them how to pray, Jesus shared His Father with them and ultimately with us. In **Mathew 6: 9-13** Jesus gave the world a prayer that has become known as the Lord's prayer. Before this Prayer Jesus has been talking about many things that we know as the Sermon on the Mount. Then suddenly He started talking about "Your father". He used the expression "Your Father" eight times to His listeners including His disciples. Then in verses 9-13, He enacted the Prayer. He told them that when they want to pray, they should call on God, their Father, and pray thus, "Our Father in heaven Hallowed be thy name. Note His collective use of the term. "Our Father". Jesus is saying that not only is God His Father, He is also the Father of all who choose to come to him and ultimately His father.

When Jesus gave the world that prayer, He established us all in a relationship with God the Father. Jesus wants everyone to have a relationship with His Father. He wants everyone to appropriate God as their Father. He also wants everyone to tap into the resources of God the father, by praying to God as the Provider of their needs. Jesus repeated use of Father also sensitizes everyone to the fact that there is a Father above all Fathers and He is God the Creator, the Supreme Deity. He presented God to us as Our Father and presented us to God as His children. He shows us how to pray to Him. But there is just ONE condition to fulfill the step into that position. God is the Creator of all the 7 billion people of the world today. All are creatures of God. Satan has no creative powers, so no one is created by Satan, even those who have submitted to him. But it seems the Fatherhood of God is reserved for those who have a personal relationship with Him through His Son Jesus Christ. God is not what we will call a Universal Father. (He is not the Father of all). To claim God as Father, **John 1:12** says we must receive Jesus. It is then and only then that we have the right to become the Children of God.

Galatians 3:26 says we are sons of God through faith in Christ Jesus. **Galatians 4: 6** says because we are sons and daughters, God sends the Spirit of His Son into our hearts, the Spirit that makes us call out ABBA Father. In **2 Corinthians 6:18,** God said that He will be a Father to us and we shall be His children. The overall purpose of Jesus on earth was to restore and reconcile humanity to the Father. At the end of His ministry Jesus said in **John 20: 17** I am returning to My Father and Your Father. Even till the last moment Jesus still let the people know that His Father could also be their Father. An interesting aspect of this Fatherhood is that the religion of Islam in the **Qur'an 23:91** vehemently says that God has no children, "Never has God begotten a son", therefore Jesus is not the son of God but the Prophet of God. Anyway, some Christians deny the virgin birth of Jesus and so deny God as Jesus Father. That is why I say that God is not a Universal Father.

Who is a Father? To understand God as "Father" we need to draw some parallels with our human understanding and perception of father. The title "Father" tells us not only what some aspect of God's character but also what God does as a Father. A father produces and procreates. The biblical assumption is that people come from the "loins of the man". If God has created all of us, forming the man from clay and the woman from his ribs, then we have all come from "His loins". If God is procreatively responsible for us and we have all emanated from Him, He is our source. He is our origin. He is our Creator. He is our Father. We are His children. We belong to Him. He belongs to us. That is why we can call Him ABBA Father as **Romans 8:15** tells us.

A father is one who loves. **John 3:16** tells us that God so loved the world that He gave his only beloved Son Jesus, to the whole world, the ultimate demonstration of God's love. Earthly fathers love, but God loves more. Our earthly father's love pales in comparison to the love of our heavenly Father. God loves us so much that even when we are yet sinners, in His love, He brought us out of darkness into His marvelous light. A father provides. He supplies the basic needs of his children, food, shelter, clothing for survival. God provides for us. He allows the sun and moon to shine on all. The Bible describes God as **Jehovah Jireh** the one who provides. Remember God's provision of manna and quail to the children of Israelite for forty years. The Bible says that we receive daily of his benefits. God is a God of abundance who shares His riches with His children. A father protects. A father ensures that no harm comes to his children. As father, God protects us from all ills. He shields us under His banner. David in **Psalm 27:10** says though my father and my mother forsake me the Lord will take care of me. **Isaiah 49:16** tells us that we are all engraved us on the palms of His hands. This means that we are constantly the object of His focus. We are not lost in the crowd. We are not insignificant.

Father/child (both sons and daughters) relationship is bidirectional as we say. We have looked at God's responsibilities as Father, what are the responsibilities of the children in that relationship. Firstly, knowing God as our Father and relating to Him as Father affects the way we live. This relationship shapes our morals, affects our attitude, our heart, and our responses to Him. It affects the way we make decisions. It moves us into a warm and rich relationship which is the basis of our worship, our praises and our adoration of Him. It is in all these that we surrender in total abandon to Him Our Father. It also affects our response to pain and hardship. Do we perpetually worry? Or do we derive strength in Him? Do we stay courageous even when we are outnumbered? Above all do we walk in the hope that it is well with us because we are God's children?

Scientifically children inherit some genes from their fathers that is why many children have some traits, abilities and skills which have come from their fathers. If God created us in His image, this means that we are genetically connected to God. This means we have some of his DNA. If we say that God is our Father, in what ways can we say we are like Him? Do we love like he loves? Do we care like He cares? Do we give like he gives? Do we forgive like he forgives? Yeah! I know some of us will say we can never be like God. But the Bible tells us that the purpose of our journey is to be like His Son Jesus and ultimately be like him. What efforts are we all making in this area? As collective children of God we need to help each other in all ways so that we can all continue each day to grow to be more like HIM. Amen.

Jesus says "He who has Ears to Hear let him Hear": Mathew 13: 9

In **Mathew 13** Jesus told Seven parables about Sowers, about Seeds, about Soils, about Weeds, about Treasures, about Reapers, and about Kingdom of heaven. These are well-known stories that have been told at Sunday school level and have been preached from time immemorial with various interpretations by different preachers. Hence the contents of the parables are not the focus of my reflection. My focus is on what Jesus said after the parables. I advise you to read the stories which are quite interesting and illuminative.

Mathew 13:1 tells us that Jesus went out of the house and sat by the sea. Jesus saw a massive crowd that have come to him. Knowing why they have come, of course to hear from Him. Jesus saw the need to effectively position Himself so that He is accessible to the people He would eventually be talking to, His hearers. For everyone to hear Him, verse 2 says Jesus stepped into the boat and sat down. The boat became a sort of pulpit from where the multitude would have full access to Him. The massive crowd stood on the shore facing Jesus. They were ready to absorb all that Jesus has to say. Jesus knowing that they are ready with receptive hearts, verse 3 tells us that He began to speak. As an Instructor I will tell you that this is a very important dynamics in Classroom Engagement. Jesus was ready. The multitude was ready. With the communication rules and dynamics of engagement in place Jesus began to speak.

Communication dynamics is bidirectional. It contains the Speaker and the Hearer. The Speaker is the One who has something to say and the Hearer is the one who needs to hear and understand what is being said. In the process the Speaker can be verbal, using words, numbers, signs, images, video. The Speaker can also employ non-verbal symbols like body language, hand gestures, facial expressions to convey what he/she has to say. The Speaker uses the symbols that he/she believes will be most helpful for the Hearer to understand what is being conveyed. It is therefore very important that the Speaker's message is well framed to ensure comprehension on the part of the Hearer. In receiving the message, it is also important that the Hearer is able to understand and interpret the message. The Hearer's job is to try to give meanings to the symbols being presented by interpreting the message as a whole. Effective communication is therefore achieved only when the message is received and understood in the way it is intended. Otherwise there will be misunderstanding when there is no synchrony between what is being conveyed and what is being received. There will also be distortions when the Hearer's understanding of a message is a different from what the Speaker is trying to convey.

Jesus did not attend School of Communication, nor did He do relevant courses in Communication Studies. But He understood Communication Dynamics. In His own case Jesus has a unique way of communication. He uses Parables which are stories and powerful symbols to illustrate concepts to His hearers. Jesus used hundreds of parables in His ministry. Verse 34 says "Jesus spoke to the multitude in parables and without a parable He did not speak to them". However twice in this chapter in Verses 9 and 43 Jesus made a significant statement "He who has Ears to Hear let him Hear". In my NKJV Jesus used the word "Hear". 95% of all the Bibles translation in the world also used "Hear". Only, one or two used "Listen". In communication dynamics, Hearing and Listening are not the same thing, although they are at times used interchangeably. Hearing is an act that involves merely absorbing of what is being heard. While in listening one is required to pay attention, reflect, contemplate, interpret, concentrate, translate, make meaning, understand and at times to respond and remember what is being said. Jesus injunction is to "Hear".

As was His practice, after each parable Jesus would give the interpretation of the parable, thereby explaining the meaning to His hearers. At a point His disciples asked why He does that. Jesus knew that the act of understanding is hard and tedious for all us. In verses 13, Jesus explains, "seeing they do not see and hearing they do not hear, nor do they understand". However, throughout the chapter Jesus explained ALL His parables to the people. After having fulfilled his part as a Marvelous Teacher, Jesus in verse 51 asked them "Have you understood all these things"? The people replied, "Yes Lord".

In this passage, Jesus did not request that people *listen* He just wants them to *hear*. As was His practice Jesus gave the interpretation of the parable to His listeners. He told them what the parable meant. Of course, Jesus did this all the time. He would tell a parable and He would go on to explain the meaning of that parable. Jesus knew that the act of listening and interpreting is hard and tedious for all us. It was one of the reasons why the Bible says of Jesus that when He speaks, the people marvel. Jesus was a Good Teacher.

At Jesus transfiguration, God told Jesus disciples to "hear" Jesus. "This is my Beloved Son, **hear** Him". God the Father in His love for His Son wants us to hear what Jesus has to tell us. The Father speaks through His Son. Jesus always has a lot to say about many things: about His Father, about Himself, about the Holy Spirit, about love, about life, about death, about our neighbor, and about our behavior and so on. As a follow up, Jesus expressed His desire for all of us to "hear" what he has to say at any given time. In return, Jesus also wants all people to hear what he has to say. Many of us do wonder if Jesus still speak now that He has returned to His Father, the Creator. How can we hear, when we do not even know whether He speaks, or not? The answer of course is "Yes". Jesus still speaks. Jesus has always spoken. He has been speaking from the beginning of time. Jesus spoke to His disciples and followers. Jesus is still speaking to His people, to all of us through the Holy Spirit. Jesus will continue to speak till the end of time.

Now that we know that Jesus speaks, how does He speak to us today? (a) Of course, Jesus speaks through God's Word. **2 Timothy 3:16** tells us that All Scripture, is God's word given by the inspiration of God. It is profitable for doctrine, for reproof, for correction, for instruction in righteousness that we may be complete, thoroughly equipped for every good work. God's Word sometimes gives us a warning, a word of encouragement, or a lesson for life. That means God at times "whispers", and at times "shouts", His Word, giving us instructions and principles for life. (b) Jesus also speaks through other Believers. He may use a friend, a teacher, a parent, or a preacher to convey His message of truth to us. Their words may come as a warning, a blessing, or as a prophetic truth about our lives. Whether we choose to hear it or ignore it depends on us. (c) Jesus speaks through God's Spirit which is "God's still, small voice". God's Spirit is in everyone because He has created everyone. However, as Christians when we accept Jesus as God's Son, Jesus speaks to us through the Spirit of God. When we are tempted, that same Spirit warns and nudges us to do the right thing. We are supposed to depend on God's Spirit to give us direction. In fact, the Bible tells us that we will hear a voice from behind us telling us which direction to go. (**Isaiah 30: 21**). (d). Jesus also speaks to us through Prayer. We may not know how to pray, but **Romans 8:26-27** tells us that God's Spirit makes intercession for us. We may not hear God's literal voice, but His Spirit confirms a certain direction or answer for us.

Do we hear Jesus speak? Jesus says in **John 10:27**, "My sheep hear my voice, and I know them, and they follow me". **Psalm 100: 3** tells us

"Know that the LORD He is God. It is He who made us, and not we ourselves; and we are His people, the sheep of His pasture." **Psalm 95: 7** also affirms this statement. It says, "For He is our God and we are the people of his pasture, the flock under his care." The verse now adds "Today, if only you would **Hea**r his voice". The Sheep know who Jesus their Shepherd is. They belong to Him, and they recognize Him by the sound of His voice. Hearing Jesus is the first level of our discipleship, of our followership. The second level is getting an interpretation of what is being said. The final level is understanding what is being conveyed. How can we follow Jesus if we do not hear what He has to say to us? How do we situate, locate or position ourselves to hear what Jesus Our Master, our Friend, our Lord and our Saviour has to say to us at any given time? The truth is Jesus is no more sitting in the boat while we stay on the shore to hear Him. In fact, verse 53 tells us "When Jesus has finished these parables He departed from there". Jesus has left the boat. When Jesus was leaving the earth, He promised that He would to send Someone to teach us, Someone to explain things to us, Someone to interpret things to us. And He did. He sent the Holy Spirit at Pentecost.

In addition to the Holy Spirit, Jesus gave the Church the five-fold ministry. Jesus speaks to His Church through those He has called to those positions. **Ephesians 4:11**, says "And He Himself gave some to be (1) Apostles, (2) some to be Prophets, (3) some to be Evangelists, (4) some to be Pastors/Priests and (5) some to be Teachers. Not only does He call people to those positions He empowers them. He gives them His Word and the tongue of a ready writer to pass on His Word to others. Above all He uses them to shepherd His Sheep.

Finally, when Jesus said, "He who has Ears to Hear let him Hear", it is not enough for us to have two ears sticking out on the sides of our head. Everybody has those. Jesus is referring to another kind of ear that He wants all of us to have: the "spiritual" ear that recognizes that God's Word is crucial, compelling and transforming. He wants us to have the "spiritual" ear that will hear and distinguish Jesus voice amidst the cacophony and innumerable voices of the world. Are we always positioned to hear what Jesus has to say to us at all times? Are we genuinely hungry enough to always want to hear from Jesus? Are we always ready to hear what Jesus has to say about anything and everything? Do we understand what Jesus has to say to us each time He speaks?

I am leaving all of us with these questions I cannot answer all these questions for you. Neither can you answer them for me. But they are significant questions that we all need to ponder upon. Every individual knows where she or he is in terms of **hearing** Jesus. The most important thing is to always have a conversation with Jesus about our desire to "hear" Him, to "listen" to Him and to "understand" Him. The good thing is that Jesus hears us whenever we talk to Him. His ear is not deaf that He cannot hear us. **(Isaiah 59:1)**. I believe that our response should be the desire for that sensitivity and connectedness so that as the collective Sheep of Jesus we may always "hear" the voice of our Good Shepherd. May Jesus confirm in us the desire to "hear", the choice to "listen" and the ability to "understand" what He is saying to us at all times. Amen.

Jesus In and Out of Boats: Peter Walking on Water: Mathew 14:22

I was reading some Bible passages when it occurred to me that the Bible contains many verses and places describing Jesus in and out of BOATS. I decided to explore "Jesus and Boats". Jesus started His ministry when He saw two brothers, James and John in the Boat with Zebedee their father, mending their nets. Jesus called them to come follow Him. They immediately left their father Zebedee in the Boat with the hired servants and went away to follow Jesus. From then on Jesus and Boats became a constant picture. Jesus preached from Boats. After preaching to the people, the Bible says "He stepped out of the Boat".

Jesus spent time a lot of times with His disciples in the Boat. He was always comfortable in the Boat. Some of His miracles are linked to Boats. There was a time when Jesus was in the Boat with His disciples and there was a severe storm, but Jesus was sleeping and his disciples were really scared. They woke Him up and He commanded the storm to stop. His disciples wondered what type of man He is that even the sea would obey Him. Jesus disciples had seen Him work miracles and watched Him do many acts of healing around the sea and Boats. We also read that Jesus after being told about the death of John the Baptist, departed from where He was by Boat to a deserted place to be by Himself. **Mathew 14** however has a focus on Peter one of the disciples stepping out of the BOAT to walk on water with Jesus. After feeding the five thousand Jesus made His disciples get into a Boat to go before Him to the other side. He sent them away in a Boat hoping to join them later. Jesus stayed behind. He then went up to pray on a mountain by Himself and He was there till evening. As Jesus was finishing His prayers there was a severe storm. Jesus saw that the Boat the disciples were in was in distress, so Jesus decided to go out to rescue them. Instead of taking another Boat to sea Jesus decided to **walk** on water to the Boat in distress. Wow!!!! what a remarkable sight that would have been. When the disciples saw Him, they were stricken to the point that they thought He was a ghost. Jesus assured them that it was He and not a ghost.

Peter the bold one said if it was really Jesus, He should invite him Peter to come and join Him. Jesus immediately invited Peter, with a simple "Come". Peter responded. He then stepped out of the Boat without thinking, into the water and walked on water for a few seconds before he realized what he was doing. The wind became boisterous; Peter became afraid and shouted, "Lord Save Me". Jesus caught his hand and they both went into the Boat. After that the severe wind ceased. Let it be noted that Peter was NOT the only disciple in the boat. Why was Peter the only one who asked Jesus to invite Him to come to Him? Why was Peter the only one who actually stepped out of the Boat to go and meet Jesus? Peter was different. Peter is the most vocal, the one who asks questions of Jesus, the one who would always reject the idea that

Jesus would one day leave them. Peter had a different perspective of the whole incident of Jesus walking on water. It took only one word from Jesus for Peter to jump overboard from that Boat. There was something about Peter that made him so courageous as to jump out of the Boat to respond to Jesus invitation? Peter was just an ordinary man, who did an extra ordinary thing by taking a leap of faith. Peter is the only one in the Bible who achieved that feat apart from Jesus. It's a remarkable story. I am sure the experience stayed with Peter for the rest of his life. Peter knew the glory of walking on the water.

But what gave Peter that courage? I think it is Peter's knowledge of Jesus. Peter had been with Jesus from the beginning, so he knew Jesus from deep within Him. In his relationship and interaction with Jesus, Peter has learned some significant things about Jesus. When He once told Jesus that He was the "Son of God" Jesus told Him that flesh and blood did not reveal that to Him. Peter's action on this occasion demonstrated that he was totally a believer in Jesus. This single act of Peter made him stand out among all the disciples. I have always wondered about the remaining disciples in the boat. Why was there no significant reaction from them as regards Jesus invitation to step out of the Boat and come to Jesus? They were watching all that was happening with curious interest. They behaved like spectators of a show. They were equally Jesus disciples. They knew Jesus. They too must have learnt something from their interaction with Him. Why were they indifferent to Jesus invitation? Why did they not jump into the sea like Peter? What type of faith did the other disciples in the boat have? What strength of character did they demonstrate by refusing Jesus invitation to come and meet Him on the water? We would never know.

The other disciples missed the opportunity of a unique experience by not being adventurous like Peter. They stayed put. They became lethargic. They never got out of the Boat. What could be going on in their minds? What were they thinking? They were probably thinking "This Peter again" some of them might think he was deluded to want to walk on water like Jesus. Peter did not think twice. He **just did**

it while the other disciples were busy rationalizing. At times people get motivated when they see somebody do something that they have thought was impossible. Peter's instant reaction to Jesus invitation should have spurred them into action. But it did NOT. I have always wondered why!!!!!!. John Ortberg in 2011 wrote a book titled "If You Want to Walk on Water, You Have to Get out Of the Boat".

https://www.amazon.ca/Want-Walk-Water-Youve-Boat/dp/0310340462

The book became very popular because the tittle of the book is a fundamental truth. For me, my interpretation is If you want changes in your life you have to do something different. If you want to experience the power of God in your life, you've got to take a step of faith. However, there are always some factors that can prevent people from taking steps of Faith like Peter did? Factors that would make them get stuck in one spot like the rest of the disciples?

One of the factors I believe could be **Fear.** Fear of the unknown. Fear of what is happening around. Some people live in perpetual fear of everything. Remember there was a storm and it was dark. But Peter did not flinch. Peter chose to respond to Jesus. Peter did not focus on the circumstances around Him. His focus was on the One who invited Him. Fear paralyses. Fear prevents us from fully trusting God and therefore experiencing what God has in store for us. The Bible in many places tells us that Fear is not of God. **2 Timothy 1:7** says For *God* has not given us the spirit of fear; but of power, and of love, and of a sound mind. **Isaiah 41:10** says Fear not; for I am with you. **Psalm 27:1** says "The Lord is my light and my salvation; whom shall I fear? The Lord is the strength of my life; of whom shall I be afraid?" Fear is not justified.

Another factor could be our **Boat** which may be our comfort zones. We get stuck in one corner and we never dare to step out. At times many people feel so safe and comfortable in their Boat and may NOT want to get out of it. Our Boat may be our house, our car, our job, our money, our position at work, our relationship, a bad habit or addiction, our tradition, our friends, our family, or anything that make us feel comfortable. Anytime we refuse to step out of our boat to do something that Jesus is calling us in faith to do, we are missing some other blessings that the Lord has in store for us. We can only respond if we clearly hear the simple Invitation from the Lord like it was said to Peter. The other disciples probably did not even hear the invitation. They were too comfortable in the Boat to pay any attention to Jesus invitation. When we learn to discern the calling of God in our lives and respond with a resounding YES and get out of the Boat, we really do experience God's power in our lives. When people decide to get out of the Boat, they are **never** quite the same.

Many of us will have a million reasons for wanting to continue to stay in the Boat. Reasons like: "I have many other things to do". "I will come out of the Boat when my life is better". "I will leave the Boat when it is no more dark, when the storm is over". It was dark in the night and the storm was still raging, yet Peter still got out of the Boat. Most people would not have the guts to step out of the Boat in that weather, even in the face of Jesus beckoning to them.

Jesus has performed extraordinary things while in the Boat. He has calmed the storm when He was in the Boat. However, this time, Jesus was giving opportunity for His disciples to do the extraordinary. Jesus was Outside of the Boat. I am sure Jesus stepped out of the Boat not to be dramatic but to prove to them that His powers are not limited to locations and situations. Since this incident Jesus has been sending out invitations to people to step out of the Boat to come walk on water with Him. Some have responded. Walking on water may not be doing big things. It could just be doing little things for Jesus like: feeding the poor, visiting the shut-in, being there for somebody else, and being a son or daughter of encouragement like Barnabas, offering a word of comfort to someone in distress, saying a prayer or two for someone in the shadow of death. It could be one of a million things.

Today Jesus is still looking for people who will get out of the Boat. I don't know what this means for you. When we have the faith to get out of the Boat, some things do change. Remember, Jesus was not IN the Boat. Jesus was OUT of the Boat. But Peter was IN the Boat. Peter then stepped OUT of the Boat. It was OUTSIDE of the Boat that Peter experienced the saving grace of Jesus. Peter was rescued from sinking. Sometimes to receive the blessings that God has for us, we must be ready to step OUT of our Boats because our blessings may be OUT in the water and not IN the boat. Jesus is inviting you reading this Reflection to step OUT of the Boat and walk on water with Him. Will you have the same boldness that Peter had? This is the time to ask Jesus for the courage to respond to His invitation. It is also the time to ask for help to be more obedient to Jesus, to always step OUT of our Boats as often as Jesus requires it of us. Amen.

Holy Cross Day: Significance of the Cross. Why I wear A Cross

The Church annually celebrates the Holy Cross Day to remind us about the significance of the Cross. The Cross is a symbol of Death. In the time of the Roman Empire the government used hanging on the cross as a form of punishment for crimes. When people committed crimes, they were hung on the cross till they die. Of course, we all know about the death of Jesus on the Cross. When Jesus was accused of crimes that He did not commit, He was sentenced to death by hanging on the Cross. Jesus was hung on the cross with two thieves also on the cross It was after the death and resurrection of Jesus on the Cross that the Church adopted the Cross as symbol for Christianity. The Cross a Symbol of Shame was turned into a Symbol of Triumph. The Cross which was a symbol of Death became a Symbol of Life, through Jesus victory over death is. The Cross is also the means by which Jesus act of love was accomplished. The Cross tells us about the Love of God for humanity. The Cross is a symbol of Salvation, through which we are saved and have access to eternal life. The Cross is also a symbol of Hope, the hope that we have in Christ. The hope of a future of eternal life.

Why do people wear a Cross or carry a Cross in their pockets? The practice of wearing crosses around the neck dates from the Early Church. The precise reason why Christians began wearing crosses has to do with martyrdom, specifically beheading. In the early centuries of the church, when many Christians were put to death as a result of confessing belief in Christ. The wearing of the cross about the neck was an open confession of the persons faith and his/her commitment to Christ even in the face of death. Many denominations hang the Cross at the altar to remind people of the presence of Jesus in the place of worship. The Catholic church uses the Crucifix that is the Cross with Jesus on it. Some denominations do not believe in using, displaying or wearing the Cross. My Anglican denomination opts for the Cross without Jesus on it. We have the cross in all our places of worship. Some countries do not allow an open display of the cross. Some offices and institutions do not allow people to wear the cross at work. There are many views about the cross out there.

In England, The Daily Telegraph of October 19 2006 The Archbishop of York, Dr John Sentamu, defended the wearing of crosses by Christians when British Airways said that staff should not wear crosses to work. He said: "The cross is a symbol used by Christians to remind us of hope. It is the hope of light overcoming darkness, victory over death and good triumphing over evil." He added: "For those of us who wear a cross, there is not only hope but also a responsibility. The responsibility that goes with claiming the name of a Christian. The responsibility to act and to live as Christians.

https://www.telegraph.co.uk/news/uknews/1531786/Cross-is-our-symbol-of-hope-says-archbishop.html

Archbishop Timothy Cardinal Dolan of New York in an interview with New York Times affirmed "Jesus on the cross is what matters. It is the ultimate act of God's love for us. In the busyness of my daily life I need to be reminded of that and reminded often. The Cross around my neck serves as a reminder of God's love for the world, but particularly God's love for me".

https://www.nytimes.com/2012/01/08/nyregion/timothy-dolan-new-yorks-next-cardinal.html

Many people wear the cross. Some people carry the cross in their pockets. I for one have been drawn to the cross ever since I was small. I have always had a cross to wear, because my mother gave me a golden cross as a young girl which I still have up till now. As an adult I have some personal reasons why I wear the cross. The Cross is my Symbol of God's Love. I wear a cross to remind myself what true love looks like. My Cross reminds me always of Jesus love for me. Jesus died for me. Jesus is risen. Jesus is alive and remains accessible to me. The Cross inspires me to take up my cross daily. The cross is a reminder of the challenge Jesus made to His disciples, the challenge He makes to me. **Luke 9:23** "If anyone wishes to come after me, he/she must deny himself/herself take up his/her cross daily and follow me". To be a follower of Jesus; I must exalt the cross; I must walk the way of the cross; I must embrace the cross. In addition, like Paul says in **Galatians 6:14** my boast must always be in the cross of our Lord Jesus Christ.

As a Christian I am also called to be a Witness for Christ. Who I am in all my ways, my speech, my actions must bear witness to Christ. It means that I will accept the responsibilities, the benefits, and even the pain and challenges that may come my way because of my free decision to follow Jesus. The Cross is not a jewelry to enhance my dressing. It is not a fashion statement. But I do want others to see it. Not because I want them to think I am "holier than thou". To be a Christian is to live differently following in the footsteps of Christ. I want people to know that I try to live my life differently as a Christian, and if I don't, I want to be called out for it. The Cross that I wear is the symbol of my religion that I am always excited to share with others.

I thank God for the significance of the Cross. I thank God for the message of the Cross, for the purpose of the Cross. I always reflect on Christ, the reason for the Cross. I thank God for those of us who have responded to the Cross. I thank God for those who are living for the Cross. I honor those who have died for the Cross. May we all continue to be guided by the goals of the Cross. I am aware that there are some who have rejected the significance of the Cross, I pray for those struggling with the message of the Cross, that they may be drawn by the Power of the Cross. I pray that the Lord may use those of us who have believed in the message of the Cross to be a conduit for carrying on the message of the Cross to those seeking the reason for the Cross. I pray that at all moments may we be granted healing at the Cross. At the end may we all be saved by the Cross. Amen.

Jesus says "Peace be with You": John 20: 19, 21, 26

Usually after Easter, we read about Jesus post Resurrection appearances. With the doors locked Jesus appeared to His disciples and at three different times. At each time, we hear Jesus say "Peace be with you": A very significant greeting and pronouncement. The word **Peace**" usually evokes many images, which vary from person to person. Individuals tend to relate what they regard as "peaceful" conditions to their own circumstances. Hence there are different expectations about peace shared by many people. Whatever culture, or race that people have come from, everybody yearns for some sort of personal peace in their lives. Jesus was very aware of that. He knew that His Apostles were troubled by the way of His death. He knew they have been frightened by the many incidents that have followed. He knew about their reactions, He knew about those who have denied Him, those who have fled, those who are still mourning his death. He certainly knew about His mother's grief after his death etc But He knew that the only gift that would bring comfort to their souls was His **Peace.** It was for this reason that He pronounced **Peace** on them.

Like the Apostles, all of us, even as Christians, are not immune to various problems and issues: poor health, money issues, relationships issues, spouses issues, children, friends, lovers, family, workplace, unsafe neighborhoods, break-ins, and worst of all, the unseen enemy. All these result in lack of peace for many, which can be marked by mental exhaustion, anxieties, depression, sadness, worry, stress, pain, guilt, fears and loneliness. In this fast-paced world of today, men and women now find it harder and harder to live within the framework of twenty-four hours. The pressures of modern living have brought frustrations to many, creating a state of peacelessness. Therefore, many people are longing for peace, but unfortunately at times many do not know how to obtain this peace.

Every Sunday when we come to church, at a point during service we greet each other with the Greetings of Peace. We go around holding each other's hands, giving each other a hug, a smile and whispering the word **Peace be with you** to each other. Some of us believe that once we escape into the sanctuary of the Lord we will find peace there. Jesus pronounced Peace behind closed doors in an environment similar to Church setting, in a congregational setting. Jesus pronounced peace in a state of peacelessness to His disciples. After that pronouncement Jesus breathed on them and imparted the Holy Spirit on them. Then the disciples became transformed, they became emboldened, they became empowered to go out and do the work He had called them to do.

When we greet each other with the "Peace Greetings" we are **not** merely observing a ritual put in place by the church. We are doing what Jesus did. We become Jesus hand extended to each other. We are saying to each other what Jesus wants for us, His Peace upon us. We do it with expectations. We do it to receive what Jesus imparted to His disciples behind those closed doors. Is it not marvelous that each week we all have the opportunity to pronounce wellness on each other, to wish each other goodness from the bottom of our hearts, and to express affection to each other? It is so precious, that we later go home feeling grateful that we have been touched by the Omnipotent hand of Jesus.

This gives us the strength that we need to face the week ahead. Then we come back again and again to be touched by the Lord. We remain in the assurance that Jesus is in our midst, in the many hands that we extend to each other. What comfort!!!. Something inside of us tells us that this important ritual has significant meaning for us and we thank God for it.

In our Bible, King David with his innumerable (many) problems, a people to rule, wars to fight, Saul's hatred, his sons' open rebellion against him, his own sins of adultery and murder, did not fret, instead in **Psalm 4:8** he says "I will lie down in peace and sleep for you O lord make me dwell in safety". David knew with certain reality and confidence that all He needs for equilibrium and balance in his life is the Peace of God which **Philippians 4:7** says passes all understanding. What about us? What about you? What about me? Peace is not only a situation, it is also a journey. How do we individually find our personal peace? How do we search for peace to help us cope with the pressures of life?

Psalms 34:14 states "Seek peace and pursue it," meaning look for peace and go after it. Jesus in **Matthew 5:9** in His sermon on the Mount says "Happy are those who work for peace; God will call them His children". In **Isaiah 57:21** God says, "there is no peace for the wicked'. Which means that Evil thoughts and actions lead to restlessness and peacelessness. No one can experience inner peace until they experience inner cleansing. Pope John Paul's in his message of World Peace Day 2005 connects peace with "doing good." He refers to Saint Paul's letter to the **Romans 12:9** that says, "Flee what is evil and hold fast to what is good." Verse 21: says, "Do not be overcome by evil, but overcome evil with good". which means that peace is attained when evil is defeated by good, and when we acknowledge that evil is unacceptable and we proclaim peace as an option for good. A spiritual sage says; to attain Peace, we must practice Peace. In the home, it is kindness, In business it is honesty, In society it is courtesy, In work it is fairness, Towards the unfortunate it is compassion, Towards the weak it is help, Towards the strong it is trust, Towards the penitent it is forgiveness, Towards the fortunate it is congratulations, Towards God it is reverence. https://peacealliance.org/tools-education/peace-inspirational-quotes/ In doing all these we come to a place of our own peace.

Every Sunday at the end of the service one of my responsibilities as a Deacon is to make this familiar pronouncement to the congregation, "Go in peace to love and serve the Lord" What does this mean? In Jesus second Peace pronouncement to His disciples He said "Peace be to you, as the Father has sent me so I send you". It means that when we have attained that equilibrium, that internal Peace which is usually bestowed to us and which we have bestowed on each other by the power of Jesus in our "Peace Greetings", it means that Jesus now wants us to go out into the world to move others to peace. He wants us to share with others what we have received. He wants that we should go and genuinely speak words of peace to others in our homes, in our neighborhoods and our wider communities around us. Going in peace to love and serve the Lord also means we are enjoined to be kind, compassionate to one another, forgiving each other, just as God forgave us. My prayer for all of us is David's prayer found in **Psalm 29:11:** "May the Lord give all of us His people His Strength; May the Lord bless all of us His people with Peace". Amen

Jesus Healing Ministry: Called to be a Healer: Isaiah 35: 4-6

Isaiah 35:4-6 reminds us of the prophesy about Jesus coming and what he would do when He comes. The reading has a specific focus on Jesus impending Healing Ministry. It reads "Say to those who are fearful hearted, be strong, do not fear." We are told to not be afraid. There are many things in the world today that would make us grow faint, fearful and weary. Isaiah reminds us that the Great Healer is coming only with healing in His wings. Specifically, He will come and save us, the eyes of the blind shall be opened, the ears of the deaf shall be unstopped. The lame shall leap like a deer and the tongue of the dumb shall sing. God is coming to rescue us and relieve us of every pain and discomfort. This is a message of Hope, of anticipation, of expectation.

Mathew 11:3 then took it to a higher level. John the Baptist sent a message to Jesus to ask if Jesus was the One, the Messiah, the Deliverer, the Healer that everyone was expecting. Jesus response was quite cryptic. He did not go rambling like some of us would. He simply told the emissaries sent to Him to go back to John and tell him what they have seen, thereby leaving John to make his own conclusion as to whether Jesus was the Messiah or not. He told them to just report what they have seen. With Jesus, actions speak louder than voice. He told them, to report that the blind did see, the lame did walk, the lepers are cleansed, the deaf ears were opened and they could hear. Even the dead were raised, and the poor have the gospel preached to them.

Isaiah 61 tells us that Jesus at the beginning of His ministry went to the Temple picked up the Holy Scriptures and opened the Book of Isaiah and read from it a proclamation of what He was supposed to be doing. Jesus said, "The Spirit of the Lord is on me, because he has anointed me to preach good news to the poor. He has sent me to heal the broken hearted, to proclaim release to the captives, recovering of sight to the blind, and to deliver those who are crushed". It is one thing to predict an event, it's another thing to see the fulfillment of that thing. By the time John the Baptist was making enquiries about Jesus, Jesus was already in the ministry fulfilling the prophesy, doing what he was supposed to do.

Healing was central to Jesus ministry. It was a major part of His mandate and He fulfilled it. However. Jesus Healing Ministry was dramatic, very wide and quite diverse. The Bible tells us that Jesus healed all sorts of people, men women, children, the young the old and lots in between. Jesus cured a variety of diseases. From the accounts of the Bible, we know that Jesus specifically cured blindness, paralysis, bent-back, which we call scoliosis today, fever, epilepsy, leprosy, dumbness, demon possession, flow of blood, and even raised the dead.

Jesus motives were unique to Him. Jesus healed mostly out of compassion. In many cases, Jesus made the first move without the people asking Him. In some cases, those who needed Him, called or even shouted out to Him and He responded and healed them. At other times, some would walk up to Him and asked if he was willing to heal them. Jesus would lovingly respond and would tell them that He was willing to heal them and He would heal them. Jesus even healed by proxy. He did not have to be in physical presence of those He healed. The Bible says He would pronounce healing to the person not present and the person that needed healing would be healed wherever they were. Cooool!!!!

At times Jesus forgave sins before healing was received. At other times Jesus demands faith before proceeding to heal. Like Jesus told the woman with the issue of blood that her faith has made her whole. Jesus used things to heal. He used sputum. He used clay. Jesus healed any time of the day, He healed in the morning. He healed at noon. He healed in the evening. He healed on the Sabbath Day to the consternation of His critics. He even healed at many critical moments. My favorite one was when at the time of His arrest in the full glare of His enemies who have come to arrest Him, Peter in anger sliced off the ear of Malchus. Jesus simply picked the ear and said "permit me even just this last one" and He stuck the ear back to Malchus. Jesus knew that His miracles were some of the sore points for some of the people. It was an annoying factor for them and that was why when they came to arrest Him. Jesus did not cowardly back off. He did not cringe. Instead He boldly and stylishly performed one more healing in the presence of them all to the glory of His Father. Jesus even threw out skeptics and doubters before performing miracles, like when He raised Jairus dead daughter back to life. We know how some people become suspicious of unfamiliar things. Unbelief is an impediment. "Without skeptics and doubters in the room, Jesus brought the little girl back to life. There are times when we need to get rid of scoffers in our lives in order to get things done.

We can go on and on about Jesus various styles and methods of healing. But what did Jesus do next. In **Mathew 10:1** we were told that Jesus called unto Him His Twelve disciples and He gave them power against unclean spirits, to cast them out, and to heal all manner of sicknesses and all manner of diseases. From then on the Bible says that the apostles went out, anointing with oil many that were sick and they were healed. This means that the Apostles who have been mentored by Jesus equally now have the mantle of healing, so they did what they have been prepared to do. We can imagine Jesus delight when he saw his men in actual demonstration of the power that had been bestowed on them. They lived up to Jesus expectation. And of course, after Jesus death they continued in the demonstration of that power. Remember Peter at the beautiful Gate with that beggar who could not walk but asked for money and Peter said "Gold and silver I do not have but what I have I give you. Rise up and walk". At a mere command, the beggar rose up and walked and was jumping for joy.

In **Mark 16: 17-18** Jesus included an addendum. He said, "Preach the Gospel, Baptize those who are saved and Signs shall follow them that believe". Jesus said in His name among some other things, they shall lay hands on the sick and they shall recover. This is where you and I come in. Jesus said all those who believe, people like us, shall lay hands on the sick and they will recover. You and I know that physical healing has become controversial. We see a lot of shows on the television, so many people do not know what to make of the them all, they do not know what is real from what is staged. Hence, some people have become skeptical, some have become suspicious, some have even become disenchanted. Some say that divine healing was for that era. Some say if God heals why are there still so many sick people in the world, even in the Church. The controversy rages on.

However, I believe that Jesus still heals today, and that He heals through people who have been bestowed with the gifts of healing as one of the spiritual gifts mentioned in the Bible. I also believe that Jesus still heals in very many ways just like He did when He was on earth. I also believe that healing happens through prayers, anointing of oil, and laying of hands. I have many testimonies to that effect. But I also know that Jesus in His life time did not heal ALL the people of this world that needed healing. Why I do not know. But I do not think that it is because He could Not. I know that at times Jesus chooses who to heal. At the Bethsaida Pool where there were throngs of people, Jesus chose to heal only one paralytic and left. Why I do not know. Just like Jesus healed for different reasons, Jesus is still the Ultimate Decider of who, the person to heal, where, the place to heal, when, the time to heal, and how, the method of healing. However, whether we believe or not in supernatural healings, Jesus the Great Physician has called all of us to His Healing Ministry.

Just as Jesus has commanded His own disciples to go to the world to continue His work, He has urged us the Christian Community, to go out and bring His healing touch to all peoples. Carrying out Jesus command to heal may not be as dramatic as Jesus own but it can take very many forms. Just as the intervention of a Surgeon in surgery brings healing, the laying of hands on the sick would be a loving touch that can help the dismayed and the broken hearted. A caring gesture on our part can bring peace to the emotionally sick person. The ordered guidance of a psychiatrist, psychologist or a counsellor can bring healing to the mind. The sympathetic listening to someone else's private torment can bring immense relief. The careful management of a sensitive family physician can work miracles. Jesus did not forbid Science which is also a gift from God. After all Luke was a physician and he was also a follower of Jesus using his skills to help many. The deliberate humane legislation of law makers can bring relief and solace to many through the Medical Institution. The strivings of an activist for Social Justice, Equal Rights for all, Peace in a violent world and Movements against wars can bring healing to distressed societies. The love, the patience and attention of committed parents can bring refreshing to a troubled teenager.

The sonorous voice of a Singer plus the music of Skilled Musicians on many instruments can bring calm to the soul which would be like having the "**Wings of a Dove**" (**Psalm 55:6**) (Courtesy of a dear friend). A measured word in season from the Clergy, the Bishop, the Priest, the Deacon, and the Laity can soothe pain, restore Hope, bring Peace and promote Joy. At the same time, the toxic sharp tongue of a Christian, the uncaring attitude of an ascetic can bring hurt and pain to others. This means we can all be Healers if we choose to be. Jesus is calling us to be Healers in our families, in our homes, in our workplace, in our communities, in our general environments, among friends, in our church, in our neighborhoods. **James 5:6 also** tells us to pray one for another. Michael Jackson has echoed Jesus call in the lyrics of his song "**Heal the World**" *There are ways to get there, If you care enough for the living, Make a little space, Make a better place. Heal the world, Make it a better place, For you and for me, And the entire human race, There are people dying, If you care enough for the living, Make it a better place, For you and for me.* https://www.google.com/search?q=michael+jackson+song+heal+the+world+lyrics&rlz Let us pray to always be guided, to have the eyes to see, the sensitivity to feel, the nose to smell, the ears to hear where healing is needed and the strength to go there. Amen.

Supernatural Healing in Today's World: Heal me O Lord and I shall be healed: Jeremiah 17: 14-16

Once in a group discussion, someone suggested that Christians are at times reluctant to tap into the supernatural power and abilities promised in the Gospel especially in the area of healing through intentional prayer especially with the increase of diseases all over. However, let me state categorically, I am one of those who believe in the physical, supernatural, divine healing, that is why I write this reflection.

However, I think the problem with supernatural healing is not the underutilization and minimal exploration of spiritual healing powers. It is the disenchantment that people have. Spiritual gifts have been perverted by quacks and charlatans who deceptively manipulate and exploit innocent and unsuspecting victims, making false promises with the powers that they do not have.

Secularization is also at the heart of it all. Religion is competing with rational science, modernization, technology, sports, politics, mass entertainment and various other interests. While different dimensions of scientific knowledge in human societies have taken great leaps and bounds, real and true spiritual development continues to lag far behind. Spiritual power is at times not perceived in its right dimension. The power of God promised in the Gospel is at times misrepresented. With the increasing preference of drugs, surgery and high-tech medicine for those who can afford it, the spiritual component of healing is at times pushed back. Throughout time, supernatural healing through the power of prayer has been questioned by science. Scientific researches on the benefits of healing prayers have at times produced contradictory results. There are the skeptics and doubters who say that the gift of healing has been taken away and that there are **not** people today who have that special power to heal. Some even add that it is naïve, archaic and unrealistic to expect to be healed supernaturally. Even though science and religion continue to be at logger heads, there are those who believe that Science and Spirituality enhance each other. After all Albert Einstein stated that "science without religion is lame and religion without science is blind" https://www.theguardian.com/science/2008/may/12/peopleinscience.religion. All religions Christianity, Judaism, Islam, Buddhism, Hinduism, Traditional Religions and New Age Spiritualities believe in some form of prayer for healing. In churches, mosques, synagogues, healing rooms, temples, coves and shrines, millions of people offer prayers daily for healing for each other. Alternative medicine therapies emphasize healing from a holistic mind, body and spirit perspective. Traditional healers abound everywhere for those who believe in them.

As a Christian, it is however heartening to note that prayer for healing is making a medical comeback. A recent article published in the Church of England's newspaper on August 17, 2010 affirms that Healing Prayer works, confirming the findings of a US study. Another study published in the American medical journal reports that proximal intercessory prayer when one or more people pray for someone in that person's presence with physical contact has been found to have remarkable results in healing the sick. Some recent Gallup Poll indicates that 75% of patients think that their physicians should address spiritual issues as part of their medical care. Nearly 50% percent want their physicians to pray not just for them but with them. That provides a positive indication that the waning interest in spiritual healing through prayer is being revived.

Divine healing is taught in the Bible as wrought by the power of God bestowed directly upon the individuals. Spiritual healing power is available and has always been available for all. For example, Jesus in His final instructions also said that His followers will cast out demons in His name. Jesus in the pursuit of healing has cast out demons to restore people to both physical and mental wellness. In today's world the connection between demon possession and some physical illness is controversial. The Gospels record that demon possession has produced some physical ailments such as deafness, muteness, bodily deformity, blindness, epileptic seizures and a range of antisocial behavior that could manifest as mental illness. This is not to suggest that all ailments are caused by demon possession. The scriptures described demons with various names, unclean spirits, evil spirits, deceiving spirits, spirits of error. Popular culture sees demon possession as fantasy or science fiction. At times one does not know what to make of the various **Exorcism** movies out there. Modern psychiatry and psychology see symptoms and behaviors once thought to be related to demonic possession as disturbances in the brain chemistry. However, some Charismatic movements have continued to explore deliverance and exorcism to restore health. Both however remain controversial in some circles.

We all know that we can be sick or have ailment in our minds and in our bodies. We also all know that doctors' error can kill, so in prayers of healing, people pray for the doctors that manage their health. However, let us sound a note of caution here, we must remember that Jesus is not a magician. *Abracadabra.* Jesus is a Healer, the Great Physician. He heals in His own way and in His own time. Only Jesus knows and understands the outcome of His healing process. Some outcomes may not be what we want or expect. But personally, I believe Jesus heals all the same.

How do we receive healing? **James 5: 15** says that the prayer of **faith** shall save the sick. This as we know is a highly controversial concept. Yes, I know what you are thinking: Faith Indeed! Do you mean that millions of people who have died through illnesses do not have faith? I do not think so. We have said that God heals when and how He chooses.

Ephesians 2:8 also tells us that faith is a gift of God. **Hebrew 11: 6** reminds us that if we come to God, we must believe that He is a Rewarder of those who diligently seek Him. This means the one who is in need of prayer must be in agreement, in accord with the one who is praying. They must be unified in their minds as regards the prayer. That is why Jesus threw out the skeptics when He wanted to raise that young girl who had died. He knew that they were not on the same page with him. They were already sneering as soon as Jesus arrived. **Mathew 18:19** says again, truly I tell you, if two of you on earth agree about any matter that you **pray** for, it will be done for you by my Father in heaven. In **Acts 1:14** we read this about the apostles "they all joined together constantly in **prayer**". In **Acts 4:24** we also read about the people, it says "And when they heard this, they lifted their voices to God with one accord"

James 5: 14-16 instructs suffering men and women what to do in case of sickness: "Is any sick among you? Let him call for the elders of the church; and let them pray over him, anointing him with oil in the name of the Lord: and the prayer of faith shall save the sick. The effectual fervent prayer of a righteous man avails much" verse 16 also tells us to pray for each other so that we may be healed. This means we need each other's support. We need to be there for each other. Problems are tough to deal with alone. It is hard to have faith, when we are weak or unwell. We need others to stand with us and do battle with us and for us. It is not enough that we have compassion for each other, we are needed to go to battle in prayers for each other. The interesting thing is that even while we are hurting, we are asked by the Lord to pray for healing for others. It is in praying for healing for others that we too are healed.

In **Luke 5:18** we read about the paralytic whose friends had faith to bring him to Jesus for healing. With the heavy crowd at the inn where Jesus was, they dropped him from the roof. Jesus was impressed with their faith. We thank God that in our church we have a list of people that we pray for week in week out during the time of Intercessory prayers. People continue to submit the names of people they want to be prayed for because they believe in the collective prayers offered to God. We also have our Healing Chapel manned each week at a point in our service, that people can come and be prayed for when they feel burdened. In **Mark 1:40-42** a leper came to Jesus and said. "I know you can heal me if you are willing." Jesus said then, as He is saying to us today "Yes I am willing, always willing" What a comforting response. In **Mark 16:15-18** after His resurrection, Jesus said "for those who believe, in My name they will cast out demons; they will speak with new tongues, they will lay hands on the sick, and they will recover". It is common to hear Christians talk of their favorite cure, the things that they have used for cure, copper bracelets, concoction taken, effective medical system, surgeries, doctors' prescriptions, etc but we seldom hear them ascribe healing to Jesus. Jesus is telling us that Supernatural healing is still available. For those of us who know and believe in our hearts that healing prayer can and does work, let us continue to tap into the power resting on God's assurance that the prayer and effort of faith shall always save the sick and heal the broken hearted. Above all let our prayer continue to be as found in **Jeremiah 17: 14-16** "Heal me O Lord and I shall be healed. Amen.

Jesus says "Lead us not into Temptation but Deliver us from Evil": Mathew 6:13

Of recent there has been some controversies about a segment of the Lord's Prayer which says: "Lead us not into temptation but Deliver us from evil". Even Pope Francis had openly waded into the discourse. The segment looks at the concepts of Temptation and Evil. What is temptation? It is an enticement or inducement, it is being lured to do something immoral, something evil, something that we are not supposed to do, something that violates our own moral code. Temptation is also being presented with the opportunity to violate God laws. What are some examples of what we can be tempted with? Temptation to take what does not belong to us, temptation for revenge, temptation to be unforgiving, temptation for sexual immorality, temptation for many things that we cannot name here. The truth is we are all surrounded by temptation everyday and every second of our lives. Temptation itself is not a sin.

However, this particular segment has always been puzzling. It is a prayer that raises many questions. Does God lead us into temptation? Does God bring temptation our way? Does God tempt us? Can God tempt us? Is God responsible for the ones who come to tempt us? What do you think? I decided to wade into the controversy with my own thoughts about the issue. As usual I go into the Scriptures. The answer is actually found in **James 1:13** that says "let no man say when he is tempted I am tempted of God. For God cannot be tempted of by evil nor does He Himself tempt anyone". Essentially it is saying that temptation originates from man, from us. God does not tempt us. Verses 14 and 15 now expands to tell us the stages that we go through before we finally yield to temptation. It says but each one is tempted when he is drawn by his own desires and enticed. vs. 15 then says when that desire has conceived or has formed it gives birth to sin and when that sin is fully grown it brings forth death, spiritual death. What it is saying is that people can be lured by their own desire, by their own lust, by their own deep yearning for something that they gravely or seriously want, whether good or bad. When that desire has been formed in the head, or in the mind of the individual, that individual becomes enticed that is, his or her will becomes weakened and then the person yields to it, which at times could be the violation of the law of the society, groups, communities, country, or even the laws of God. When the sinful act has been committed then there is death. This does not mean physical death, but something dies in that individual. There is shame, guilt, regret, anger as a result of yielding to temptation because resolve had been weakened, desire has actually come to fruition. The person has been ruled and taken over by their lust, desire or want. I know some may not agree with this analysis.

I think what that prayer is saying is "May God not allow us to be overcome by temptation". When we say lead us not into temptation, we are asking God to keep us from sin, from a process that will lead us into doing something wrong. The issue for all of us is what do we do with all these temptations that assail us or surround us every day of our lives? How do we fight it? Do we resist it? Do we yield? Do we blame the devil? Do we blame God? Or do we take responsibility for our actions. How we respond to temptations says a lot about us. Are we strong in the face of temptation or are we weak? Being tempted is one thing, knowing what to do with that temptation is another thing. So essentially, it still boils down to the choices we make. God has given all of us free will, so God is not responsible for the choices that we make when we are tempted. What we do rests solely with us. It is also about our perception of what we have been assailed with.

1 Corinthians 10:13 says temptation is common to man (it recognizes that we are naturally prone to temptation, that temptation is an intrinsic part of life) however it adds that God is faithful, He will not allow us to be tempted beyond what we are able to bear. He then says but with temptation, God will make a way of escape that we may be able to bear it. Is that not amazing and comforting. Is it not assuring that not only does God not tempt us; God is able to help us ride through temptations when they confront us. Of course, from what we have heard there are major and minor temptations. Nonetheless no matter how small and how big, it is still temptation and we still need to know how to respond to it. I am sure that Jesus was aware that temptations will come our way and they will pose problems for us that was why He included that portion in His prayer. In **Mark 14:38** Jesus actually told us what to do with temptation. He said, "watch and pray that we may not enter into temptation". The spirit is willing but the flesh is weak. We may not always want to yield into temptation but as humans we are very weak and so we need God's help to get us through.

The second segment of the prayer says Deliver us from evil. What is evil? The dictionary says Evil is something that is bad, wrong, sinful, wicked, causing harm or injury to others, corrupt, vicious, and malicious. It is the opposite of good. People talk of evil eye, evil mind and the Evil One. Evil is painful, it is deprivation, evil is suffering. Evil is a little child being run over by a drunken driver. We live in a world where evil abound. Many would say we live in a dangerous world. Yet we will all agree that it is still a beautiful world. Why? When God created the world, He said it is Good. If the world that God created is so good, where did all these evil come from starting with Cain killing his brother Abel out of jealousy? The Bible also has an answer to that question. **Jeremiah 17:19** says that the heart of man is full of evil**. Mark 7:21** says out of the hearts of men proceed evil thoughts and goes on to give a list of the bad thoughts that come from us. Evil again comes from our minds. We are the ones who construct evil in our minds.

However evil is not only something that people can do to us, it is also what we can do to others. **Romans 12: 21** says "Do not be overcome by evil but overcome evil with good". Evil thoughts can develop in the minds of all of us, no matter what good intentions we have. People at times have the desire or the urge to hurt others. People love to hate, people despise other people. People can be vindictive, full of bitterness, resentment, jealousy. People can be stubborn, wicked, proud and arrogant, people can be spiteful, and people can misuse their power. People can be unforgiving. People can be mean to others. People can actually love evil. People can treat others unfairly, people can deny other people of their rights, people can say things that are not true about someone else, people can ignore the needs of others around them, people can be selfish and self-centered. All these are evil. We live in a world where not all the people we know or surround us are our well-wishers. There are seen and unseen enemies, people who will actually go out to do things against us. Friends betray friends, family members betray family members, and co-workers betray and malign each other. So how do we deal with all these evil around us?

1Peter 5:8 says the devil is roaring around seeking whom to destroy. Jesus in **John 14:30** calls Satan the ruler of the world. Remember Satan came to tempt Jesus when He was most vulnerable. If Satan can tempt Jesus he can also tempt us. Jesus knew that temptation and all forms of evil can come at us and that is why he urged us to pray the prayer: "Deliver us from evil". **James 4:7** says **resist** the devil and he will flee from you. We live in a world that is divided into good and evil. As human beings we have free will to choose one over the other. How do we resist and overcome evil? One simple gesture of love, pity, forgiveness, kindness, goodness can build resilience. Not that simple I know. Making the effort is all we need.

In **1 Chronicles 4:9-10**, there is a story about a mother who named his son Jabez because he caused her too much pain giving birth to him. Jabez in return now prayed what has become known as **Jabez Prayer** (**verse 10**) to God. He says "*Oh that you would bless me and enlarge my border, and that your hand might be with me, and that you would keep me from evil so that I may not cause pain!*" Jabez must have known the intensity of pain from his mother. He must have been told how much distress he had caused her. Of course, pain is a natural part of giving birth. However, on his own Jabez made a choice that he does not want to willingly or unwillingly cause pain to anybody else in his life again. What a choice. What a decision. He then composed that prayer. How remarkable!! How sensitive!!!. I think Jabez provides an example of someone with a mind of Christ. Personally, I want to be like Jabez. I do not want to willingly or unwillingly cause pain to anybody in my life. Hence, I want to adopt Jabez prayer as part of my daily routine in addition to the one that the Lord gave us: "Lord I pray that you would keep me from evil so that I may not cause pain!" Amen

Reflection on Living Hope in Christ 1 Peter 1:3

Sometime ago at one of our Clergy conferences our Guest Speaker, a Bishop brought up the issue of hope, a complex concept. I then decided to delve into it in my own reflection. What is hope? My dictionary describes it as an expectation, that which one desires will happen, a person or thing in which one places confidence, something that we anticipate, expectation of something better, desire for a positive outcome, something to look forward to. In everyday life we say things like I wish this will happen, I wish that will happen. I wish that a situation will change. I wish that a discomfort that I am having will disappear. I wish someone will change his/her mind about something. We wish we know somebody in power to help us change a situation. We wish we have friends in high places to effect some desired change. There are million things that we wish for each day. We wish winter will just stay away and we continue to enjoy summery weather. All that is good. It is good to look forward to things, to changes even when they do not look plausible.

We all have hope for good health, financial security, peace of mind, safety for our families and friends, fulfilled lives for our children. Our lives are filled with expectations. **Hebrews 10: 23** says "Let us hold fast the confession of *our* hope without wavering" So what is the confession of our hope? **1 Peter 1:3** says "Blessed be the God and Father of our Lord Jesus Christ! According to his great mercy, He has caused us to be born again to a **living hope** through the resurrection of Jesus Christ from the dead". I cannot say that I fully understand this "Living hope" thing. However, Hope seems to be the only Christian concept that is directly linked to Christ. We have love, peace, joy, faith, but hope is the only concept that directly links us to Christ our Lord. His death on the cross and resurrection gives us hope of eternal life. He says since he was raised from the dead we too have the hope of being raised to eternal life. That is the principal assurance that we have. Hope in after life. Many religions talk of reincarnation. But our religion talks of having an eternal life in Christ; there is life after death in Christ. Which means that our life is not just eat, drink and be merry for tomorrow we die as Paul says in **Corinthians15:32**. Hope in life after death is not vague. Our life consists of hope of a future of a life in Christ even after death. But before we die what hope do we have?

King David through the Psalms helps us to come to the reality of the hope that we confess in our Christian faith. **Psalm 46: 1** says God is our hope and strength, a very present help in trouble. **Psalm 119:114** You are my refuge and my shield; I have put my hope in your word. **Psalm 119:116** Sustain me according to your promise, and I will live; do not let my hopes be dashed. **Psalm 130: 5** says I wait for the Lord, my soul waits and in His word I put my hope. Wow!!! King David surely knows about hope. Our life is a life of hope, a life of anticipation, a life of expectation. It is also a life of anxiety. We live in anxiety of what will be. What will tomorrow be like? Because we do not know we have anxiety. But the Bible is clear that we should not worry about anything. **Psalm 31: 24** says Be strong and take heart, all you who hope in the Lord. **Psalm 33:20**: We wait in hope for the Lord; he is our help and our shield.

Hebrews 11:1 says "faith is the substance of things hoped for the evidence of things not seen". The bible now links our hope with our faith. Faith and hope obviously go together. We cannot just have wishful thinking about anything, but we have to hope that someone is able to bring things to pass. However, there are times when our hope is shaken or can be shaken. When we are confronted with situations that are overwhelming, situations that make us waiver, situations that make us wonder, situations that make us fearful, what do we do? Some people actually lose hope. They lose hope in everything that they have confessed, everything that they have believed in. Some even lose hope in God. They lose hope in God's ability or willingness to deliver. Some even lose hope in their own ability to continue to believe anything. They become despondent. Because they have waited for so long for that which they wish to happen and it has not happened, they simply give up and stop believing. Life is always like a roller coaster, at times up and at times down. As one problem is being solved, another one rears its ugly head.

Hope as a vital part of our life that drives and motivates us. Hope gives us the power to endure in hard times and excel in good times. Without hope we might as well be dead. Many of the scriptures that we have looked at tell us that through faith we can have hope even in the face of desperate situations and hardship. Hope however is a word that is on the lips and minds of many people. Alexander Pope a well-known poet says "Hope springs eternal in human breast"

https://www.goodreads.com/quotes/10692-hope-springs-eternal-in-the-human-breast-man-never-is Some people speak of having hope, some of losing hope, some talk of gaining hope. Others urge friends not to lose hope. There is false hope, there is real hope. Some speak of hope against hope. Hope, hope everywhere but there is not enough of it. Hope in unending in all of us. Our verse says, "we are born again to a **living hope** through the resurrection of Jesus Christ from the dead". David in **Psalm 71: 14** says "as for me, I will always have hope". How does David do that? I wonder. How can our hope be constant and consistent? All over the world there are people living by hope, hope in Christ, hope in His return and hope in the eternal life with Christ. I do not have the answer to all the questions about hope. But all I know is that Hope came to the world at Jesus birth. Hope came again at His resurrection, so we cannot be without hope. My prayer is King David's prayer in **Psalm 33:22**, May God's unfailing love continue to rest upon all of us, even as we continue to put our hope in Him. Amen.

Reflection on Friendship with Jesus John 15:13-16

Jesus in **John 15:13** says Greater love has no one than this, than to lay down one's life for his friends. This reflection about friendship with Jesus is an expansion of the Lenten Reflection of Jesus as Friend. It is one of the significant times when the word friend is used in The Bible. It is also one of my favorite reflections. So who is a friend? The dictionary describes a friend as a person who knows and likes another, who supports and favors a companion, a person who belongs to the same side. Friends are different from family. Friends we choose. Family we have. Although there are no written rules about friendship, we all wade through it.

In friendship there are expectations like loyalty, camaraderie, companionship, commitment, intimacy, not necessarily sexual, but intimacy in the sense that you share with each other, things that you will not tell somebody else. There is acceptance of each other's, strengths and weaknesses. There is giving as a token of friendship. There is interdependence on each other for support. Friends talk of being there for each other and watching each other's back. There is mutuality and reciprocity. The phrase "my friend" gives us a sense of belongingness, that we belong to somebody and somebody belongs to us. It is a bidirectional relationship that is very fulfilling.

So how do we become friends? We meet; essentially in various circumstances or fate brings us together, in school, in church, at play, in the workplace, through somebody else, through networking. When friendship is good, we feel good about it. There are different types of friendship. We talk of childhood friends, lifelong friends, short term friends, loyal friends, friends who have betrayed us. We also talk of friends who are closer than a brother as the Bible puts it. Some of us even include friendship in our marital relationships. We hear people say I am married to my best friend or my husband or my wife is my best friend. Friendship is great. It is good to have a friend. In the Bible, the word 'friend' is not used glibly. God did not use it glibly, Jesus did not use glibly. The word is used for a few people in the Bible. In **James 2:23** Abraham was called the friend of God. **Exodus 33:11** says God speaks to Moses face to face as a man speaks to a friend. In **John 11:11** Jesus called Lazarus His friend, must be for a very good reason. The only time Jesus wept was because of Lazarus, His friend. In **John 15:15** Jesus called His chosen Twelve who have served Him faithfully "friends".

In this reflection, I try to explore Jesus' perspectives of friendship. At the beginning of His ministry, Jesus called many to follow Him. We do not know what parameter Jesus used to choose them. "Come follow me" was what He said to all of them. As we know Jesus received all sorts of responses to His call. Some rejected His calls; some gave various reasons why they could not follow immediately, but others instantly dropped whatever they were doing and followed Him. Jesus accepted those ones and they became His Followers. From then on Jesus developed a relationship with them, teaching them, praying with them, spending time with them, performing miracles in their presence, mentoring them and preparing them for greater work.

Many people always assume that once they are saved and begin to follow Jesus, or once they serve Jesus, they think that they have become the friend of Jesus. I know that we all like to sing those quaint songs that talk about being friend with Jesus. However, Jesus clarified that. In **verse 14** Jesus said: You are my friends if you do whatever I command you. At a point they were no more Followers, they became Servants involved in His ministry. Jesus upgraded them and the relationship to another level and another status. It seems that while Jesus was mentoring them. He was also evaluating them. Again, we do not know by what criteria they were judged but at a point Jesus decided they were ripe enough to be promoted to the next level. That was when He said in **verse 15** No longer do I call you servants, for a servant does not know what his master is doing, but I have called you **Friends** for all the things that I have heard from my father I have made known to you.

At this point I want to remind us of what Jesus said about these servants who have just become friends. Jesus said in **verse 16** you did not choose me, but I chose you and appointed you that you should go and bear fruit, Very significant!!! Very poignant. We always all chose our friends based on different criteria. Right! But there are times when people choose us to be their friends and we respond to that call if we feel comfortable with it. In this case Jesus was the one who initiated that relationship. He chose the men, He went after them, He called them and mentored them. In the process, Jesus was watching them all, observing their ways, how they were comporting themselves, their behavior, how they were interacting and attending to the numerous people swarming around Him. He was taking note of their commitment to Him and His work. He was also watching to see if they were on the same page with Him as we say in modern world. They were all under His scrutiny. Obviously, Jesus liked what He saw, so He gave them a pass mark and decided to move them up. Hence, we can conclude that the servants were loyal, obedient, and compliant to their Master's will. They performed well.

At this point if I ask if you reading would you like to have Jesus as your friend I am sure you will say Yes!!!. Very Good!!! For all of us what will friendship with Jesus entail? What will it look like? From the story, Friendship with Jesus assumes three stages. The first is the **Followership stage**. When we become Christians by the power of the Holy Spirit, we responded to Jesus call, Come follow me. At that point we become His followers. This is the first level of our walk with Jesus. Jesus becomes our Savior. We accept what He has done for us. We confess our sins. We are brought out from darkness into His marvelous light. We are removed from the miry clay and our feet are set upon the Rock to stay. We come out of the world and we become a peculiar people, adopted sons and daughters of God, members of God's household, brothers and sisters to God's first Son, aliens to the world, peaceful people, God's ambassadors and children of the Most High. Justified, we become the Redeemed of the Lord. We learn a new language. Old things pass away, new things come to stay. We invite Him into our lives. We surrender to Him and we are baptized by His Spirit into His Body. It's all exciting at this stage. That for us is the beginning of the journey. At what stage do we get promoted to the next level? This did not happen in an instant to the disciples. They worked hard at their relationship with Jesus.

The second is the **Servant-hood stage**. The disciples served. That was their specific involvement in His ministry. Jesus calls us all to servant hood. Christianity is not only about **following**, it is also about **serving**. At this stage we all decide that we do not want to be bench warmers in His kingdom, we want to be participants in His work. We become aware of the gifts that we have and can put to use. The beautiful thing about servant hood is everyone has gifts bestowed by the Father, our natural abilities to use. In addition, God says in **Joel 2:29** "on my men-servants on my maid-servants I will pour out my spirit". This is the stage that Jesus adds spiritual gifts, to whatever we have. He then expects us to stir them all up and use them all for the good of the Body, not put them in the closet. Thankfully we know that many people are at this stage, using their gifts, serving in one capacity or the other, in their congregations, in various ministries, administration, music, church work, Sunday school, prayer groups, caring and giving and also in their communities, making themselves available for others, on their jobs, in their families, for friends and so on. We Thank God for that. Interestingly, it is at this stage that many of us think that we have arrived. We tell ourselves that we are serving Jesus, we are doing fine and that we will just keep on doing that until our Lord comes. Little do we realize that there is still another level to go.

This is the **Friendship stage.** Most people have always assumed that when they are saved, they become friends with Jesus. We all sing those quant songs "What a friend we have in Jesus", "There is not a friend like the lowly Jesus." "I love Jesus, I love Jesus, He is my friend He is my friend". We forget that Jesus chooses His friends. Has Jesus called you to friendship? Has Jesus promoted you to that next level? Have you done enough to merit that promotion? As for me I have always tried not to be presumptuous about my friendship with Jesus. Of course, I have always desired to be a friend of Jesus. I would like Jesus to see me as a friend. I have always told Jesus that I would like to be His friend. I have always wanted to qualify to be His friend. Being a friend with Jesus is a great privilege. But it goes beyond having the desire. What does it take to be Jesus' friend?

Jesus Himself gave the answer in the passage of focus. He gave the condition for friendship with Him. Jesus talked of **Obedience**: **John 15:14** You are my friends if you obey me, if you do all that I command you. It's one thing to be a follower, another thing to be a servant, but absolutely and entirely something else to be a friend. You can be a follower of Christ and not walk in obedience. You can also be a servant of God serving dutifully but not walking in obedience. Obedience is having a moral relationship with Jesus. It means making His divine law supreme. The moral law of God does not say we may or may not, it says "Thou shall not". The moral right and wrong comes only from God. The moral law of God is not just the Ten Commandments as we have them, there are so many angles and deeper explanations to the laws. The call to Friendship with Jesus requires that we fulfill and live in absolute obedience to those laws.

Many of us take advantage of our relationship with God. We take advantage of His goodness, His kindness, and His faithfulness. We say He is a good God, a forgiving God, and so we continue in presumptuous sins and disobedient lifestyles. We however forget His severity and His requirement that we obey. Our Lord and Master does not insist on obedience because He is a taskmaster or a slave driver. He allows us to operate our free will, we have choices. However, we all know that submission and obedience are easy between two people who have genuine regard for each other. Jesus obeyed His father and submitted to His will. Do we choose to obey at every turn or do we find excuses for some of our acts? After all, He knows we are humans, we say. Obedience is being in harmony with God's laws. The beautiful thing is that God does not leave us to our senses. He comes in with the Holy Spirit power that helps us keep His commandments. Do we make use of this power at all times? In Him we have the ability and the power to overcome sin. Why then do we still disobey? We do because we allow the virus of disobedience and lawlessness to infect us. **Revelation. 22:14** says "Blessed are they that do His commandment that they may have the right to the tree of life and may enter through the gates into the city".

We know that some of us Christians discount obedience. "There is no condemnation for those who are in Christ Jesus" **Romans 8:1** we quote. We say that salvation is by grace and we have that grace. We want an easy relaxed life style, a disciplined life of obedience at every point is unacceptable to us. The world has become spiritually and morally permissive, that when people are told that they have to be accountable and take responsibility for their actions, they say, "Thank God you are not God". In **Ecclesiastes 12:13** Solomon the wise man says, "The whole duty of man is fear God and keep His commandments". These commandments are not grievous in any way. Our obedience results in sanctification and holiness. God in **1Peter1:16** says Be holy because I am Holy. Holiness is absolute purity. God knows and we all know that we cannot attain that purity in our flesh, we are only required to make an effort.

Of course, as I said, the key is Does Jesus consider us to be His friends? Have we qualified for that description? How exciting it would be when we can claim Him to be our friend because we know for sure that He has designated us to be one. Is that not worth working towards? Today Jesus is making that call to all of us. He wants us to be His friends. He wants to call us to a higher level. Paul in **Philippians 2:12** says as you have always obeyed, work out your salvation with fear and trembling. We all belong to different statuses and different levels. I do not know the level that you are in, neither do you know mine. But you know and the Lord knows. I cannot speak for you and you cannot speak for me. Those who need Salvation, need to heed the call and accept

Jesus as their Lord and Savior. Those who have accepted Jesus as their Lord and Savior and are at the Followership stage need to go up to the Servanthood level. Those who are already Servants, working for the Master, need to go to the next level, the Friendship level. We are free to relate and locate ourselves where we think we are.

Personally, I think I am at the servanthood stage. I want to be upgraded to the Friendship status. I want to be one of those that Jesus can confide the Father's secrets to. I want to be the one to know what is on Jesus' heart and mind. I want the Ultimate. What about you? I am sure you do too, so that when we hear that inner voice that tells us that we are Jesus' friend we can confidently sing that song. "I love Jesus. I love Jesus. He's my Friend, He will never leave me. He is my friend". Amen.

Reflection on Growing Old in Christ Psalm 71:18

This reflection is to celebrate Old Age. An Irish Proverb says, "Do not resent growing old. Many are denied that privilege". We live in a world where people are consumed with the fear of growing old. Everybody wants to live long, but nobody wants to grow old. Youthfulness is idolized. The media message is all about staying young forever. There is nothing wrong wanting to be young and remaining young forever if that is possible. However, the reality of life is that we are all programmed to grow older. George Burns (1896-1996) said, "You can't help getting older, but you don't have to get old."

I was invited to speak at the Ten years anniversary of "Bernadette Swan Social Care Foundation", an association that is set up to help the Seniors in the community. The Bernadette Swan Foundation is about extolling old age. It is about saying you do not belong to the archives once you have reached a certain age. It is about saying that you can continue to be useful in life until the very end. As an Adult Educator, we always say that learning is life-long, from birth to death. Bernadette

Swan Foundation has continued to provide the opportunity for seniors to continue to enjoy what the French call the *joie de vivre,* the joy of living. The Swan Foundation has taught us that as long as we are alive, we must continue to live our lives not as if there is no tomorrow as some people will say but as if there is indeed tomorrow and it is quite rosy. The Swan Foundation teaches us that as each day moves us to the end, each day reminds us of the strength that we have had, each day reminds us of the better days that we have had, and each day reminds us of how we must live each day that is left and granted unto us fruitfully.

The organization also celebrates Grandparents. Young people are asked to nominate some old people essentially, for whatever virtues they have seen in them. This for me is grand. It is very endearing to note that young people do not see Old people as "irrelevant". The Grandparents that were nominated have been able to make impact on the lives of the young people who have nominated them. In my area of work, this is significant, considering the level of ageism, and the discrimination that old people experience each day. A world where older people are discounted and dismissed as not Cool enough, as being out of touch, where some would say of them "they just don't get it, they just do not understand, they are just so disconnected from certain realities". The Grandparents Award Recipients have shown that that there is life after life. That it is possible to connect with young people even though we all live in very different worlds.

To prepare this speech I chose to reflect on what one of the wisest and most perceptive people in the Bible has to say about Old Age. In the Book of **Ecclesiastes 11 and 12** King Solomon whose wisdom is legendary to all people, regardless of their religion was reflective about Old Age. Solomon says youth is good. He describes the days of youth as the Days of Light, He then encourages us to live our lives to the fullest before we grow old. In fact, Solomon asks us to rejoice in our youth before the difficult old days come. Solomon then refers to the days of old as the Days of Darkness. Interestingly, Solomon did not extol one over the other. In fact, in one of the verses Solomon tells us that the Morning is the time of our Youth when we must sow our seeds. He says we must work and do all that we need to do to prepare for later years. Sow the seeds and wait for the fruits. Solomon then adds that the Evening is the time of Old Age when we must not withhold our hands, we must not cease to keep busy, we must not stop contributing to life, and we must not desist from being relevant in the world around us. As Solomon says, we do not know which one will turn out to be better, the Days of Youth or the Days of Old. He says in fact that both may even be very good.

In my reflection, I thought how nice it would be to have a glorious impactful Youth and an equally significant Older life. How many of us desire that balance?. I do. How many of us tell ourselves "Never say Never Again", to borrow the tittle of one of James Bond Movies, and Justin Bieber's "Never say Never" concert movie in a world that is full of all possibilities? Solomon is definitely not naive about old age. He talks about when the sun and the moon are darkened, when the arms and hands shake and become feeble, when the shoulders, legs, and back slump when the knees buckle, when the back gives up. He also talks about the time of scarcity of the teeth, about the thinning of the hair, about when the vision grows dim, about when the arms are no longer long enough to hold reading material. He even talks about the loss of hearing, and about how we struggle to sleep and how we struggle to wake up early. He talks about when our voices quiver and weaken, and when people around find it hard to hear us.

In spite of all these limitations, Solomon is not fatalistic about old age. He tells us that old age can be glorious. He says that our years of old age can be an inspiration to countless others. He tells us that we can genuinely enjoy life. He tells us that our spouses, our friends, our neighbors, our community members, our children, and our grandchildren can still see some good about us and still have some remarkable things to say about us. He also tells us that we must not refrain from sharing good memories with those around us, instead of becoming grumpy old people, who only have tales of woes to share.

How can we not enjoy old age, which certainly comes with many benefits? To start with, many researchers found that contentment comes with old age, because that is the age when we accept things the way they are. That is the age when we are confronted with the stark reality that we do not live in a perfect world, and so nothing is perfect, and so we must just accept life as it is. Old Age also comes with immense privileges, one of which is that we all have the freedom to say and tell things the way we see them, to also do things in ways that are most convenient and most comfortable for us and not bother about what others think about us. People's opinions cease to matter anyway after some time especially if we are convinced that we are on the right track.

As individuals, we all see things differently, we all interpret meanings differently. King David, King Solomon's father talks about the things that we do when we are young and the things that we do when we are old. One stage of life leads to the other. One stage is a stepping-stone in the building blocks of life. The truth however is that we all grow old, if we do not die young. Since Old age is a reality, does it not make sense to give ourselves to reflection about it? Self-Introspection I think it is called. Old age starts at different ages in different countries and in different cultures. In Canada, Old Age starts at 65 when you become a Senior Citizen. My question for all of us is "What do we want our lives as old and older people to look like?". Have you thought about it if you are not yet there? If you are already there What does attaining Old age means for you? Let us hope it is much more than thinking about Old Age Pension.

At the event we heard about how the Awardees Grandparents have managed their old and older age. How they have contributed immensely to the next generation and how have put their marks on the sands of time. We also heard about how they have begun to reap the benefits of building very strong relationships from when they were younger. Glowing reports do not happen instantaneously. They are cumulative reports of lifelong investment in people and in good works. It is the reward for good seeds sown earlier that have been watered and tended for a long period. Old and older people usually have lots of free time, what have you been doing with yours? These days I see many retired people volunteering in various places, in hospitals and in many community organizations in the city. I say Kudos to them. With this shifting world around us, everyone has different thoughts and feelings about getting older. Overall, many old people say that life slows down but they also claim that it is the time to enjoy themselves, enjoy their lives because it is the time that one gains a deeper meaning of life and learns to enjoy the things that are really important.

Solomon tells us that there is more knowledge and more respect from others in Old Age. He also adds that there is increased wisdom, and great achievements. Solomon then tells us that instead of concentrating on just "adding years to our lives," we must focus on "adding life to our years". This he says would be a priceless contribution not only to our own life but also to the lives of those around us. Solomon therefore says that we must live our lives to the full. He says in Old Age, we must not put undue pressure upon ourselves when making significant decisions. Solomon also says old age is the time to remove grief, anger, and pain. It is the time to make each day count. It is the time to live purposefully and meaningfully so that at the end we can say that it was all worth it. At this point I want all of us to start reflecting about our Old Age. What legacy do we want to leave behind? What would the people in our lives say about us? Like the Awardees of today let us remember that we can still make hay while the sun is shining. We can still guide many others along in the journey. We can still influence many others for good. Eric Hoffer says, "The best part of the art of living is to know how to grow old gracefully." Are we growing old gracefully? Have we put away those things of youth, marching on in the elegance of Old Age? I sincerely hope that none of us is in denial about Old Age. I also hope that none of us is prone to looking mournfully into the past.

Queen Elizabeth of England has become the longest reigning Monarch in the history of England. What a glorious life she has had!! What elegance!!!! What beauty!!!. She has ruled Britain to borrow a

Biblical expression with "skillfulness of hands" and "integrity of heart" (**Psalm 78:72**) She has been quite influential in all aspects of life that in addition to all things the media even talks about her sense of Fashion at well over 90 years old. Wow!!! We can be role models at any age, if we do not fall into the trashy mold of today's world.

In closing, I would like to share some thoughts about my mother. My mother passed away some years ago. She was a teacher and later became Principal of schools. My mother was indefatigable. After my father passed away, she spent some years with us in Canada but lived more in Seattle with some of my siblings. My mother passed away at 89 years old. At 80, she became a viable member of the Central Area Senior Centre in Seattle. She learnt to use the computer. She learnt to send emails. She learnt to surf the internet and send to us articles that she found interesting especially if they are about **health** and about **religion**, her two main passions. She joined an Aqua swimming exercise group. My mother studied Frobel and Montessori in Australia, so she has a way with children. As soon as my mother had learnt to use all these modern technology and means of communication, she put on her teacher's hat once more and started teaching the other Seniors in the Center. She became the ultimate teacher at the Centre. On her 89th birthday the Senior Centre in Seattle floated a very big party in her honor as the oldest member of the center. She passed away suddenly a few months just before her 90th birthday. On the day that she died, she went for her aqua exercises, attended the adults' midweek Bible study in her church, and stopped to buy Kentucky Chicken, her favorite fast food. She got home, had supper, had her shower went to bed and did not wake up in the morning. What a way to go many said!!.

At the memorial, service that we held for her in Seattle, before we took her back to Nigeria for burial, the Seattle Senior Center gave us a big plaque, which they called **Resolution,** a Commendation of her contribution to the center. It says in part "Helen Olulanu Banjo was a dedicated member of our Central Area Senior Center, Seattle Washington USA and supported our vision to provide activities and services for the recreational intellectual, social, physical, and mental health and well-being for seniors within our community. Therefore the Board in appreciation for her passion, dedication and support gives this Resolution to her family in a commemorative manner". It was handed to me as the oldest of her eight children. As I received it, my mother's life flashed before me from the time when I was three years old and I went with her to the school where she taught for nine years. I also remembered how all of us her eight children went to the school wherever she taught. I have always said that I have a role model in my mother.

However, for me it was quite significant that she would relocate to Seattle at a very advanced age and she was still able to make a mark in that community. I share these words with you not just because I am proud of my mother. But because I have learnt through her that at any age, all of us have the potential to make life better for all the people around us and that we are all able to make life worthwhile for the next person, for the sake of entire humanity, starting with our immediate domain. I want to leave you with the words of actress Lucille Ball which says: "The secret to staying young is to live honestly, eat slowly, and lie about your age" Although I would not recommend the last one. (Smile). There is nothing to be ashamed of about one's age. But I will substitute that with in the words of an Anonymous writer who says: "Instead of aging, start living". King David's prayer in **Psalm 71:18** which says "do not forsake me when I am old and gray" resonates well with me and should be our collective prayers. Amen

Imitators of Christ in this Generation: 1Corinthians 11:1

I was invited by CUNNA to speak at an event on the "Imitators of Christ in this Generation". I wondered which generation CUNNA had in mind. The world has produced some definable generations since society started labelling generations. Starting with the one known as the Greatest Generation, those who fought in World War II, as well as those who kept the home front intact. This generation is conventional, possessing confused morals, but desiring faith, and for women, desiring both a career and a family, that generation saw the emergence of the Feminist Movement which gave power of participation to women. This generation also saw the emergence of the Movies industry. Then we have the **Baby Boomers** whose teens and college years were part of the 1960s counterculture. Out of it came The Hippie Subculture that created their own communities, listened to psychedelic rock, and embraced sexual freedom. This is the generation of Miniskirts, Elvis Presley, the Beatles, and high-heeled shoes. This generation later became conservative compared to the generations that came after them. Coincidentally I belong to that generation. Generation X is the generation of young adults who are influenced by fashion trends, music, and slang terms and witnessed the rise of Mass Communication. The Y Generation is known as a Culture War "battleground" with growing disagreements between Conservative and Progressive perspectives. Generation Z is the "Internet Generation" at times called the "Google Generation", the point at which the whole wide world has been changed.

At the point of preparing my Reflection, I wondered when we talk of **Imitations**, which generation is going to provide a model for us? The world today still has some representations of all these generations listed above. They all have their strengths and achievements but in terms of providing model for anybody, they are all deficient. Models set parameters of behavior and since I could not find a Perfect Model in all these generations, I decided to settle on the One Role Model that is Eternal and Everlasting, the same yesterday today and forever. I settled on **Imitating Christ.** I think being called to be Imitators of Christ in this ever-changing world is a great challenge. Paul in **1 Corinthians 4: 15-16** says "For though you might have thousand instructors in Christ, yet you do not have many fathers, for in Christ I have begotten you through the Gospel. Therefore, I urge you to Imitate me". Paul affirms this again in **1Corinthians 11:1** when he says, "Imitate me just as I imitate Christ". What a bold claim. Paul asserting that he is imitating Christ.

Imitate as defined by the dictionary means try to be like, follow the example of, act, make or do something like. In **Ephesians 5:1** Paul even tells us to "Be imitators of God". In another verse of the Bible, we are told to be perfect like God. This I thought is a very tough command. It sounds and looks impossible. Usually our parents, extended family members, society, model for us the format to follow. We are required to behave like them assuming they are godly role models. However, that also may not be enough because even our parents have shortcomings. When Paul urges us to imitate Christ, it has nothing to do with trying to merit eternal life. It has to do with our journey of growing in godliness and how we are required to live our lives. The life of Jesus Christ gives us a supreme example, a great model to follow. So, what are things that Jesus did that are worthy of emulation?

Jesus in His post resurrection appearance gave His disciples what is known as The Great Commission found in **Mathew 28 vs.19-20.** He says: "Go therefore and make disciples of all the nations baptizing them, teaching them, to observe the things that I have commanded you". Jesus spent His entire time teaching and modelling for his Apostles what he expects them to do after He has departed. Therefore, it is not surprising that His Commission would demand that they do what He has taught them. Imitating Jesus mean that we will be perfect image of Christ. While it is not possible to be Jesus perfect image, we do not want to be poor photocopies of Him either, to borrow from President Leopold Senghor's of Senegal's description of what the French tried to achieve in their effort at the Assimilation of Colonized Nations. We want to look as if we have been produced on **Sharp** photo copy machines, not some blurred copies that are at times unreadable. We have to be good and acceptable copies of Jesus to influence our world, our generation. If we are going to be models for others, we cannot afford to be distorted, otherwise we will unleash our distortions into the society, who will in turn copy our distorted version and spread it round. We then become part of the problem of society, of our generation. Apostle Paul was confidently able to urge the Corinthians people to imitate him because he was confident that he has been viable Imitator of Jesus and therefore a near perfect Image of Christ.

What about all of us living in a new world that has become largely secular. How do we influence that world? To start with Jesus said that we are in this world but NOT of the world, which means we have to live a life that is distinct from the patterns of the world. Our motto cannot be "if we cannot change them, join them". Jesus in **Mathew 5: 48** now urges us to be perfect just as our God in heaven is perfect. Very tall order. How do we become perfect in an imperfect world? How do we make crooked paths straight in our world? It is quite a challenge, but we must try. The good thing is that we live in a world of technology. we have quick access to information, we have apps for everything. Technology can be used for good and for evil. The choice is ours. However, the best thing that we can do is to build our lives around Christ. This means copying Him, doing things the same way He does things, the way he thinks, the way He speaks, the way He acts and reacts, essentially putting our foot in the same place where He puts them, following in His Footsteps, overall is having the same lifestyle as Jesus. Of course, some would say that we are human and so we cannot achieve that. Jesus belonged to a Generation which He impacted to the point that over 3 billion of the 7 billion people of the world today are following Him. He was only 33years old when He did all that. The truth is all of us are constantly surrounded by people who are watching us, who are using us as parameters for good or for evil, whether we are aware of it or not. They may be younger people, people the same age as we are, and even people older than us. That is why it is important for us to do things right, so we do not become flawed models for some innocent unsuspecting people. Then we become responsible for their failures.

It is like students who spy on others to cheat in exams. Of course, if the person they are spying on gets the answers wrong, they too get the answers wrong. Jesus in **Luke 6:39** and **Mathew 15:14** talks about the blind leading the blind, they are all going to fall into the ditch. How do we not become the "blind leading the blind"? Societies have what we call "copy-cat tendencies" This means that people copy each other, follow each other, imitate each other without questioning each other's ways. That is how and why bad beliefs, bad behavior, bad utterances, bad ways, spread fast in our world and become absorbed into the culture. That is how the abnormal becomes normal. Unfortunately, many of the so called models are flawed, selling flawed values and morality, projecting flawed images about life to the society and many others in the society are absorbing them.

Let us look at some of the things that we can do in our attempt to Imitate Jesus, which will make us acceptable models for others in our generation. The primary condition for imitating someone is to be around that person. We cannot imitate someone we do not spend time with. To borrow the young ones lingo, we have to "**hang** out with Jesus", this means being in His presence, in His company, in His house, in fellowship with Him and with one another. We must stay in His presence to develop His character and His traits. It is in our constant fellowship with Jesus that some of His qualities and essence rubs on us. In my line of work, Differential Association Theory essentially says that we become like those we associate with.

Imitating Christ is also making ourselves **available**. It is one thing to hang out with Jesus it is another thing to find the time to be in the company of other people. Jesus did that. He spent time with His disciples also spent plenty of time with other people, 4000 people, 5000 people. If we are not available to spend time with other people how are we going to influence or affect our community, our generation. We have to start with developing relationships with people. Jesus told a guy called Zacchaeus that he was coming to his house and he did. That way He established a relationship with Zacchaeus, which provided the opportunity to talk, which provided the opportunity for conversion. The bible tells us that from Jesus visit to Zacchaeus that day, many became converted. If we remove contact with some people, if we discriminate against people based on our perception of them, our "*holier than thou attitude*" will not provide the opportunity for us to impact them. Some people have used **2 Corinthians 6:14** that says, "Be ye not unequally yoked with unbelievers" to alienate or segregate themselves from some people. I have heard one of the TV evangelists say that Jesus said we should love our neighbors he does not say we should live near them. Wow!!!.

Acts 13: 36 tells us that after David has influenced his own generation by the will of God, he fell asleep. David fulfilled a purpose in his relationship with his generation, worthy to be mentioned. Jesus as our role model is not a difficult sell, because all believers long to connect with Jesus in some way, to share some part of him. Some want the heart of Jesus so they can know what it means to truly love. Some want the eyes of Jesus so they can see others as He sees them. Some want the wisdom of Jesus so they can know truth. Some want the feet of Jesus so they can walk His path. Imitating Christ will surely be a great adventure for us. If we are imitating Christ, we are certainly manifesting acceptable traits for our generation. Are we ready to go on that journey? I hope we all are. Let us all put on our girdle and start off. May we all be empowered on the journey. Amen.

Reflection on Bearing much fruit in Christ: John 15:4

There are three usages of fruit in the Bible (1) fruit of the womb, (2) those physical juicy things that we like and eat, (3) the Fruit of the Spirit. In **John 15:4** Jesus says if we abide in Him, we will bear much fruit. This I believe applies to the first usage, Fruit of the womb, that is bearing children, having offspring. Does our walk with the Lord produce off-springs, not necessarily our biological children, but offspring for the Lord that would later be adopted into the kingdom as sons and daughters of the Most High? How many sons and daughters have we brought into the kingdom? Jesus expects us to bear much fruit in that area.

In **Mathew 21:18-22** on His way back to the city, Jesus was hungry He saw a fig tree and went near it to pick a fig but there was nothing on it, so He cursed it, and it withered immediately. In **Luke 13:6-9** Jesus told a parable of a man who planted a fig tree and in three years the tree produced no fruit and so he ordered that it should be cut down. In **Mathew 3:8** Jesus said that every tree that does not bear should be cut down. The fruit when they are beautiful and juicy will draw men nearer. Towards the end of summer all over the city we see apple trees with fruits hanging down on them. I see people always drawn to them because the apples look juicy and everybody wants a taste. What type of fruit do you and I bear? If the fruit is good, people will come near us to taste of it. It is a law of natural tendency. People are naturally drawn to good things. As people are drawn to us, we begin to recruit an army of potential followers for the Lord.

The third usage is the **Fruit of the Spirit** which Paul talks about in **Galatians 5:22-23**. These are nine traits, nine attributes, nine characteristics of God which we are expected to have. These are love, joy, peace, patience, humility, kindness, goodness, faithfulness and self-control. Let us quickly look at the scriptural meaning of each of this fruit. Love is close to the heart of God. It is agape, strong yet tender, ardent, compassionate devotion to the well-being of someone. Joy is an expression of inward rejoicing. It is rapture, delight, gladness. Peace is a state of inner equilibrium, quietness, rest, security in the face of turmoil. Patience is endurance, steadfastness, forbearance, longsuffering. Humility is meekness, and gentleness. Kindness is having compassion. It is love in action. It is a disposition. Goodness is excellence, of perfection. It is a state of being virtuous. Faithfulness is worthy of trust, keeping a promise, loyal, constant, being true to a person or to a cause. Self-control is temperance, moderation in indulgences of appetites and passions. It is the ability to check, to regulate, to restrain, and govern self in all aspects of life, it is a discipline.

All put together, the fruit is simply evidence of the Holy spirit in our lives. It is the godly attributes of those who walk in the Spirit. How do we develop these traits? Just as natural fruits take time to grow and ripen, the same way developing these nine traits takes time. It is a process. In **John 15:1** Jesus said we should bear much fruit to prove that we are His disciples. In **Mathew 7:16** Jesus also said that people will be known by their fruit. The Fruit of the Holy Spirit affects believers' relationship with God, with others and self. As we grow in our relationship with the Lord, we develop unselfish love, true joy, lasting peace. As we build relationships with others, we reflect God's patience, kindness and goodness. As we mature spiritually, we develop an inner strength which results in faithfulness, gentleness and self-control. Overall, We will have true love, we will have peace which passes all understanding, we will have joy unspeakable, we will be patient, we will be kind, we will start growing in goodness, we will be faithful, we will be meek, we will be humble, we will be temperate, we will have self-control.

When we manifest these attributes in our relationships with others, others, neighbors, friends, fellow brethren, family members, co-workers, even strangers will perceive that we have these qualities, they will see them in our lives and experience them and benefit from our practical demonstration of them. Which means we will love our neighbors, we will deal with them in joy, we will pursue peace and seek peace with them. We will be patient with all because God is patient with us, we will be kind and good to all because God is good to all. We will be faithful in our relationships because God is faithful in all His relationships. We will be meek and humble because Jesus is meek and humble. We will exercise temperance and self-control because that is an attribute of Jesus.

Above all, in our relationships with God, as Jesus said to love God, when we love God, we will be at peace with Him. We will appreciate the importance of waiting on Him and waiting for Him. After all **Isaiah 40: 31** says "Those who wait on the Lord shall renew their strength". We will develop the inner strength that results in our being faithful to God. Do you know that there are times when we carry our abrasiveness to God. If we fear God, not only will we hold Him in awe and reverence, we will also hold in reverence things that pertain to God. May we have the desire and the Love of God to do all these. May we grow rich bearing much fruit. in Christ. Amen.

Food Security in a Hungry World: Jesus Feeds the hungry: Mathew 14:13-21

First of all, we want to thank all of you for your continued support and contributions to PWRDF through those blue envelopes and your coin boxes. May our Good Lord, the Ultimate Provider continue to bless you all. Amen. PWRDF is alive, well, growing and moving on with its programs. It is a privilege to be your Parish Representative at the Diocese level. Through this position I have come to know a lot more about the inequities in the world that we live in both locally and globally and more so about PWRDF activities and its relentless efforts to address many of these problems. Last year Dr. Geoff Strong the Diocesan Coordinator for PWRDF came here to talk to us about the activities of PWRDF. I am sure some of you may be wondering why we need to talk about PWRDF again. Actually, PWRDF each year sets aside a time for deep reflection on whatever concept they choose to deal with. They have in the past talked about Aids, Homelessness, Poverty, Racial discrimination, other Development issues. This year PWRDF has chosen this Lenten season to reflect on **Food Security**, our topic for today.

Food is what people, animals and plants consume to make them grow, survive and keep them alive. Essentially without food there is no life. **Isaiah 55:1** says something interesting about food, it asks everyone who thirsts to come to the waters and those who have no money to come and buy wine and milk. How can people buy anything to eat, when they have no money? Great question but this is the reality of life. Today there are many people in this world who have no money to buy the most basic necessity of life, food. Some years ago, The Band Aid Musical Group comprising of Bono, Bon Jovi, George Michael, Sting, Boy George, Paul Young, Phil Collin, and Simon Le Bon and others sang that classic soul inspiring song **Feed the World, Let them know it's Christmas time.** The Band Aid at that time chose Christmas, a time of plenty, to focus on food. PWRDF has a chosen the Lenten Season a time of less consumption to focus on Food. How ironic!!!

The message essentially is that food security is a perennial problem for many people all the year round. Coincidentally and interestingly in today's Gospel we read that Jesus our Lord and Saviour, the Son of God needed food for sustenance in His corporeal body. In His visit to Martha and Mary they gave a dinner for him. Even Lazarus who had been raised from the dead also ate. He too needed food for continued survival. Jesus demonstrated to us in physical sense the importance of food. Lent is a time of prayer and penance, a time when we prepare ourselves for the coming of Easter. It is also a time of abstention when we fast, when we go without food for some parts of the day, or when we give up or deny ourselves of something that we like. In **Isaiah 58:7** God tells us the type of fasting that He expects of us. In addition to some other things God says I want you to share your food with the hungry and to welcome poor wanderers into your homes. Mary and Marta did that for Jesus. They welcomed Him in their home after His long foot sojourn. They fed Him and made Him comfortable. This verse definitely asks us to take the focus away from us and shifts it to the "**others**". We are required to reflect on those who have food in abundance and those who do not have enough. It then asks us to be generous about this most basic need of human existence.

Food, food, food everywhere but not enough to eat. For some, especially in this part of the world, access to food is so pervasive and abundant that people do not give thoughts to food. People just eat. Adele the Executive director of PWRDF shared her experience. She says In Canada, people tend to greet one another with some variation of "Hello" and "How are you?" In some other parts of the world, she said that the standard greeting is "Have you eaten today?" For those people food is a rarity, the absence of food is the norm, mere access to food is the luxury. Canada has social services such as food banks, school lunch programs, soup kitchens and so on to assist those in need. In other places people's nourishment generally depend solely on the crumbs that fall from the tables of some other people.

In advanced countries people know that component of good health is good nutrition, hence people talk about balanced diet, healthy food and so on. People even make their food choices based on their preferences or necessities maybe due to allergies or intolerances. Hence people eat special diets, ethnic foods, organic foods, local foods, diet foods, and vegetarian food and so on. Here people cook with recipes, with spices to keep the food experience interesting and enjoyable. These days people even talk of Slow Food cooking to emphasize the importance of pleasure and taste in food consumption. On the other side of the world, people are just happy to eat the same bland food day after day, food without any variety, food that is taken like medication just to survive. In the advanced world, people actually get bored with their food if there is no variety. People even discuss food from exotic perspectives; people talk of gourmet, haute cuisine, a la carte, table d'hote (I know these because I went to school in France). People talk of culinary arts, dining out, soup of the day, chefs' recommendation, buffet, pot luck, all you can eat, take away, home delivery, food shows, food network, Wow!!!!. In some parts of the world these phrases and expressions simply do not exist in the people's vocabulary nor in their lingo. The people do not have the luxury of all these extensive choices. Most times they face food shortages because of inadequate supply.

In the land of plenty Food waste is the problem. In Canada; the stores are often stocked with more than sufficient supplies to last extended periods of time. Hence people buy a lot of food that is wanted but not necessarily needed. People have food stored in their homes for both short and long-term consumption. People hoard so much food that at times gets spoilt before they can be eaten. Many leftovers and forgotten foods get thrown out. Supermarkets discard one third of food for not being fresh enough. Restaurants throw out unsold food with the trash. With opportunities for bulk purchases of food, many people simply buy more than need only to toss them out into the bins at a later date. In some parts of the world all these are simply unheard of. People do not even have enough to eat not to talk of hoarding or of tossing out. They purchase only what they minimally need at any given time.

While school feeding programs exist in Canada, in other parts of the world, children could go to school hungry. School children who are hungry cannot learn; cannot concentrate because the hunger pains are distracting for them. Talking of hunger pains, for those who go without food during lent, not eating can be difficult. Right! It boils down to struggling with temptation with all the food that one is surrounded with. It takes the grace of God to keep it up during Lent. While secretly lamenting about how tough fasting can be, how many people give thoughts to those who are required to go on forced, full or part time fasting all the year round. In this part of the world most peoples' pattern of eating is 1-1-1, (representing three meals a day) while for some others it could be 0-0-1 or 0-1-0 or even 0-0-0, the zero representing no food.

Canada and other developed countries have people called food producers, large scale farmers, who are saddled with the responsibility of producing enough food for the population that they cater to. In some other parts of the world there are no food producers; there are just food planters, people who survive on what they have been able to grow for themselves or what they have traded with their neighbors. Can you imagine how tedious it will be if you and I have to plant and grow everything we need to eat before we can eat them. Uh!!!!! In this part of the world food is brought to the communities for people's consumption. But over there, people have to go in search of food. All over the world we hear that food prices are increasing. However, many people in advanced world are still able to eat because of low cost of food. In other parts of the world, as food prices increase, hunger increases and so does crimes and conflict over access to food. The poor without access to basic necessities like food are more likely to resort to all sorts of violence which can lead to social malaise. The Bible calls it the violent taking it by force.

We cannot talk of food security without reference to poverty which is simply the inability to provide oneself with basic needs. Poverty impacts what people eat, it impacts people's ability to grow or purchase food, it impacts the quality of food that people eat, and how much people consume. Poverty can be caused by many factors like inequities, unjust systems, lack of social structures, lack of access to education and health care, which can result in hunger and malnutrition. The root causes of poverty are also the root causes of food security problems. The cycle of poverty can be devastating. All over the world, money is given for work done and that money in return is used to purchase commodities, including food. Canada is blessed with legislated minimum wages so that needs are somehow met. In some parts of the world where unemployment and underemployment are rampant and governments are infinitely corrupt, money is not easy to come by; hence, food purchases are not achievable for some. In some individualistic environment people simply focus on themselves. Those who have simply do not care about those who do not have. At times people just do not see the hungry around them.

I have deliberately taken us through a journey of contrasts and contradictions for effect. I have focused on some of the things that we take for granted in this part of the world. I have also exposed the anomalies that exist in those other places, all to increase our awareness about **Food Security**. The good news is that PWRDF is not unmindful of these problems and so it has chosen to do something about it. PWDF has resolved for the next three years to address the issue of Food Security in some parts of the world. PWRDF is not the only organization in this world offering support in underdeveloped areas of the world. But PWRDF is an Anglican initiative and that is why it is of importance to us. We know that our money is being put to good use. However, PWRDF cannot operate in a vacuum. They need us all. We all are PWRDF!!!!!!!!

Once again, we thank God for the opportunities and the desire to help and the provision to do the same. I am sure we are all ready to give again to the work of PWRDF. Of course, there is inequality everywhere. I sometimes hear people say that there are hungry people in Canada too why should we bother with those abroad. Max Ehrmann in his Desiderata (1927) says "if we compare ourselves with others there will always be people who are better or worse than us".

https://www.desiderata.com/desiderata.html Here we are talking about people who are in general worse than those of us in Canada, the people who need our help. Let us come to the rescue of these people in any ways that we can. We can choose to spend the time analyzing how and why there is so much inequality in the world or we can choose to help collectively in any way that we can. I believe enough awareness has been raised about how "the other half lives" Courtesy Susan George. Remember Jesus talked to His disciples about those who gave him food when he was hungry and those who did not. They all claimed they would never have done that to Jesus. But Jesus calmly told them that as long as they do or do not do it for others they are doing it to Him. In **Luke 6:38**: Jesus asks us to give, surprisingly with assurances of benefits and rewards.

Finally, as much as PWRDF wants us to give money, they also want us to pray. Pray without ceasing, pray always pray we are urged. As we pray let us reflect on this world of plenty and abundance, yet a world where many through no fault of their own are victims of the various lopsided systems that they live in. Let us in our personal thoughts and prayers continue to remember the many millions of people all over the world who are oppressed, deprived, and marginalized, those who cannot have food in the various fashions that we have talked about and so must go to bed hungry. Let us pray that God may touch the hearts of the various leaders of this world that they may pay attention to the needs of their people. Let us continue to pray for PWRDF and all those who are out there in the field helping out in ways that you and I cannot. Above all let us pray that all of us may be Jesus hands extended to all these other people that Jesus equally loves. Amen.

The Gift of Water: Jesus by the Well: John 4

Last year our PWRDF Lenten reflection focused on Food Security. This year, the focus is on The Gift of Water. I do not need to recount the uses of water in our lives. Water is life, they say. Water is also a powerful sacred symbol for us as Christians. It is used for baptism of course and at the Eucharist playing an important role in our life of faith. As much as water is needed for all, it is sad to say that there is an **uneven** allocation and distribution of water in our world. Canada for example is blessed with the least expensive water in the world. It is abundant and accessible. But surprisingly while millions of liters of water are daily wasted in the urban areas, there are many isolated **First Nations communities** who despite their belief that water is a sacred gift from the Creator are living in places where this basic necessity of life is absent, so says a report. Also, beyond Canada in many other parts of the world like in Asia, and in Africa people have to walk miles to get water for their daily needs. This is why PWRDF, makes allocation of water the key to some of its programs helping to raise funds for water projects working to bring, fresh, clean safe water to the villages by drilling boreholes deep into the ground. Anglicans across Canada continue to be part of these life-changing projects when they donate to PWRDF.

In the light of this **topic,** I want to look at Jesus specific discourse on water. Jesus had various engagements with water, starting with His own water baptism, turning water into wine in His first miracle, calming the stormy seas, going fishing with His disciples, and washing His disciples' feet with water. However, a point came when Jesus had a **personal** need for water. He experienced thirst. The story is found in the Book of **John 4** about Jesus encounter with a Samaritan woman. There are many theological positions about Jesus interaction with this woman. Some have focused on the **gender** differences between Jesus and the woman, some on the cultural differences, Jesus being a Jew and she being a Samaritan, some even on the **sexuality** of both of them, Jesus being a "Celibate Preacher" and she a "Serial Monogamist" with several marriages under her belt.

Personally, all I see in the story is a woman who refused to give water to a Stranger in spite of the stranger's request and promptings. I see a woman who missed the opportunity to do good. The story is that Jesus came to a city of Samaria, and Jacob's well was there and Jesus was wearied, tired and thirsty from walking, and so He sat by the well. A woman of Samaria came to draw water and Jesus said to her "Give me a drink". This unnamed woman of Samaria instead of responding to the stranger's thirst and need of water, went on some rambling about the cultural differences between them. She said how is it that you being a Jew ask a drink from me a Samaritan, for Jews have no dealings with Samaritans. What recalcitrance!!!. I thought. Must there be cultural **harmony** before people can respond to each other's need. If Jesus was shocked at her insensitivity, He did not show it, instead He tried to shift her focus back to the issue at hand. He said, "if you know who is asking you for water you would have asked Him to give to give you water and he would had have given you living water".

Of course, either she did not know who Jesus is or did not recognize Him. At that point one would have expected her to change position and respond to the physical need of the Stranger before her. Instead she went on another round of rambling. She said, "you have nothing to draw water with, where then do you get that living water"? Questioning and more questioning!! As of now she still has not addressed the need of the Stranger. I am sure by now Jesus was getting thirstier, while this woman continued with her irrelevant rambling. When Jesus then explained to her that whoever drinks the water that He has to give, will never thirst again**;** this strange self-centered woman in her response in shifted the focus to herself and said to Jesus. "Sir, give me this water so that I may not thirst again". Is it not remarkable that the one who was supposed to give water became the one begging to be given water? What paradox!!!!Jesus gave this woman the opportunity to be humane, to reach out, instead she became self-focused, not responding to the need before her. She was not even coy at asking Jesus for water when she herself had not given Him the water that He had asked her for.

Is this not typical of us humans, we always act primarily in our own self interests. Our own needs soon become our primary focus: Lord, bless my father, bless my mother, and bless everyone around me so that they can bless me. Uh!!!

The same way in our own relationship with Jesus, we at times treat things that pertain to Jesus in some perfunctory manner, and yet we never think twice before we impose on Him. At times we even choose to ignore Him, but we are never afraid to ask for His favors when things get tough for us. Like David in some of his Psalms we scream "Lord Make haste to help me" "Jesus, I need you!!!" I know I do that whenever I am in a desperate situation. He always responds anyway. I always know that He will.

Has the Lord by the promptings of the Holy Spirit ever asked you to do something, to help someone or reach out to someone and instead of just rushing to do it, you keep rationalizing in your heart and mind why you should do it, trying to justify your way out of it. Of course, we have a **Saviour** who does not deal with us as we deserve, the Bible says. Instead He is forever patient and compassionate. Jesus interaction with this woman is an example of His great patience. He did not rail at her for ignoring of His need. He did not condemn her insensitivity to His plight. Instead Jesus simply revealed Himself to her hoping that would change her behavior. "If you know who I am, you will ask me for water". Still she did not reverse her neglect, neither did she offer that much needed water to Jesus. However, Jesus continued in His magnanimity and love towards her. Jesus loves. He never let us go, He never blames us for anything, because He knows our weaknesses, our frailties. He is always drawing us to Himself. What a privilege!!!

Personally, I would not want to be like this Samaritan woman. She missed an opportunity to be kind to Jesus. We would never know what **else** Jesus would have rewarded her with, apart from the offer of that spiritual water. Jesus always has something more, something better for us. I **Corinthians 2: 9** says "Eye has not seen, nor ear heard, nor has it entered into the heart of man the things that God has prepared for those who love". I never want to miss that. Today Jesus is asking us to give Him water to drink, not only for Himself but for all those marginalized communities that do not have access to clean drinking water. What is going to be our collective response? I know that it is always very tempting for people to blame the poor. Why don't they help themselves? Of course, they would like to. Remember we live in an unequal world. George Orwell in Animal Farm says, "All animals are equal, but some are more equal than the others". Jesus said the poor will always be with us. The song writer says, "the steadfast love of the Lord does **not cease**, His mercies **never** come to an end, they are new every morning". If this is true for us in our own lives, then we must not be weary of extending goodwill and good actions to others.

This period let us all be on the lookout for **where**, **when** and **how** we may be of assistance to those in need not just of **water** but other necessities that may be brought to our attention. My prayer this day is that when Jesus will appear to us in various forms, even like a thirsty, wearied traveler and asks a favor of us, we will not to be diverted and distracted to the point that we fail to attend to His needs as well as respond appropriately to Him as expected. Amen

Growing in the Knowledge of Christ. 2 Peter 3:18

People's New Year Resolutions usually range from the mundane to the very serious. Personally, for me I always try to center my resolutions around my spiritual walk, not because I am "holier than thou" but because I know that I need to keep focused, I need to be centered, to monitor my progress and to be motivated as I go along. However, like most people I do not always achieve the goals that I set. But I keep on trying. Most times, I roll over my resolutions to the following year, which makes me human! This year while reflecting on my resolution, my thoughts shifted to **2 Peter: 3.** In it Peter talks about many things, people who want every evil thing that they desire; those who say the wrong things to confuse people. He talks about Jesus coming back and how some are wondering whether He is really coming back because it looks like it is taking so long. He adds that Jesus is delaying His coming so that more people can be saved. He now adds that while we are all waiting for Jesus to come back, "we must all grow in the grace and knowledge of our Lord and Savior Jesus Christ" (**verse 18**). That caught my attention and so I decided that my focus for this year would be "Growing in the knowledge of Christ".

Growing means moving from one stage to the other, increasing in ability and or becoming greater. Our natural life is a life-long process of growth. We start to grow from when we are born and continue until we die, moving from stage to stage. We grow physically, mentally, emotionally and in many other ways. As we grow, we learn to do different things. Each stage of life comes with different responsibilities and abilities. As we go along, we learn what each stage entails and we try to master them. Some do a good job of it, some do not. Nonetheless, that remains our natural physical growth process. However, the question that confronts all of us is "Do we grow in our spiritual lives as we grow in our natural lives?" The Bible talks about how Jesus grew in knowledge, wisdom and understanding. If Jesus grew, we too must grow. For our lives to be well rounded and balanced, we must grow spiritually as we grow physically. The Bible talks about baby Christians who drink milk and meat Christians who are mature (**1 Corinthians 3:2**). This means that we are required to grow, to increase because as the Bible says that there are deeper depths and higher heights to attain. We are not born to be static, stunted and glued to one spot. We must evolve and increase.

Growing in the knowledge of someone means knowing more about the individual, which leads to having a better understanding of the person. In all our personal relationships, we try to know our family members, our friends, our partners, our spouses, our children, our colleagues, our neighbors, even our fellow brothers and sisters in Christ. As a continuous process, we make the effort to learn and understand each other more, which deepens our relationships. When people have a very good relationship, we always say that it is because they know and understand each other. Nevertheless, if they do not know and understand each other, the relationship begins to crack and very soon, it comes to a "sudden death" as in soccer.

I try to identify what this growth in the knowledge of Christ would look like. To start with I know I must increase the information that I have of Him. Of course, we all know the stories, we know about how Jesus was born. We have just celebrated Christmas. We will soon celebrate Easter and then we will hear more about how He died. Growing in the knowledge of Jesus is more than having that mere information about Him. It is about having a deeper understanding of who He is, what He has done, what He is doing and what He will do. Jesus life is a perfect model for study, an adequate teaching material. His life of utterances, teachings, and actions are all recorded in our Scriptures, the greatest source of information about Him. From experience, we all know that when we read any material more than once, we pick up something new each time we go through it. Deeper knowledge of Jesus is not instantaneous. It is a process. The more we read about Jesus, the more we know and understand Him by the power of the Holy Spirit who illuminates our minds. I know that I must be as the Bereans that Apostle Paul talks about in **Acts 17:11**, who were zealous in their desire to know more of the scriptures, and so they read more and investigate more what they have heard.

Secondly, I know that I must "hang out" more with Jesus to use the youth lingo. Spending more time with Jesus in prayers, at His banquet, the Eucharist, in worship, in adoration, not skipping the set times for these activities, because of some lame excuses, which many of us are prone to will deepen my knowledge of Him. The more time I spend with Him, the more He will reveal Himself to me. **Mathew 13** tells of Jesus speaking to the multitude in parables and how in private He would explain the meanings of those parables to His Apostles. One of them asked Jesus why He always spoke to the multitude in parables. Jesus response was astounding. He said; "Because it has been given to you to know the mysteries of the Kingdom of heaven but to them it has not been given". Therefore, if I want to be part of that inner circle, I must spend more time with him, to learn more from him. Jesus still makes Himself available to teach us by the power of the Holy Spirit if we find the time to sit at His feet like Mary, His friend Lazarus' sister.

Thirdly, to grow in the knowledge of Jesus, I must put my feet where He puts His. Jesus as a model does not just say things, He does things. He then asks us to "go and do likewise". A tall order, I would say. But I need to start from somewhere. I need to have that "measuring rod" mentioned in **Ezekiel 40 t**o evaluate my progress as I go along. Some of us are born into our faith; some of us are converts into the faith. Hence, we are all at different stages of our spiritual walk, like those workers in the Bible employed by the rich man; some came in the morning, some in the afternoon and some in the evening. It does not matter when we started; the same reward awaits us all. We will all grow by doing some of the things that Jesus demands of us. I intend to do more this year.

Finally, Jesus knew Himself. He knew why He came to the world. He knew His purpose on earth. He stayed on course until the end. He was not diverted, nor did He allow Himself to be distracted. Growing in the knowledge of Christ requires that I know more about myself, so that I can stay focused and learn to do away with those things that may stand in my way. Jesus deserves that I have a worthy knowledge of Him. I do not want my relationship with Him to become stale and static. I want to achieve what one of my favorite songwriters says: "Day by day oh dear Lord, three things I pray, to see you more clearly, love you more dearly, follow you more nearly". To achieve this, my theme song this year is "New every morning is the love". I want Christ to make all things new in my life. This year. I want the old things to pass away. I do not want to continue to do things the same old way and expect a different outcome. I want a new heart, a new mind, new thoughts, new attitudes, new values, new feelings and new priorities.

Like the Potter's clay, I want to be remolded so that I can love more, forgive more, show more mercy, manifest more grace and be more obedient. I want to be filled with humility, to be gentle, meek and mild like Jesus. I want all my rough paths made straight. I want to shun evil, to lay aside every sin and weight that can easily beset me. I want to be more sensitive to the needs of the people around me. I want more oil in my lamp so I can keep burning. Like Barnabas, I want to be more of a "daughter of encouragement" (**Acts 4:36**). In the words of St. Paul to the **Philippians 4:8**, I want my heart to be set more on "those things that are true, noble, just, pure, lovely, of good report, of virtue and praiseworthy". Above all I want to continue to follow more after the things which make for peace (**Romans 14:19**). I am very aware that I will not achieve all these this year, but I am prepared to try. Making resolutions is easy. Keeping them is the challenge. Making the effort is good but trusting God for empowerment is the best part. Will you come along with me? Let us journey together.

Growing in God's Wisdom: Job 28:12

I was reading the Book of Job when **Job** in **28:12** asks where wisdom can be found. Where is the place of deep understanding? Somehow, I wondered why Job brought that up. I guess he must have needed Wisdom at that moment of his deep anguish and sorrow That sets my thoughts on Wisdom. What is wisdom anyway? The dictionary describes wisdom as having knowledge and good judgment and applying that knowledge in what is true and right, demonstrating sound judgment in deciding and acting, having profound thought and understanding. Job's response to his own question is found in **Job 28: 23**, he says God alone knows the way to wisdom and where wisdom dwells.

In **1Kings 3:4-14** God appeared to Solomon in a dream and asked him what He should give him. Solomon said "you have shown great mercy to me and you have allowed me to become king after my father who was a great man, But I am little child I do not know how to go and come and I have this your people to rule, a great people too therefore give me an understanding heart to judge your people, to discern between good and evil" In short Solomon asked for Wisdom. God said because you have asked for this, I will not only grant it to you, I will in addition give you honor and riches. There will be no one like you. Solomon was following in the remarkable steps of remarkable man, his father, King David. He was young and perceived himself to be inexperienced he was saddled with the responsibility of leading God's people, a people who had shown themselves on frequent occasion to be stubborn rebellious and hard on their leaders. Solomon had just emerged from a messy fight over succession to the throne, with his brothers trying to snatch the throne from him. There was a lot of intrigue surrounding that succession even with members of his own family and their supporters. Solomon had reasons to be wary. He knew he has a great challenge ahead of him. He was not naïve, he knew that only God could help him through. The Lord was delighted with Solomon's request. Consequently, God granted him wisdom beyond the measure that Solomon had anticipated. I think it was not so much Solomon's request that impressed God, it was what he was going to do with it. Solomon was very perceptive.

Proverbs 2 deals copiously with the concept of **Wisdom.** It says, "The Lord gives wisdom and from His mouth comes knowledge and understanding". God's wisdom is a gift to be possessed. Why do we need wisdom? Verse 5 says it will help us understand the fear of God and find the knowledge of God. Wisdom teaches us the awesomeness of God. Only with divine wisdom do we understand. Spiritual wisdom helps us to discern the power of God in us. Divine wisdom reveals the activities of God to us. What happens when we have wisdom? **Vs 10-11** say when wisdom enters our heart, discretion will preserve us and understanding will keep us. Wisdom will help us navigate each day of our lives as we relate to God, seeking Him to know His intent for us in our lives.

James 3:13-18 now gives his own perspectives about wisdom. He makes a contrast between wisdom that is worldly and the wisdom that is from God. In verse 13 he says he or she who is wise and understanding among us should show it by good conduct and our actions which should be in done in humility. James makes it clear that what makes us wise is not what we know but who we are. He says let the wise man or woman show his/her wisdom by his/her good life by deeds done in humility that comes from wisdom. James defines wisdom differently here. For James wisdom is the expertise or the ability to do a job well. It is the skillfulness in dealing with life, the capacity to live life well as it ought to be lived. The wise are those who when they live life as it ought to be lived have something to show for it. They have accomplished something eternally worthwhile.

James 3:17 now tells us what wisdom from God looks like. It says: The wisdom that is from above or from God is first of all pure, then peaceable, gentle, willing to yield full of mercy and good fruits, without partiality and sincere. It is not puritanical. It is not strictness, severity and distaste for joy and pleasure, but love for all that is good and true and beautiful. Wisdom is not harsh but fragrant and agreeable. and compassions. It understands the heartache of a lonely cold marriage or a rebel child, and weeps for the hardness of the world. It knows the pain of physical ailment and overwhelming debt. It understands the scars of neglect and humiliation. **2 Cor. 5; 16-17** says Wisdom from God views all people as neighbors and loves them with the impartial, unprejudiced love. Wisdom from God is not hypocritical, it is sincere, it does not deceive, nor deal in false humility. It is honest, unpretentious, transparent.

Time is an essential part of growing in wisdom. We grow wise slowly. It does not happen in an instant. We can grow and we will grow as the wisdom is given from above. And as we practice what we have been given a deep thirst will awaken in us for more and more and more will be given. **Mathew 13: 12** say whoever has more will be given more and he will have in abundance. Most of us live fairly unremarkable lives. We are not miracle workers, nor are we noted for anything in particular. We are not important in the sense of the world nor are we essential to the world order. We are just plain ordinary people. But if we are heavenly wise or heaven minded we will never worry about being irrelevant in life. James says when we are wise, we will sow the seed of righteousness. Paul says we will be God's aroma of Christ among those who are being saved and those who are perishing (**2 Corinthians 2:15**). The wise do not have to press and push, the lasting legacy of the wise is the way they make their mark in the world around them. I believe this should be more important to us in our various situations than the pursuit of an attention seeking life.

James 1:5 says If any of us lack wisdom; let us ask God who gives liberally and without reproach and He will give it to us. God gives without taunting us for our shortcomings nor does he embarrass us for our lack of it. Let us ask for wisdom if we think we need it. It will help us to navigate our everyday lives and make us stronger and help in our interactions with people. Sophocles the Greek writer says, "where wisdom is, there happiness will crown a piety (meekness) that nothing will corrode". Wisdom is deep rooted. Wisdom is desirable. Let us all ask God individually for this wisdom. I do not know what measure of it you need neither do you know what measure I need. But I am sure we all need some measure of wisdom. Let us ask our God of every good and perfect gift, let us ask in faith for God's promise of wisdom to meet our lack and our needs every day of our lives. May those qualities that define wisdom be granted unto us, we pray in Jesus name. Amen.

Jesus on Hierarchy in the Kingdom: Mathew 13:10-11

Mathew 13 10-11tells of Jesus speaking to the multitude in parables and how in private He would explain the meanings of those parables to His Apostles. One of them asked Jesus why He always spoke to the multitude in parables. Jesus response was astounding: "Because it has been given to you to know the mysteries of the Kingdom of heaven but to them it has not been given". Jesus just affirmed hierarchy, the *inner* and the *outer* circle as I call it. In fact, there was a time when Jesus told His Apostles that they were no more servants but that they have been upgraded to become friends, a more privileged position.

Hierarchy is a difficult concept. Most people do not like hierarchy. But we live in a hierarchical world. Hierarchy is needed for governance, for structure, for functioning and for allocation of responsibilities and resources. In all organizations, both secular and religious, by virtue of their positions, some people have more privileges than others. That should not be surprising to us because there is hierarchy in God's kingdom. That is why there are archangels and angels. Hierarchy comes with intrinsic and inherent power, which may not be bad in itself. I think the problem is how people choose to use that power. Power is the ability to do. Power exercised by an individual is labeled as either good or bad depending on its use. In a positive sense, power is perceived as valuable when it enables the holder to achieve goals but viewed negatively when used as a weapon of tyranny, ruthlessness, deviousness and for upholding undemocratic processes.

In the Bible, Lucifer used power negatively. He became overly ambitious and said "I will ascend into heaven. I will exalt my throne above the stars of God. I will be like the Most High" (**Isaiah 14**). Paul used his power to oppress the early Christians, but he had a change of heart when he encountered Jesus. In our world, hierarchy is used as an agent of oppression, of marginalization, of domination, in the work place, within the family, in the community, everywhere. It is also used to play god in some instances where life and death decisions are cruelly made for others. Power is used to deprive others of their personal and innate rights. In many cases the powerful demonstrate little or no sensitivity to those perceived as powerless. Jesus used hierarchy for the empowerment of His disciples. He invested a lot of time training them. However, bestowed with privilege and power, there were times when the disciples would attempt to over step their boundaries, like when they would try to prevent some people from having access to their Master or when they tried to forbid someone using Jesus name to cast out demons. But Jesus would always disallow their over handedness. Jesus carried hierarchy to the next level, when He selected Peter to be first among equals. He told him, "when you have been converted, strengthen the brethren". That sums up the godly use of power. Pass it on, let others benefit from what you have. But at times power corrupts and absolute power corrupts absolutely.

Just as hierarchy could be a source of discouragement and disillusionment, it could also be a motivating factor; an opportunity to strive for upward mobility, a determined effort to be greater and not stay at the bottom. Hierarchy is a very delicate issue to broach. Can the powerful be more mindful of how power is exerted? Should the powerless live in perpetual fright of the weight of power over and above them? Jesus affirmed hierarchy on earth as it is in heaven in demonstration of the right use of power. His own are expected to appreciate the blessings of being placed at the top of the hierarchy. They must use their privileged position not to lord it over, but to empower others as Peter was instructed to do. My prayer for God's kingdom on Earth is that all those who have been endowed with Power, Position and Privilege develop the sensitivity to be mindful of the Powerless of this world among and near them. Amen.

Jesus as Co-Feminist: International Women's Day: March 8th

At another annual celebration of International Women's Day, I decided to look at Jesus relationship with women, Jesus as Co-Feminist. Ah! Ah!! Ah!!! I know what you are thinking. How dare she use that highly demonized name for our Lord and Savior. You love the Lord, I love the Lord and so do thousands of feminists who actually applied that cognomen to Jesus. What is feminism? It is the philosophy that men and women should be treated equally and should have equal access to opportunities and resources. Feminists are the women who organize on behalf of this principle. They are not a homogeneous group; some are liberal, socialist, radical and multiracial and some are theologians. Feminist theologians abound in all religions of the world. They also all recognize that there are men who are sympathetic towards the issues of inequities between men and women and so they work tirelessly to advance the "cause". It is for these men that the feminists coined the phrase "Co-feminist".

Religion has the potential to empower women, but ignorance, media propaganda, and misinterpretation of religious texts have all allowed religion to marginalize and alienate women from the center. Patriarchal interpretations of religious texts are indicated and observed in all religions. Women of all religions have been denied their rights in the interpretation of scriptures. Yet in addition to having high family responsibilities, women are important stakeholders when it comes to religious issues. Many of the exclusionary practices used against women, are at times not only scripture-based, but cultural norms, interpreted by men, and then accepted by women who lack the knowledge and confidence to challenge the interpretations. Yet many women in the past and present are known for their great moral and spiritual authority which have given them a high status and much prestige within their own communities. In churches, it is women who organize fund raising events, education programs, revivals, kitchen responsibilities, bazaars, harvest events, charitable outreach for prisons and outcasts who need to be brought into the fold.

So how was Jesus drawn into this discourse? As we all know, Christianity has come from a patriarchal age. Interestingly most feminists, in fact all feminists, even the most hardened of them all, find no fault with Jesus the Author and Finisher of the Christian faith. Jesus is always tagged as a **Co-Feminist** because He was not in any way discriminatory against women. They always cite Jesus as a perfect example of a man who love women and treat them equitably. They say nowhere did Jesus put women down. The New Testament has profound accounts of Jesus relationship with women. They played a major part in His life and work. Women followed Jesus everywhere. Women were great companions for Jesus. Jesus befriended women. He protected them. He healed them. He helped them. He defended women. What a Great Friend of women!!!

Some feminists have questioned why there was no women among the Twelve. They argued that if Jesus loved women so much why did He not appoint at least One as one of His Apostles. The response is that Jesus had many women as His disciples and companions. See what He did with women. He entrusted Himself to women. He accepted their hospitality to Him. Women who always cooked for Him. Women looked after Him. **Luke 8:1-3** tells us that Jesus also accepted financial provision from various women who followed Him. Jesus allowed many women to mill around Him and he allowed them to spend their substance on Him. He did not feel too superior to allow women to attend to him. Jesus was a "Ladies-Man" if we could put it that way.

During His ministry, Jesus featured a lot of women in His parables, the woman who took three measures of meal till it was leavened, the woman who lost a coin and went to a great extent to find it, also included are the parable of the foolish and wise virgins and so on. In **Matthew 23:14** Jesus denounces the Pharisees for oppressing widows and taking their properties. This demonstrates Jesus sensitivity to women. He uses women in His parables so that the women in His audience may identify with the characters. Jesus expressed this sensitivity to the Syro-Phoenician woman whose daughter was sick. He understood her heart as a mother. She would not give up. Jesus not only appreciated her loyalty as a mother, He commended her for her obstinate faith. It was a poor widow with meagre contribution that Jesus singled out for praise. He commended the poor widow for her generosity with her mite. Nothing was too little for Jesus to notice about women, even this poor insignificant woman.

Jesus compassion to the outcast women usually considered sinners was remarkable. He treated them with utmost consideration. He did not condemn the sinner at Simon's house who wiped His feet with her tears and her hair. Jesus defended the woman, reminded His guests and others that she has performed the common courtesy due to any guest. While the men were questioning in their minds why He did that, Jesus publicly forgave her sins and used the occasion to teach love, forgiveness and faith. In **John 8:3-11** Jesus had no words of condemnation for the woman taken in adultery. When men were going to stone the woman, Jesus asked for her accusers and proclaimed that the one without sin among them should cast the first stone. Jesus did not only rescue her from death, He freed her from all her sins to the amazement of all the men around, reminding them that they were all sinners.

Jesus did not recoil at contact with women. The custom of those days was that women did not just go near men in public. It is still like that today in Arab countries. In **Luke 8: 43-48** Jesus disciples were outraged that the hemorrhaging woman, the one with the issue of blood, would go near Jesus to touch the hem of His garment possibly to defile Him. There was no reproach for her. Jesus did not condemn her. Instead Jesus commended her faith and dismissed the rigid Jewish taboo as irrelevant. She was dramatically healed.

In **Mark 10:13-15** Jesus showed gentleness towards the mothers who wanted to bring their children to Him and could not get past His disciples. Jesus showed love for the woman who was crippled for many years by touching and healing her. In **Luke 7:11-17** we read that during a funeral procession, Jesus demonstrated compassion for the widow of Nain whose only son died. Jesus moved near without being asked and raised the boy back to life giving immense joy to the mother. In **Luke 13:10-17** Jesus also showed compassion to the crippled woman who had been bent for 18 years. She was going along when Jesus called to her "Hey woman be healed" and she was healed. Women's healings were usually spectacular. In **Mark 5:21-23**Jesus raised Jairus' daughter when some people were laughing and deriding that He did not know that the girl was dead. Jesus threw out the skeptics and raised the young girl to life.

Jesus did a lot on the side of women. He gave women opportunity to proclaim the Gospel. **In John 4:7,** With the Samaritan woman at the well, Jesus initiated a conversation, the only time He revealed His identity was to this woman. He asked the Samaritan woman by the well for a drink, a taboo, nevertheless it was only to her that He revealed Himself as the Messiah, which gave her the opportunity to go and spread the word. At His Resurrection Jesus appeared first to a woman Mary Magdalene the one from whom He had cast out demons. She remained a faithful and passionate follower of Jesus. After the arrest of Jesus when all the men had fled, she lingered all the way to the cross to watch the crucifixion. She was the one who carried the spices to prepare the Lord for burial. She was the only one who came to see the burial site when everybody had left. She was the one who discovered that the stone had been rolled away. Jesus richly rewarded her faithfulness when He now appeared to her and told her to go tell the Apostles that He had risen. What a sensitive Lord! You can imagine her joy at seeing Jesus alive again.

Jesus harsh words were never for women, they were for the powerful male establishment. Jesus actually rejected the patriarchal power structure of His day. Jesus did not in any way uphold the male establishment. It was the male religious leaders He called "hypocrites" (**Luke 11:44**). It was a male political leader He denounced as a "fox" (**Luke 13:32**). It was the greedy businessmen trading in the house of God He called "thieves" (**Luke 19:46**). Jesus did not call into His fellowship, the righteous, the pious, or the highly influential persons of the community but He invited those who did not belong, the tax collectors, the sinners, and the Women. He promised God's kingdom not to the rich, the established and the pious, but to the poor of whom women are usually the poorest. No wonder the women loved Him so much that even after one of His Apostles betrayed Him and another denied Him, the women were there for Him.

Over all, Jesus, championed the cause of women who Paul described as the "glory of men" (**1 Corinthians 11:7**). Jesus was even concerned about women's sexuality issues. He protected women from the lustful inclination of men by saying that men should relate to women without lust in their hearts. "But I tell you that anyone who looks at a woman lustfully has already committed adultery with her in his heart" (**Mathew 5:28**). This means that women should be treated with respect on equal basis and on their level of achievement not objectified as sex objects to be used and disposed of by men. He said adultery and fornication is not only when men sleep with another woman, it is when men begin to undress women with their eyes and in their minds. This means that men are not giving recognition to the woman's worth, as a person. But they are relating to her as object to be used for their own benefit. Any man who lusts after a woman has already committed adultery and he is guilty, Jesus said.

On the Cross at His death Jesus last thought was for His mother. He was concerned about her welfare and saw to her care by handing her over to His brethren. Jesus had earlier indicated His respect for His mother when He performed His first miracle turning water to wine at the instigation of His mother. He did not have to yield to her, but He did. After His death His mother remained a faithful follower.

It is interesting at this point to note that Paul too like Jesus acknowledged the role of women in his ministry despite some controversial things he said about women. Paul did not undermine women's important roles in the Early Church. He gave the women honorable mention. He talked about Appiah in Philemon who was mentioned as hosting a church in her house. He talked about Euodia and Syntche who labored with Paul in the Gospel. He talked about Lydia, the woman who sells purple, a prosperous woman, who heard about Paul and opened her home to him and fellow believers. He talked about Mary to the Romans, who labored much for the sake of the Gospel. He also mentioned Persis, Phoebe, Priscilla, who risked her life for Paul in Rome, also Rufus mother who acted like a mother to Paul. Tryphena and Tryphosa were all recognized by Paul for their contribution to the work of God. God used women in various ways and allowed their contribution to be retained in the Scriptures.

So how does the world today, thousands of years later, view women in various religions. Thank fully women have come a long way. Jesus has shown the way, with, of and for women. Jesus had indicated in many ways that He was against all forms of discrimination especially sexism. Jesus continues to draw women unto Him according to God's promise in **Joel 2:28-29** when God said I will pour out my Spirit upon all of you. Your sons and daughters will prophesy and even on your male and female servants I will pour out my Spirit. All women want is to find meanings for the divine presence within and around them. With Jesus Co-Feminist on their side, women have continued to revolutionize religion in various ways. Women have continued to be religious specialists. Women have continued to be religious innovators. One can say that they are on their way to attaining the prophetic dimension which Mahatma Gandhi (1869-1948) captured when he said, "The words of women will have the same authority as the Scriptures". Amen.

He (Jesus) Answered Her Not a Word: Mathew 15: 21-28

I was reading **Mathew 15: 21-28** an interesting story about Jesus interaction with a woman whose daughter was severely demonized. It is a strange story, but it is also a significant story. Many of us regard Jesus as being very sympathetic and compassionate towards women. I have recorded my thoughts on Jesus as a Co-Feminist in another Reflection. On reading this story, I was taken aback. I was really startled by Jesus reaction to this woman, hence I decided to allow my thoughts to go deeper and try to understand Jesus interaction with this woman. Jesus has just finished explaining to the people the relationship between God's commandments and men's traditions and some other issues brought up by Peter. As usual with the Lord after some long exposé, preaching, teaching, narrating parables, etc. He would leave one location and cross to another part of the city. So that others too would have the benefits and advantages of His teaching. He did not confine Himself to one location. He was always moving to where there are needs. On this particular occasion, He went to the region of Tyre and Siddon.

Verse 22 tells us that a woman of Canaan from that region came and cried out to Jesus saying, "Have mercy on me O Lord Son of David my daughter is severely demon possessed". She came because she had a problem. She was distraught over her family situation especially over her child. Many have come to Jesus for various reasons, over different personal problems, health problems and so on. Hers was a case of a mother's anguish. We all know how mother's groan when their children are ill, or when they are having severe problems, troubles, issues and challenges. The children's problems become their own. They ache and ache bearing the pain in their bodies.

This Canaanite woman came to Jesus came at an era when the world was divided into two: the Jews and the Gentiles. Traditionally the Canaanites were the enemies of the Jews. It was their lands on the other side of the Jordan that God gave the Israelites. God drove the Canaanites out and settled the Israelites there. They were the people God drove out of the promised land because of their immorality and their idolatry, the others were the Amorites, the Jebusites, the Hittites etc. You can understand why they are the enemies of the Jews. Jesus was from the Jewish tribe. But this woman came to Jesus not minding His superior race, not bothered or intimidated by the fact that she is the "other". We do not even know her name. because it was not mentioned. But Thank God nobody is anonymous before God. He knows us ALL by name. This woman showed courage and determination with her first step of coming to Jesus. She definitely must have heard about Jesus, His reputation and His good works. She cast aside any intimidation and came to Jesus. She was not to be deterred. She had a problem. She knew who can solve the problem. Emboldened by this fact, she came to Jesus. I love this woman!!!!!

Her first utterance was an acknowledgement and confirmation of who Jesus is. "Oh Lord Son of David" followed by a plea "have mercy on me". She uses Jesus special tittle "Son of David", I am sure in her mind she thought, "if I use His special tittle not to flatter Him but to acknowledge who He is, He will not resist me. If I plead for mercy, He will not ignore me, after all I have heard that He is a Merciful person., healing and caring. But see what happened. **Verse 23** says "But He answered her Not a word". This is very unlike Jesus. She was totally ignored. Jesus did Not respond to all the respect accorded, the pleading, above all Jesus did not honor her faith. It was her faith in Jesus that brought her to Him. Granted that this woman had no claim on Jesus, she was an outcast, a Canaanite, a Gentile, nonetheless she was not deterred. She was not even a born again as some would say in today's world.

All she knew was that Jesus was the Great Physician, the Healer, the Good one, but He was ignoring her, stonewalling her. Not a word from the Son of David. Have you been there before? Even King David the man after Gods own heart, in **Psalms 28 and 35** yelled unto the Lord, "Do not be silent unto me lest I be like those who go down into the pit". To make matters worse, the disciples asked Jesus to send her away. Cruel disciples!!!!treating her like an outcast. They knew she had a problem, they knew she was desperate, but they just could not stand her being pushful and so asked Jesus to send her away. I wonder why they did not do it themselves. After all they were ready to prevent even small children from coming close to Jesus. Lol.

It was then in **Verse 24** that Jesus gave a remarkable response that was like rubbing salt on an open wound. Jesus said, "I was not sent to the lost sheep of the house of Israel", meaning I was not sent to the likes of you. I have nothing that I can do for you. Wow!!!!!Jesus treatment of this woman was so contrary to who He is, to His image. This woman came in utter sincerity, desperation, and great respect not with a sense of entitlement but begging and pleading. And yet Jesus put her off with these severe words. I wonder how some of us would have reacted to Jesus response. Some of us would feel so humiliated, and lash at Jesus wondering who does He think He is. Some of us would mumble some unprintable words. Some of us will simply break down in tears, wondering what else we were supposed to do. However, this woman was not put off, was not discouraged by Jesus' response. In **verse 25** the Bible said that she came and added **worship** to her pleas. Worship to Someone who has just given you the worst brush-off anyone could receive. This woman cried deeper "Lord please help me". This time she probably went on her knees, bowed her head in in surrender, groveled on the floor in total abandonment. Jesus remained unmoved. **Verse 26,** Jesus second response was more pungent than the first one. Jesus said: "it is not good to take the children's bread and throw it to the little dogs" meaning we cannot give things meant for the privileged ones to the outcast, to the rejected ones.

Why would Jesus treat this poor woman like this? Jesus is not cruel. He is not a psychopath who enjoys heaping pain on people. After all we have been told that He is touched by our infirmities. We have been told that Jesus came for the whole world. What if we are not perfect, so what if our walk is not right. We have been told that even if our sins are as red as crimson, Jesus blood will make us as white as now. God says He will show mercy unto whom He will show mercy, God said He will never cast away all those who come to Him through His Son. Why then is Jesus not responding to this woman's pleas and cries? Many people would give up in utter resignation at that stage. If God does not want to answer my prayers, there is nothing I can do about it. They will say. But we forget what Jesus said we should do. He says we should keep on asking, we should keep on seeking, we should keep on knocking. **Luke 11 9-10** "for everyone who asks receives, he who seeks finds, and to him who knocks it will be opened".

This is exactly what this woman did. She did not give up, after all she was in Jesus Presence. She was smart. She did not walk away telling herself she will go and look for alternative to Jesus. Something deep in her heart told he that this is not denial even though it looks like it. In **verse**

27 she then responded that "even little dogs are entitled to the crumbs which fall from their masters' table". What brazen effrontery!!!!That did it for Jesus. In **Verse 28** He said "O woman Great is your faith. Let it be as you desire". Instantly her daughter was healed. Wow!!!!!.

It was then I started to think of the implications of Jesus reaction to this woman. To start with, Jesus did not instantly respond to her. There are times when we need to be tested. It was faith that brought her to Jesus. It was faith that enable her to receive what she came for. Wait on the Lord. Faith does not falter. Faith persists. Faith does not murmur nor give up. Jesus did not respond to her not because her pleas were not passionate and fervent enough, in fact they were. At times God just wants us to keep at it. He wants to see our persistence. God responds to all needs, even those we bring to Him on behalf of others. This woman's plea was on behalf of her child. She eventually got a reprieve for her. Let us keep on interceding for one another. Intercessions are valid before the Lord.

This woman understood that other things might be obstructing a positive response to her prayers. She changed focus from prayers of healing for her child to prayer of mercy for herself. "Have mercy on me. Lord, help me". When Jesus seems totally silent and it seems that nothing is happening, we wonder if it is sin that has separated us from Him. David in **Psalm 66: 18** knows that if he regards iniquity in his heart the Lord will not hear him. That was why David penned his Psalm of confession **Psalm 51 "**Have mercy O Lord on me according to your loving kindness, according to your tender mercies, blot out my transgressions wash me thoroughly from my iniquities. And cleanse me from my sins". Prayers of forgiveness, prayers of submission do work. Also, it seems Praise and worship at times work together. The woman started with praise to Jesus then she added worship. Praise and Worship of the Lord could be offered no matter the circumstances. This may be hard I know. This woman offered both despite Jesus negative reaction to her.

However, it was this Canaanite woman last response that impressed Jesus. She said, "even little dogs eat crumbs from their masters table". There was no sense of entitlement. Lord I do this I do that, I walk in your ways, I obey all your commandments, therefore I deserve all that I want or need. As you read what is your desire? What are you desperate about? Bring it before the Lord and be rest assured that in His own time he makes all things beautiful just like He did for the Canaanite woman and her daughter. Amen

Jesus' visit to Mary and Martha. A different perspective: Luke 10: 38-42

This was a message I once shared at Christmas, a time of visits, family get together, cooking, fellowship, entertainment and of course with a focus on the Reason for the season. I shared about Jesus visit to His friends' house and how He was entertained by them. This Passage found in **Luke 10: 38-42** tells us that a female whom I will call Sister Martha welcomed Jesus into her home. It was then mentioned that she has a sister called Mary who sat at the feet of Jesus to hear His word while the older sister was preparing food to entertain Jesus and His entourage. We do not know whether Sister Martha invited Jesus to her home or whether Jesus simply stopped by informally when He entered this certain village called Bethany on His way to Jerusalem. Either way it was a privilege for those two women to have Jesus come to their home. How many of us would like Jesus to just stop by our home at Christmas season? Personally, would set me into a frenzy.

Jesus showed up and these two sisters went into a frenzy of different kinds. To start with Jesus did not arrive alone. He never went anywhere alone. He had His twelve friends who were always around and many other followers who always tagged along out of curiosity and out of genuine interest. So Jesus showed up with many people. Secondly Jesus did not show up in an SUV or a private jet for that matter as some religious leaders of today would. Jesus did not even arrive on donkey.

He walked. These walks could be tiresome, tedious, because of uneven terrain, no paved roads, no sidewalks. These walks could make one tired, hungry, thirsty and beat as some might say in local parlance. These two sisters recognized that Jesus and His entourage had both physical and emotional needs to be met.

Sister Mary was very welcoming. A good host or hostess would pay attention to a distinguished guest, welcoming, fawning over the guest providing companionship to the guest so that the special guest is not left alone or made to feel ignored. In my culture a good host/hostess would sit awhile with the guest especially one who had come from afar. You would ask how the journey was, did you travel well, hope you did not encounter any difficulties on the way. you will say I am very glad to see you, even though unexpected. This way the visitor will not feel guilty for stopping by without notice. The guest will feel at ease. You will even ask about people back home, people that you know, even family and friends and neighbors too. You will exchange information and try to catch up on old time news. Then your guest would tell the host/hostess that it was good to be in his/her house. This is what we call doing the emotional labor, the expressive role that ensures your guest has emotional comfort and wellbeing.

I would say that it was in this process of Mary performing this expressive emotional assignment that Jesus too began to what He does best, teaching, preaching, talking about Himself, about His Father's Kingdom, His ministry and his fellow workers and travelers on the road. Of course, Mary naturally became absorbed and so engulfed. Who would not be? The Bible tells us that when Jesus speaks people wonder. Mary sat at the feet of Jesus lapping up every word that came out of His mouth. I am sure Jesus was pleased to have such a captive and attentive audience in Mary.

There was also sister Martha who was quite sensitive to Jesus' other needs, His physical needs. Having travelled on those long dusty roads He and his men would need food in their stomachs and so she swung into action. Strangely enough there were no women among this particular entourage. The story might have had a different dimension. Martha went into the kitchen to start preparing nutrients for Jesus body. So both sisters were doing what women do best and at most times are very good at it. It would have been gross negligence and irresponsibility for both of these sisters to go off together in the same direction, either to both to sit at Jesus feet keeping Him company, interacting with Him, and just savoring His words. Jesus would have loved that. But then it would have been inappropriate not to remember that He would need to be shown some hospitality. At the same time, it would be rude and it would amount to ignoring Jesus and His company if both had disappeared in to the kitchen cooking with no one out there with Jesus to hear what was on His mind. There was a good gender division of labor. Both sisters were fulfilling some gender roles. Both sisters complemented each other's role.

So, what was the problem? The Bible tells us that after some time Sister Martha came out from the kitchen to complain and told Jesus to reprimand Sister Mary for not helping her with the kitchen chores. When she complained to Jesus, we were told that Jesus gave her what has been considered Jesus most significant and **controversial** response. Jesus said "Martha, Martha, you are so worried and troubled about many things and Mary had chosen "the good part". Some translation calls it "the better part". I have heard people preach on this story before and most times it has always been about extolling the role and responsibility and the part played by one of these women over the other. It has always been about making a choice between being a Mary or a Martha. And I have always wondered where does that leave the man? After all Lazarus the brother to these two women was Jesus very close friend. Where was Lazarus when all these was happening? Hanging out with the men. The bible had nothing to say about Lazarus helping out in any way with the needful things to be done when one has guests. Not serving the drinks, not setting the table. We were not told that he contributed anything towards entertaining his best Friend. He left it all to the women. Gender negligence. I call that

Why was Martha so upset, with her baby sister that she had to complain to their esteemed Guest. It was not sibling rivalry as some have called it. Martha was just overwhelmed with what she was left to do That is evidence of the stress and burnout that women suffer when others in the house refuse to participate in the household chores. Also why did Mary not deem it fit to help her sister at some point, as a woman knowing that their guests would need to be fed. And with so many men to cook for, which would mean a lot of work. Even with modern gadgets and equipment that the modern woman would have, it is still a lot of work.

In the traditional times both then and now, preparing meals would involve fetching water, kneading dough to make bread, grinding manually some of the needed items, possibly fetching some firewood and the actual cooking of the meal and serving. Martha was surely overburdened and so she complained out loud. But it looked as if Jesus sided with Mary commending Mary's sitting at His feet and listening to Him. Do we then take it that Jesus did not appreciate Martha's effort at providing hospitality? I have always maintained that Jesus was always sensitive to the plight of women. Do we then assume that Jesus undermined Martha's role? I do not think so.

Many people have used this story to depict Martha as the practical one and Mary as the spiritual one. The story has also been used to reinforce a hierarchy of spiritual engagements over secular ones. It has even been said that it is much more important to engage in spiritual pursuits than to engage in secular ones. The implication is that only religious works, religious activities, religious exercises are of much importance. Secular tasks are devalued, forgetting that some secular activities are needed for everyday survival. I personally think it would NOT be appropriate to characterize Jesus words to Martha as establishing a hierarchy or creating a dichotomy between the sacred and the secular. I am sure that Jesus knows and is very mindful of the fact that we need both for our survival. I do not also think that Jesus does not appreciate the fact that there are some needful and necessary things that we need to do in this world. After all Jesus at another time observed that we are in this world, a great reality. In **John 17** Jesus has some lengthy explanation and affirmation of His presence and our presence in the world. God has put us in the world for a purpose. Which means that we are part of the world, we exist in the world and so we need to survive in the world.

In all these I think the issue is not whether Mary was spiritual and Martha was physical. I think the issue is the keyword used to describe Martha. In **Luke 10:40** Martha was described as being "**distracted**" in some translation. I think I like that. Jesus in verse in **verse 41** said "Martha, Martha you are too worried and troubled about many things". The dictionary described distraction as something that prevents someone from giving full attention to something else. It is also mean to be encumbered with, over involved in, engrossed with, too pre occupied with, over focused on, paying too much attention on, too burdened by, overly concerned with I could go on and on and on to describe Martha's state. Aren't we all at times, both men and women get seduced by **distraction**, which takes away our focus on things that are needful, things that matter? We all know about the cares of the world, a life to live, a job to do, children to care for, at times parents to look after, spouses to help, vulnerable family members who need our undivided attention. And many others who impose on us and we ourselves who need to attend to our own needs. All these take so much of out of our time and effort that we get **distracted** from the important things.

As much as some of these things that we engage in are useful they become great diversions from things that are important. Distractions and diversions from what I ask. At times as people of religion we have some basic responsibilities and rites to perform. At times we are not able to perform them as we have become too distracted with or by other things. Some Christians cannot go to the house of God even on their designated days, because they have some chores to do or games to watch on TV, or sports to take children to, dogs to walk, or work to go to. At times as husbands/wives, fathers/mothers, politicians/citizens, teachers/

students., religious leaders/followers, professionals/clients, are not able to fulfill their responsibilities because they have become distracted by many other things, that they lose focus on their primary responsibility.

In this story I think both women Marta and Mary have their plusses and their minuses. However, both are guilty of negligence. Martha was too engrossed in the kitchen to ensure that the Guests were alright. Mary too was distracted and singular focused. She ignored Jesus and His men's physical need. They both lacked the needed **balance**. The bible say we shall not live by bread alone. We cannot live nor survive by eating only spiritual bread without the physical bread. Neither can the soul survive if we eat only the physical bread and no spiritual bread. We need both for our wellbeing.

Ultimately it is about **combining** Martha's traits with Mary's traits. It is not an either one or the other issue. It is about being diligent in our day to day responsibilities and still being faithful in our relationships with God. This is the challenge. We cannot fulfil one to the detriment of the other. It is about being both in the kitchen and at Jesus feet. It is not a choice between one or the other. It is being both. Afterall Jesus did not only preach and teach. He fed the people with both physical and spiritual food. As much we need to be responsible enough to meet our daily physical obligations, we must equally be diligent enough to pay attention to our spiritual needs. Unfortunately, no one can achieve that balance for us. It requires individual adjustment on the part of each one of us. There is no one size fits all to this pervasive and perennial problem of distraction that plagues many people.

Finally, there is no divide between our physical self and our spiritual self. They are integrated. One feeds the other. They are both emmeshed together. The good part is when well blended they both function in unison, in consonance and in mutuality. At Christmas or any other celebration Jesus may not be stopping by unannounced. He may not be showing up with His numerous friends, we must remember that Jesus in His Omnipotence actually lives with us and within us. He does not go and come at will. He is an Ever Present God. Which means we cannot be looking to be Mary on some days and Martha on some days. It is being Martha/Mary on all days. Our prayer is that all of us are effectively in composite rolled into the one who our Lord wants us to be. Amen

Jesus' Modus Operandi for Today's Woman

In our Prayer Meeting we did a series on Jesus Manner of Operation. We always say we want to be more like Jesus, but the question has always been how do we achieve this? Following Jesus Modus Operandi is living according to His will. It is the ability to interpret things from His perspectives. It is understanding things in the light of His wisdom. Jesus said we can do all these things and even more through Him by the power of the Holy Spirit. We decided to look at how Jesus operated, some of the things that He did and the practical manner in which He did them, so we can learn from them. We identified some of Jesus **Modus Operandi** that we think today's woman will find useful.

Jesus was a Problem Solver: Do you know that everything that God created is a solution to a problem? Every gift that God gave is meant to be a solution to somebody's issue. To start with God established the golden thread that links creation. God wanted a love relationship; He created Adam, when Adam was lonely, God created Eve. When both of them did not know what else to do with themselves they figured out how to make babies!!!! Jesus calling was to achieve a purpose. Jesus was a problem solver, most times whenever Jesus saw or identified any problem, He would immediately move to resolve that problem. He always knew where He fitted in and where He could help. When people are burdened with guilt because of their sins, Jesus offered forgiveness. When people are spiritually starved Jesus says I am the Bread of Life. When people were physically hungry Jesus fed them. When people's bodies were riddled with sickness and diseases Jesus healed them. When people are possessed with evil spirits, Jesus delivers them and set them free. When people appear to be ignorant Jesus offers them wisdom. Jesus says My words are Spirit and life. Jesus sat for days teaching the laws of God and how to have extraordinary relations ship with God and with other people. Jesus is still giving of Himself. Hence how can we all explain our survival in this hard world of ours? But for His grace. If our assignment in life is to help people solve problems, to bless someone. We must build our lives around someone elses' lives. There are needs everywhere, there are needs in the church, in our communities, in our workplace, around each one of us. Do we see these needs or do we close our eyes and pretend they are not there or do we just not see? Do we open our hearts, our eyes, our minds to these needs and addressed them with the gifts that we have? We must look for ways to do something in somebody's life. We must pray to be always guided, to have the eyes to see, the sensitivity to feel, the nose to smell, the ears to hear where we are needed and the strength to go there.

Jesus was always available: Jesus went to where the people were. Jesus ministry was not a localized one. He did not sit and wait for people to come to Him. Jesus was itinerant. He went from place to place, to the highways, to the byways, to people's homes, to their celebrations, to their marriages, to their synagogues, to the pool where they were recreating and having fun and wanting to be healed. Jesus was reachable. He did not confine Himself to one location. He walked into the lives of those who need Him. Some people are born extroverts. They are outgoing people. But some are not. People who need us may not want to come to us or may not be able to come to us. We have to go to them so that God's purpose can be achieved. We should not be afraid to connect to people. At times in the process of reaching out we may be rejected, we should not be afraid of rejection. After all some people criticized Jesus for going into sinner's house to eat. If he was in a place and was told that He was needed somewhere else, He will quickly wrap up what He was doing and move to the location when He was needed. He was somewhere else when He was told about the death of the young girl, he quickly went to the girl's house. When he was told about Lazarus illness, He wrapped up what he was doing and travelled miles to be with Lazarus sisters. We live in a small world, a global village as some scholars will tell us. Let us get out of our comfort zone and go somewhere, call on some one, reach out to someone. We must not be hermits. We must not confine ourselves to our weenie little world. The world is our oyster. God has given us the world let us explore it. We never know who God will use us to achieve His purpose in us and in the lives of others. In Christ we are all interconnected.

Jesus knew what He has to offer, His gifts.: Jesus has confidence in who He is and what He has to offer. If you are a salesman or a saleswoman and you have something to sell, if you do not believe in what you have to sell, you cannot promote and market it to people. Before you can recommend it to someone you must believe it in it. You must believe that it works. Jesus believed in His products. He believed that His product will change people. In **John 4:13-14** Jesus said to the woman at the well, Whosoever, drink of this water, that is water in the well, he says he shall thirst again but whosoever drink of the water that I shall give him shall be in him a well of water springing up into everlasting life. What makes us believe in our products? I think it is the knowledge of our products. In **John 10:27** He says my sheep knows my voice so when they hear it they follow me. What confidence! Jesus knew what He had to offer. Do you know your **gifts**? Do you even know how to put to use the gifts that you have been given? A great challenge, I would say. The Bible talks about the gift of the Father, the Gift of the Son and the gifts of the Holy Spirit. We are all endowed with some gifts that will help us to achieve the purpose of the Giver. It is our responsibility to know the gifts we have individually been given and look for opportunities to put them to use. Jesus did. How else would 5000 men without the women come looking for him. Jesus was always giving of Himself. Like Paul says in **1Timothy 1:6** we all need to stir up the gifts that we have been given to be relevant and effective in our lives.

Jesus knew His beneficiaries, those He has been sent to: Jesus knew the people He came to serve. He was always in their company, interacting with them. That is why He was confident that they will know His voice In **John 10:14** Jesus says, I know my own and my own knows me. The bible counsels us to know the people we work with or we are in contact with. **Proverbs 27:23** says be thou diligent to know the state of thy flocks and look well to thy herds. A pastor/priest must make concerted effort know his flock. The flock are not just people you see on Sundays glued to their regular seats on Sundays. How often do priest pastors go out of their way to familiarise themselves with their flock. That is why some people say that they can never go to any of those mega churches, because there they are anonymous. Out of all the thousands of people milling around Jesus, he picked Zacchaeus, called him by name and told him he was coming to his house. Priests and pastors may not be able to go everybody's house but must be interested enough in their welfare to know when members of his flock might need their attention. Above all he/she needs to know about their spiritual journey to know how to minister to them. A lawyer must know his clients else he cannot defend them well. A doctor must know his patients very well otherwise holistic healing cannot take place. A policeman must know his community very well to be able to protect them. A teacher must know his or her students very well to ensure good interaction and successful learning. If we want to be like Jesus it starts with the knowledge of people around us. A wife is assigned to her husband vice versa. Parents are assigned to their children. Secretaries are assigned to their bosses. Moses was assigned to the Israelites. Aaron was assigned to Moses. Paul was assigned to the Gentiles. Jesus was assigned to ALL of us. To be effective we must have a good knowledge of the people that we are required to work with. Take time to study and know them and understand them. It is vital to successful interaction.

Jesus took time to Plan: The Bible says woe unto those who do not plan. **Proverbs 24:3** says through wisdom a house is built and by understanding it is established. **Proverbs 19:9** says a man's heart plans his way but the Lord direct His steps. Jesus taught in **Luke 14 28-32,** For which of you intending to build a tower does not sit down first and count the cost whether he has enough to finish it lest after He has laid the foundation and is not able to finish it. And all who see it began to mock him saying this man began to build and was not able to finish. Or what king who is going to make war, does not sit down first and consider whether he is able to win with 10,000 men or with 20,000 men. When he finds he does not have enough men to fight, while the enemy is still a great way off sends a delegation for recommendation of peace. What is a plan? A plan is a written list of arranged actions necessary to achieve our desired goal. **Habakkuk 2:2** tells us to write the vision, make it plain upon the tablets. Nehemiah wanted to rebuild the walls. He planned towards the success of that project. God always honor those who planned. Noah planned after he was instructed to build the Ark. Solomon the wisest man who ever lived took time to plan the building of the temple. Moses the great Deliverer took time to plan the tabernacle and the direction of his journey. Planning makes us look structured. But there is a caution. We can see from Jesus movement that at times, when He has planned to go somewhere and when something new crops up, or suddenly there is a need somewhere, Jesus does not hesitate to make a detour to attend to that need. Planning does not mean becoming unduly rigid. It means having a blue print to work with. The secret of success is planning. Planning is tedious. It is laborious and many avoid it and so do things haphazardly. Planning is time-consuming but it is well worth it. Plan ahead, have in your mind what you want to achieve. **Proverbs 6:6-8** tells us to go to the ant to consider its way and be wise. Ants plan and gather food during the harvest and store it for the time of lack. They work in summer to enjoy in winter. How many of us plan? How many of us strategize? How many of us behave like fire fighters who act promptly when there is a fire because they are always ready, always ready in and out of season. They do not collect the water the day there is a fire. They always have the water ready to be used, that is how they are able to save lives. We thank God that he has given us the ability to plan. Let us put it to use.

Jesus found time to Rest: Jesus was an action man. He was always on the go, on the move. But He also knows the necessity of Rest and Relaxation. **Mark 6:31** Jesus said Come ye yourselves apart into a desert place and rest awhile. Always out of His busy schedule, Jesus found the time to rest. Jesus was tired, He even slept in the boat. Rest and Recuperation is a time of repair. It is a time for renewal. It is a receiving time. Jesus would separate Himself, He went into the mountains into secluded places to recuperate, to receive, to replenish. Work time is giving, rest time is receiving. We must have both. As women we know how we juggle between running the home, running our lives, running our children's lives, our jobs, our spouses, our friends, our extended family, helping our neighbors and doing church work. In all these, we cannot give of our best; in fact we will be performing below capacity if we do not rest awhile. Even organizations understand that people suffer from stress. that is why they grant stress leave. Jesus rested whenever He needed to. How many times have we heard about people breaking down? We cannot attain efficiency if we do not know how to rejuvenate ourselves. Jesus demonstrated judgment about maintaining a good balance between work and rest. This is a great challenge for all of us, not knowing when to stop. Then we become tired and unable to go on, then we quit and then we fall into the category of the under achievers. Studies have shown that one in five women suffer from fatigue and mental breakdown. We need to plan take time off to replenish so we can continue fulfill the purpose that Christ has set for us. I think we will all agree that some of the things that we have identified are pre requisites for success. May God guide or thoughts and ways so that we can be successful in all that we do. Amen.

SECTION THREE

Miscellaneous Social Issues Reflections

This Section contains some Miscellaneous Reflections on Some Social Issues. Some are Conceptual, some are Personal, many are Interesting. Enjoy

Contents

Celebrating the Diversity in God's Kingdom. Genesis 11

I chose "Celebrating the diversity in God's Kingdom" as the theme for 2015 Black History Month Service, which was hosted by my Parish, St. Faith's Anglican Church in Edmonton. The month of February is always a very significant month. Many events are celebrated in the month. Most universities observe the Global Awareness Week in February. World Day of Prayer is yearly observed in the month. International Development Day is marked in February. Of course, it is also the month that we celebrate LOVE in all its ramifications. I am talking of Valentine. It is also the month of Oscar awards, Hollywood's big event. The Chinese New Year celebration starts on **February 19.** In addition, of course, the Black History Month celebration is always in February. All these events mark the diversity among all peoples.

My thoughts then strayed to the story of the Tower of Babel in **Genesis 11**, which starts in verse 1 with "now the whole earth had one language and one speech". That spells uniformity, which sounds good. Unfortunately, out of it came an insidious plot by the people against God. In verse 4, they said to themselves "Let us build ourselves a city and a tower whose top is in the heavens, let us make a name for ourselves". The Bible says God read their thoughts and decided to counter their plot and confuse them. In verse 9, we are told that at Babel, the languages of the earth were confused and the people were scattered abroad over the face of the earth. However, as one of our hymns tells us "God is working His purpose out". The dispersion that started out as an intention to confound turned out into the great geographic and linguistic diversity that we see in our world today. Then fast forward to many centuries later, the same God who scattered the people at Babel began to gather them together again at Pentecost, this time creating a new community. Though different languages were again spoken, a pluralistic, international, multilingual, multicultural Church, the Body of Christ, was born.

Genesis 1:31 tells us that after creation, God looked at everything that He had created and noted that it was good. In fact, not just good, but very good the bible says. The good world that God created was not a homogenous world. It is indeed a beautiful world with rich diversity. With over seven billion people, the world today indeed comes with a fascinating tapestry and an array of different human shapes, sizes, colors, languages and culture. One cannot overlook the good that exists in the world that God has created: beautiful faces, beautiful people, beautiful places. The equally good part is that God relishes the diversity that He has created. Not only did He declare the entire creation good, **Joel 2:28** tells us God promised that He would pour out His Spirit upon all flesh, meaning that He would empower everyone one that He has created with His might, He would bestow on everyone His enabling Spirit. His favors and daily benefits would be on everyone. No one would be excluded. Great and encouraging thoughts!!!!.

In **Ezekiel 24:3** God gave Ezekiel the prophet an unusual assignment. He was instructed to put a pot on fire, to fill it with water, to add to it pieces of meat of every good cut, and to add the seasonings and to set it all to cook. He was to allow it all to simmer very well. As top chefs will tell us, all these diverse ingredients when cooked together usually melt and produce an enjoyable, fully blended nutritious meal. This in essence is how the "melting pot" analogy came to be. God initiated it, not the United States of America. The overall message in all these short stories is that God had a purpose for the diversity that He created. He could have allowed the one language, the one speech of Babel to remain. However, He created diversity out of that oneness. In that diversity, God wanted cohesion. He wanted "Unity in Diversity". Unity is a state of oneness, a state of being joined together. Paul in his letter to the **Philippians 2:2-5** reminds us what this cohesion would look like. He talks of being like-minded, having the same love, being of one accord and of one mind. Wow!!!

In essence, Unity in Diversity means that all differences would be discounted. The dividing walls would be broken down. Unity means that we will all be bound together in love; we will all have the same mind of Christ. One cannot over emphasize the benefits of such unity for the world and for individuals in the world. It is immeasurable!!!Thankfully, today we can all say that even with the immense problems that the world has witnessed, the diverse world that God created has fast been emerging as a melting pot. This we see in global travels, migration, relocation, intercultural alliances, international adoption, cross-cultural marriages, ecumenism, interfaith groups and various forms of unification that are happening all over the world. It is a promising melting pot that has continued to evolve.

Paul in his letter to the **Galatians 3:27-28** now emphasizes and reiterates this Unity in the Body of Christ. He says for as many of you as were baptized into Christ, having put on Christ, there is neither Jew nor Greek, neither slave nor free, neither male nor female. For in Christ Jesus, all are one. In this one sentence, Paul nullifies the three main stratifications that we see in our world. First, he says there is neither "Jew nor Greek", in the Body of Christ. This is about the **ethnic and racial** classification that the world likes to talk about. To start with, **Psalm 24:1** reminds us that the earth belongs to the Lord and all the people therein. We live in a world that is clearly diversified along racial and ethnic lines. We hear of the white people, the brown people, the black people, the yellow people, the red people, the mixed people, the so called people of color, and of course people classified based on their geographic origin, North Americans, South Americans, Europeans, even within Europe we have Eastern Europeans, we have Africans, Caribbeans, Asians, Hispanics, Indigenous people, East Indians, Orientals, Middle Easterners, People of the Pacific, Mediterranean people. The list is endless. We also even hear of people being categorized as majority and minority. In all these man-made categorizations, Paul is saying that in the world that God had created and more so in the Universal Church of Christ Jesus, ALL ARE ONE, all are one entity, united under God's cloak. From this podium, I can see an array of God's beautiful diversity under one tent, all of us with different faces, who have come together to celebrate, to worship, and to proclaim the name of JESUS, affirming that Jesus is the Lord.

The second categorization that Paul mentioned is neither "**slave nor free**". This is class stratification. The world system likes to impose hierarchy. We hear of the First world, the Second world, the Third world and even the Fourth world. I am not naïve about these divisions, but the occasion is to celebrate diversity. The Body of Christ and indeed the world is rich in human resources found in various cultures, racial and ethnic groups all over the world. God favors ALL that He has created. He bestows His talents on ALL regardless of where they have come from. Hence, there are gifted people of different races, and ethnicities all over the world, in the top hierarchy of Financial systems wielding immense power, the Justice systems, the Medical field, the Military, in Science, various technology specializations, the Police, Entertainment, various fields of Education, as political leaders, religious leaders, community leaders, corporate administrators. Not only are these of different races and ethnicities, they also belong to all the different faiths that exist in the World. Many are Christians, followers of Christ and many others are of other faiths. So in spite of all these world divisions, the testimony is that in God's eye, from God's perspectives, all the people that He had created are ONE.

The third category that Paul nullifies is the **male/female dichotomy**. He says there is neither "male nor female", which means that there would be no discrimination nor stratification based on gender in the world that God created, more so in the Body of Christ. After all **Genesis 1:27** says So God created humankind in his own image, in the image of God he created them, both male and female. The implication is that men and women are created equal, in God's eyes, nonetheless with some differences. **Genesis 2:7** tells us that God formed a man from the dust of the ground, which means the man was formed from "raw material". **Genesis 2: 22** then says that *God made* a *woman* from the *rib* that He had taken out of the *man*, which means the woman was made from not from raw materials but the "finished product". I leave you all to draw your own deduction from that little story. Uh!!!

However, the big conclusion is that God created the man and the woman "fearfully and wonderfully" (**Psalm 139:14**) in His image. Nonetheless, the world has continued to promote and perpetuate another narrative. I will dwell neither on "gender diversity", nor on "gender inequality", because the occasion is to celebrate diversity. Thank God that in spite of all those narratives, that we often hear, we can safely say that women have come a very long way. A Black woman has been made a Rabbi of the Jewish religion in America. Today we can proudly say that the Bishop of the Anglican Diocese of Edmonton is a woman, Rev. Dr. Jane Alexander. Suffice it then to say that the male, the female, the transgender, the transsexual, the cis-gender, the intersex, even the hermaphrodite are all the "same" in God's eyes. Paul's overall conclusion is that all fabricated categories are irrelevant in God's eyes, because ALL People can enjoy a fulfilling relationship with God and above all in Christ Jesus. Amen!!!Therefore, with all these categorizations nullified, we are reminded that the unity in our diversity comes with "responsibilities".

As individual members of this beautiful world that God has created, more so in the Corporate body of Christ, with Christ's love binding us together, we are required to utilize for the good of all, the potential, the strength, and the abilities that have been granted to us all. Paul again in **Ephesians 4:16** says Under Christ's direction, the whole body is fitted together perfectly. As each part does its own special work, it helps the other parts to grow so that the whole body is healthy and growing full of love. We live in a world that is described as a "global village", which essentially means that we are all interconnected in one way or another. The overall purpose of this unity in diversity is about serving each other. In our diversity, we are all gifted with some gifts by God, to put to use for the good of all humanity. The assumption here is that being joined and knitted together promotes the proper functioning of the Body.

This means that all of us under God's tent should be looking out for the interest, the overall health and the overall well-being of each other.

Finally, as Christians, in this diverse world, if it is of any consolation for us, Jesus the Head of the Body knows us all, He knows us by name. He knows what we are doing. He knows what we are capable of doing. The Bible says God has our names written on the palm of His hands (**Isaiah 49:16**). This should encourage our hearts to walk freely with each other, to interact freely with one another, regardless of where we have all come from. Unity in diversity is about caring for each other in our neighborhoods, in our communities, in our workplace, in our local assemblies, in our cities, in our provinces, in our countries, in our continent, and above all, in the diverse and beautiful world that God has created. It is about taking responsibilities for each other. It is an individual responsibility. It is also a corporate responsibility.

As we continue to enjoy and savor our diversity, let us always remember to thank God for the blessings of this diverse world. Let us in unity continue to allow the mind of Christ to operate in us. Let us continue to allow the love of Christ to compel us to love one another as Christ has loved us. Let us continue to allow the image of the lowly Christ to encourage us to relate to each other more in humility and compassion. People matter to God and so we should matter to each other. So while we are all savoring God's "melting pot" and enjoying the diversity in whatever form that it may be served to us, let us continue to remember that God's kingdom is not a human institution and that we are all required to live together in loving peace and harmony. May God continue to help us all to do the needful. Amen.

Fellowship in the House of the Lord: Why I go to Church. Psalm 122:1

Sometime ago I read an article in Christian Today titled "Unchurched America: by Cath Martin. https://www.christiantoday.com/article/

unchurched-america-they-pray-own-bibles-and-are-spiritual-but-nearly-half-still-see-no-value-in-attending-church/41808.htmThey pray, they own Bibles and are spiritual but nearly half still see no value in attending church. These "Churchless" people as they are called are aware of the church and even think positively of the Christian faith, but, for whatever reason, feel that actively being a part of church is not for them. My Anglican Diocese of Edmonton has a "Back to Church" program in which we are encouraged to invite people who have either become "Churchless" or who have never attended church to come to church. I once invited a self-proclaimed non-Christian friend of mine to Church. She said to give her one good reason why she should come to church with me. I responded that I would oblige her with a thousand good reasons. David in **Psalm 122:1** says, "I was glad when they said unto me; let us go into the House of the Lord". Today a growing number of people are not glad to go into the House of the Lord and so have become permanent or temporary dropouts from the church. Their reasons vary from I do not believe in God. Many others claim that they have no faith in organized religion. Some accuse the Church of being a self-serving institution. They claim that the Church does not meet any of their needs. Christianity, Religion and God bashing are nothing new. They are very common. Thanks to secularization. The Good News however is that there are billions of people who still delight in presenting themselves in the House of the Lord.

So why do people go to church? People who do, all have different reasons for attending church. I can only speak for myself. My week starts on the day of the Lord. I go into the House of the Lord to reflect on my past week, to thank the Lord for the triumphs and achievements of the week, to lay my challenges at His feet, to ask for guidance and commit the new week in to His hands. I pray, I sing, I commune with God after my own pattern, but in the House of the Lord, there is a format to follow. I benefit from it. I also benefit from being taught and led in worship by others. In the House of the Lord, I face the reality of sanctification, which helps me to continually evaluate my standing in Christ. In a world where there is a constant search for truth, because there are many voices out there, in the House of the Lord I find the ultimate expression of truth in Jesus Christ who said, "I am the Way, the Truth, and the Life" (**John 14:6**). A constant reminder of this in the House of the Lord prevents me from falling into error. I go into the House of the Lord to build up my faith. I not only hear about the faith of ancient believers, their struggles and triumphs, I also hear about the experiences of breathing, living believers, which help me to sort out my own struggles.

Like many others, I pray privately but in the House of the Lord, I also pray with others while we pray one for another. In the House of the Lord, we pray individually, and yet we pray collectively. In the House of the Lord, I participate in set prayers, I also pray extempore. Our collective prayers in the House of the Lord are an aroma, sweet and beautiful in the eyes and ears of the Lord. I live in a world that is full of distractions: work, recreation, and even my own thoughts that are at times counterproductive. The House of the Lord provides me with a conscious break, an escape, the opportunity to experience silence, and be still before the Lord. In the House of the Lord, I am subject to the awesome reverence and reminder that God lives HERE, wherever the House of the Lord may be. I am reminded that God is in His Holy Temple, let all earth be silent before Him (**Habakkuk 2:20**).

I go into the House of the Lord to enjoy the various artistic and creative expressions of worship such as music, vocal and instrumental, dancing, architecture, designs, decorations, concrete and conceptual art, all evidence of the Lord's inspiration and gifts to His people. I live in a secular culture that at times ignores God, denies the reality and Presence of God, demeans the fear of God, and de-accentuates the Beauty of God. The House of the Lord provides me with a spiritual environment that has a wholesome focus on God. In the House of the Lord, I am constantly reminded of God's love that translates into protection and provision, the daily benefits that are showered on me and all those around me, which at times we all take for granted or which at times we ascribe to our own strength. In the House of the Lord as well as in other places I am constantly reminded in the words of a songwriter that says, "All good things around us are sent from heaven above" and so I fall on my face in thanksgiving to God for His goodness and His mercy to us the children of men.

The House of the Lord is a community, a collective, a group, where we share, we give, we receive, and sharpen each other's face (**Proverbs 27:17**). In the House of the Lord, we sing in unison, "Make us one Lord" to avow that sense of community. In the House of the Lord, with others, I am reminded that we are indeed one, all under the tent of the Almighty. In the House of the Lord, I am not alone, I do not walk alone and I do not feel alone, because I am with other members of the Household of God.

Finally, I go into the House of God to fellowship with Jehovah, the Great and awesome God and His Son, my Lord Jesus Christ, my Redeemer and Saviour, my Friend who calls me precious as He bids me to come to Him, the One who has rent the veil asunder so that I can have access to Him. **Revelation 1** tells me that on the day of the Lord, John heard the voice of the Lord, saw the Lord, and was touched by the Lord. My expectations whenever I go into the House of the Lord, wherever that may be, with millions dotted all over the globe, are to hear, to see and be touched by the Lord. One thing I have desired of the Lord that I will always seek, that I may dwell in the House of the Lord all the days of my life, (**Psalm 27:4**). May my feet and yours constantly stand within the gates of the House of the Lord (**Psalm 122:2**). Amen.

Laying down our lives for "the other". John 15:13

The Easter Season celebrates the universal fact that Jesus laid down His life, for the entire world, His friends and enemies alike. Jesus in **John 15:13** said that the sign or mark of friendship is when one can lay down one's life for "the other". "Greater love has no one than this that one lays down his life for his friends". Does Jesus expect us to do the same in our relationships? I often wonder. When Peter offered to lay down his life for Jesus, his Friend and Master wondered if he knew the implication of what He was saying. However, Peter did not die for Jesus; instead he denied Him in the moment of intense scrutiny. But Jesus knew Peter's heart, his commitment, his sincerity as well as his weakness. He would eventually give Peter His greatest assignment yet, "feed my sheep". Obviously, Jesus is not asking us to commit "suicide" as a proof of our friendship or love. In **1 Corinthians 15:3** Paul calls it "dying daily". Killing ourselves daily is quite a challenge. It is bringing under control all our unruly desires, taming our wild appetites, allowing God to make something beautiful and harmonious out of the discordance of our lives. It is the ability to bridle the whole body according to **James 3:2.** One of our favorite hymns describes the slaying of self as "let sense be numb, let flesh retire."

My thoughts then shifted to how I can lay down my life for "the other". In **Luke 10** a young lawyer asked Jesus, "What must I do to be saved?" Jesus' response: "Love God and love your neighbor" ignited his follow up question, "Who is my neighbor?" Jesus responded with the story of the Good Samaritan. Jesus did not define, nor limit the concept of neighbor. He did not say we must only love people from our race, our tribe, our ethnicity, our country, our community, our church, our workplace, our social networks and our family. What about religion? He did not suggest that we must only love Christians and those of the same denomination with us. He did not ask us to despise those of other religions: Judaism, Islam, Hinduism, Buddhism, Sikhism, Zoroastrianism, Shinto, Jainism, Taoism, Rastafarianism, Goddess worshippers, WICCA, Druids, African Traditional Religion and other traditional religions, even those of irreligious systems: atheism, agnostic and secular humanism. Jesus did not indicate that we cannot love those who are below us in status, those who do not measure up to us, those whose values are not in sync with ours, and those who are downright unlovable from our perspectives. He said to love people of all class systems, the poor so we do not add to their misfortune, the rich so we are not accused of jealousy. He even demands of us to love those who not only hate us but cannot stand the thought of us.

In our world today the evidence of "not loving our neighbor" is quite stark and rampant. It is manifest in man's inhumanity to man, brother against brother, sister against sister, man against woman, woman against man, children against parents, parents against children, wives against husbands, husbands against wives, friends against friends, neighbors against neighbors, communities against communities, nations against nations, the struggles between the rich and the poor, oppressive systems of the world, injustice, inequities, deprivation, marginalization, recklessness, misappropriation of public funds, embezzlement, organized crime, thefts, racism, domination, politicized religion, erosion of accepted values, which some might say is subjective anyway, exploitation of the masses by secular and religious leaders, political correctness, decline of family systems, intimidation, manipulation, aggression, violence, kidnappings, children's recalcitrance, permissiveness, pervasive poverty, greed, in a world that Mahatma Gandhi says has enough for everybody's need but not for everybody's greed, reckless sexualization of everything that should be held in reverence, oppressive hierarchical structures, abuse of power in the work place, within the family, in the community, within the Church, power to play god in some instances where life and death decisions are cruelly made for others, deprivations and the violations of the personal and innate rights of others, insensitivity of the powerful to the plight of the powerless, the list is endless.

God chose to love us while we were yet sinners. He chose to permit His Son's death on the cross. Jesus chose to die for us. He chose to lay down His life for us. Jesus then said Love one another as I have loved you. If we truly know God we will love as He does. Loving "the other" is a choice. Laying down one's life for "the other" requires commitment. **Hebrews 13:1** says let brotherly (and sisterly) love continue. **1John 4:7** says "Beloved let us love one another for love is of God". True love is like God, just, holy and perfect. **1John 3:18** says "let us not love in word or in tongue but in deed and truth". **Romans 12:9** say "Let love be without hypocrisy, be kind and affectionate to one another with brotherly love". **1Corinthians 16:14** says "Let all that you do be done with love". How much can we choose to love our fellow human beings, who annoy us every day, who we do not think much of, whose existence have nothing to do with us. In **Galatians 19:34**: part of laying down one's life for "the other" is loving the strangers that are among us. How many of us have attitudes about the culturally different, regarding and defining them as "aliens", patronizing them because we feel superior, discriminating against them because we see them as "lesser than", exploiting them because we can. How many of us perceive refugees and immigrants as strange underdogs, wondering from which unmentionable planet they have come from, evaluating them with such unkind curiosity. **1Corinthians 13** says "love is kind". **1John 4:20** says "if a man says I love God but hates his brother he is a liar, if he does not love his brother who he can see, how he will love God whom he cannot see". Is it possible for us to love all people? How easy is it for us to love "the other?" Only you can answer that question.

Psalm 15: 3 captures some of the essence of loving our neighbor: do not backbite with your tongue, do no evil to your neighbor, do not take up a reproach against your friend. Do not be an "accuser of the brethren" (**Revelation12:10**). The Golden rule says, "Do unto others as we want others to do to us". Are we so intolerant of "others" that we do to them even as they do to us or even worse, before they do to us? Do we suffer from superiority complex that we, look down on others because we consider ourselves better endowed than them? Doing evil does not mean taking a knife to cut them into two. It starts by not giving due recognition to some people because we think they do not measure up to our standard. It is denying people their innate rights and privileges. What about taking up a reproach against your neighbor/ friend. How loyal are you? Are you the first one to expose someone else's short coming with undeserved self-righteousness? What type of friend are you? Love covers multitudes of sins.

When someone you consider guilty is down, do you jump on the band wagon of those passing judgement even before the facts are made known or do you offer support and fair play because it is the right thing to do? Jesus even adds the toughest one in **Matthew 5: 44** "For I say to you love your enemies, bless those who curse you, do good to those who hate you and pray for those who spitefully use you and persecute you." Wow!!!! We all need the Lord's help with that one. Jesus modelled for us the concept of laying down life for others. He gave His all to the world. Laying down one's life for "the other" is being noble, sensitive, thoughtful, unselfish, sincere, cheerful, loyal, warm, not puffed up, not behaving rudely, not envious, not arrogant and not spiteful. It is genuinely caring one for another and upholding each other. Are you on? Are you in?

Sex is God's Idea: Sexuality in God's Kingdom on Earth

World Health Organization says that sex occurs more than 100 million times everyday around the world. For all its frequency, sex remains a private, personal, intensely individual and complex matter in people's lives and in many cultures. God in the Garden of Eden inaugurated heterosexual relationship when He gave Eve to Adam. The Bible introduces SEX. The Bible celebrates SEX. Forget the apple narrative; SEX is given for procreation and for pleasure. All societies control sexuality. All societies have social norms that grant approval to certain sexual behavior and disapproval of others. No society grants unrestricted sexual liberties. Even as sexuality is God's gift to human beings, God places limitations on sexual practices, not to cause discomfort for His creatures but to ensure that physical relations are the most special and unique expression of love and trust a human being can bestow on one another. God's limitations on sex are positive. Without limitations, SEX becomes mere performance and everything is devalued.

However, in the fast-paced world of today, SEX seems to be on everybody's mind and lips. Malcolm Muggeridge says, "Society has sex on its brain; it is a very uncomfortable place to have it". I remember The Thorn Birds, the movie based on the novel by Colleen McCullough. I also remember Richard Chamberlain's excellent performance as Father Ralph. Many people see the Thorn Birds as a love story. However, I see a priest's intense struggle with his Spirituality (his love for God) and his Sexuality (his human passion). There is no doubt that Father Ralph loves his God more than he loves the woman of focus as he claims in the movie. In spite of his unflinching commitment to God and his vocation, Father Ralph succumbed to the lure of the flesh. For me this story represents the sexual struggles of many Christians in today's world. This led me to reflect on Sexuality in God's Kingdom on Earth.

Society continues to experience a sexual revolution that has led to changes in many areas of human sexuality. Attitudes towards sexual permissiveness have changed with people having a more tolerant view of it. The Media generally permissive with sexual content continues to portray non-marital sex as exciting, spontaneous sex as romantic, extra marital sex as normal and inevitable. Sexual issues have become so overt with the incessant bombardment and assault by the media that it is definitely always in everybody's face and thereby almost on everybody's mind, even on Christian minds. Who can resist the temptation of thoughtful engagement? Society has become permissive. It is now judgmental within the Church to discuss human sexuality from moral perspectives.

Negative views about homosexuality are waning. With celebrities, many high-profile individuals, and religious leaders coming out of the closet, homosexuality is receiving a high five. Heterosexuality is being branded as one of the "isms" (heterosexism). Families and parents are becoming more accepting of their members and children's sexual orientation when it is different from their own. Within the Body of Christ, some are saying that God loves all people and He would never alienate any of His creatures, therefore gay people should be welcomed with love in various congregations and allowed to integrate and be assimilated. This is happening. Homosexuals are claiming that their sexual orientation should not prevent them from fully serving God and therefore should be ordained by the Church. Many gay and lesbians have been ordained as Bishops, Priests and Deacons in many denominations all over the world. Many Christian homosexuals are establishing their own local congregations in various parts of the world purportedly to have the freedom to worship God in any way that they deem fit. Many countries of the world have placed the seal of approval on gay marriages. The Church is not left behind. The latest discourse is should the Church marry gay people, in spite of what the Scriptures say about homosexuality as a sexual orientation. Some Christian denominations have overwhelmingly voted for gay people to be married in the Church by the Church. Bisexuality is also receiving legitimacy among Christians with the first female bisexual Congresswoman elected to office sometime ago in the USA and many celebrities and other young people even in the Church claiming to be bisexual.

Although same-sex union/marriages, ordination of gay priests etc are receiving high profile support and validation within the Church, they are not the ONLY sexual issues being played out in the Church today. God's Kingdom on earth has continued to be plagued by other definable sexual issues. Cohabitation, which has previously been branded as "living in sin", now has legitimacy, approval, and support of many societies, governments of the world and of the Church. Many heterosexual Christians, many gay and lesbian Christians, many ordained gay and lesbians in the holy orders are cohabiting in common law relationships. This brings to mind Jesus encounter with the woman at the well. Jesus told her that she has no husband because she was not married to the sixth man she was "living with". This incidence in the Bible has been subject to many interpretations.

Premarital sex, which has traditionally received low tolerance in many cultures and in the Church, has increased in favor, even for the female. Many young Christians male and female are engaging in premarital and informal sex, with abstinence being touted as "unrealistic". Teenage pregnancy has dramatically increased even among girls raised in the Church, with many young single unmarried mothers and fathers in the Church. Many unmarried Christian adults are engaging in sex in their intimate relationships, which the Bible calls "fornication". Sexual relationships in non-marital situation have become so pervasive that it has become the norm. Marital infidelities, mistresses and sidekicks have become normal societal trends. There is nothing "shocking" about these practices in the Church anymore. They were formally regarded as plagues. Studies show that men and women, Christians and non-Christians alike are engaging in extra marital affairs with the workplace being the most fertile ground for it. Overt and uncontrolled recreational sex; certain sexual preferences like BDMS, which had previously been deemed to be sexual deviance are now being practiced by male and female Christians. Many Christians are poly-amorous. Christians male and female belong to various Swingers Clubs.

Married Christians including the so-called "Men of God", at the top of the hierarchy are struggling with the laws of attraction and are daily drawn into extra marital affairs, which the Bible calls "adultery". Many have fathered and mothered children outside of their marriages. Jesus puts a severe injunction on adultery. He says it is not just the physical violation but also engaging in thoughts about it. **Matthew 5:27-28.** Infidelity has become the most prominent reason for divorce, even among Christians. Divorce has become the preferred option with the low tolerance that human beings have for each other's violations. With easy access to divorce, many Christians are divorcing despite the fact that God says He hates divorce (**Malachi 2: 16**). Christians constitute a sizeable portion of the 50% whose marriages end in divorce. Christians are brushing aside with deep conviction their marital commitment of "till death do us part" with the right to divorce if there is no more love in their marriages and of course if there is violence. Interestingly gay and lesbian couples are already divorcing after all the efforts to secure the rights to be married.

Christians are now heavily involved in remarriages. Christian religious leaders, Bishops, Pastors and Reverends have become "serial monogamists". The Bible says that a woman is bound by law as long as her husband lives. Remarriage can only occur when the divorced spouse dies. This is no more adhered to within the Church. Remarriages and blended families are on the increase in the world and within the Church. Some Christians now practice "polygamy" which was contrary to the Church's position of "one man one wife", because their culture supports and accepts the practice. Many Christians remind us of some famous polygamous men in the Bible, Abraham, Moses, David, Solomon. What happens to a polygamous man who becomes a Christian? Traditionally, the Church has urged them to divorce the women and keep one, but which one has always been the problem. These days the Church does not impose such limitations and choices. Polygamous men proudly come to church with their multiple wives in tow, on their arms actually dressed alike for uniformity and identity.

Today, monogamy/polygamy/singlehood dynamics are being fueled and played out in various forms because of the lopsided male/female sex ratio. These are manifest in "kept women", "official mistresses" and children born out of wedlock by both single Christian men and women. Maybe there are Christian women out there practicing polyandry (one woman with multiple husbands). Who knows? Even old couples are wondering if it is Christianly to have sex at an advanced age. Does God approve? They ask. Who knows? All I know is that Abraham was 100 years old and Sarah was 90 years old when they were blessed with Isaac. Some celibate priests are struggling with their vows, claiming that they can marry and still be able to serve God effectively. The Catholic Church has been under pressure to abandon its position of "celibacy" for priests. Jesus said that some people become eunuch for the sake of the kingdom (**Mathew 19:12**). Hence, celibacy they say is a choice and has never been imposed on anybody. The Bible also talks about the merit of "singleness". Those who are single have more time for the things of God while he who is married cares about how he may please his wife. (**1Corinthians 7: 32**). However, God says it is not good that man should be alone. The Bible also counseled that people should marry if they burn because it is better to marry than to burn. (**1Corinthians 7:9**).

Genesis 2: 25 says the two shall become one. That certainly speaks of sexual relations but the Bible never limits it to one dimension. The fact is if people in intimate relationships are not spiritually and psychologically one, meaningful physical oneness is impossible. This probably accounts for the emotional estrangement and disconnect that is often seen among people, Christians as well. **Corinthians 7: 3-6** has the most important view of Christian sexual relations. Let the husband render to his wife the affection due her and likewise also the wife to her husband. **Proverbs 5: 18-19** adds rejoice with the wife of your youth ....let her breasts satisfy you at all times and be enraptured with her love. However, many in today's society rebel against the limitations on sex dismissing them as "intolerable", "dictatorial", "austere" and "old fashioned". **Ephesians 5:33** says let each one of you so love his wife as himself and let the wife also sees that she respects her husband. Today submission to one another, mutuality and reciprocity are now deemed as archaic and non-practical concepts. Church people now write their own marital vows to exclude some of these considerations with the approval of their leaders.

God's gift to humanity is its Sexuality as well as its Spirituality. Overall, sexuality has become thorny for many Christians. Paul drew attention to the perennial struggle between the flesh and the spirit. God's various commands and injunctions are designed to make life better for humans not complicated. If "Sex is God's Idea" as Earl Paulk suggests in the title of his book, why has human sexuality become so complicated?" Just a thought! Sexuality in God's kingdom is experiencing a significant, baffling, complicated, poignant shift and transition. Que faire? As the French would ask. The question some people are asking is "Where will all these lead to?" All I can say is Nobody knows. Only God has the answer. St. Augustine says that our hearts are restless until they find rest in God.

However, one thing that comes to my mind is **Revelation 7:13-14** Then one of the elders answered, saying to me, "Who are these arrayed in **white** robes, and where did they come from?" And I said to him, "Sir you know". He said to me, "These are the ones who come out of the great tribulation and washed their robes and made them WHITE in the blood of the Lamb". I am just wondering if this has anything to do with "Sexual purity". At this stage, I think I will go with St. Augustine's prayer: Lord, make me chaste, but not yet!!!.Amen. But then, If not now, then when? Only God knows. Amen.

The Challenges of being Blameless Before Men. Deuteronomy 18:13

Deuteronomy 18:13 says you shall be blameless before your God. **Ephesians1:4** indicates that we should be holy and without blame before Him. **2 Peter 3:14** asks us to be diligent to be found without spot and blameless. Paul to Timothy demands that Bishops and Deacons must be blameless. My thoughts then strayed to what it means to be blameless. John Calvin says blameless means to be free from any notorious fault. The dictionary describes it as without guilt, censure or reproach meaning to be perfect. No one is perfect except God. **Corinthians 1:8** tells us that it is Christ who will confirm us and make us blameless in the end. This means we cannot declare ourselves blameless, we will be judged blameless by another. In Isaiah God says that if our sins are like scarlet and red as crimson they shall be made as white as snow. The Book of Revelation indicates that those in heaven will be judged blameless before God. Does it mean that they have never sinned? Of course not! It means that God forgave them and granted them righteousness.

In **2 Corinthians 8:21** Paul says that we must provide honorable things in the sight of the Lord and in the sight of men. This means that there should be no question about our integrity or upright character and that we must be mindful of our behavior before God and before men, that is before each other. To me blameless before God seems less of a challenge than blameless before men. We live in a world where we are not always forgiving of each other, where seals of approval are not readily given to deserving people, where people are not always kind and gracious to each other, where we are very critical of each other, judge each other harshly, condemn each other, discriminate against one another, oppress each other, bear false witness against one other, deny each other's rights, covet one another, put each other's relationships asunder, kill each other, where self-promotion is virtuous, where the golden rule for some is do unto others what you can't stand them doing unto you. Who can survive all these without God's grace?

In **Acts 24:16** Paul says he tries his best to be blameless before God and before men. Did he succeed? I would say, before God, Yes, but before men, we only need to look at the various persecutions that he suffered. God described **Job in 2:3** as upright, one who feared Him, shunned evil, and above all blameless. Job did some introspection and in **Job 9:21** adjudged himself blameless. But Job was not spared by his friends. They did not declare him blameless. They accused him of some secret sins that turned God against him. Blameless before men is tricky. In **1Chronicles 21** we read about God's displeasure with David for taking an unauthorized census of the people. God sent Gad to David to tell him about His displeasure and to choose his own punishment out of three that God would provide. David sad to Gad "I'm in a desperate situation! But let me fall into the hands of the Lord, for his mercy is very great. Do not let me fall into human hands." David chose to be punished by God because he understood that in it all God would still be merciful. David did not want to fall into the hands of man, he knew that would be Dreadful.

However, being blameless before men is not just about how they treat us, it is equally about how we treat others around us. Are we blameless in the way we deal with people? Do we relate to people with integrity of hearts? When people hurt us, do we reach out to them or do we look for the opportunity to payback, because revenge is sweet. Do we make efforts to mend broken relationships? Or is it good riddance to bad rubbish? How often do we violate our values and take advantage of others and situations? Many a times people are presented with options that they know are not right, not appropriate, not ethical and at times downright evil, but alluring all the same. They respond because it is seductively tempting, irresistible; with the feeling of I can get away with these and no one will ever know. These offers are too good to pass, they may not come again, I will go for them. We may not always succeed at being judged blameless by others, our peers, friends, family members, workplace colleagues, church members, neighbors etc. But we may want to be deemed to have tried because there is profound peace for the one who strives to be blameless before God and before man. Amen.

God's Advocates versus Devil's Advocates

Every Easter Season we are reminded of Jesus' victory on the Cross, over death, over Hades and over Satan. "The Strife is over, the Battle won", says the songwriter. In spite of this victory, the war continues to rage. I am not talking about America's "just wars", the pre-emptive strikes, the war against terrorists both home grown and out grown that President Obama defended in Copenhagen when he went to receive the Nobel Peace Prize. I am not talking about ISIS, the war in Syria, and Afghanistan. I am not even talking about the Boko Haram war against Christians and young girls in Nigeria. I am talking about the war that had been raging since the creation of the world when in **Genesis 6: 11** we are told that the earth was filled with violence. I am talking about Satan's rebellion against God when he said in his heart "I will ascend into heaven, I will exalt my throne above the stars of God… I will be like the most High" (**Isaiah 14:13**). I am talking about the war in heaven when Arch Angel Michael fought the dragon, "and the dragon and his angels fought, but they did not prevail, nor was a place found for them in heaven any longer. The great dragon was cast out, that serpent of old, called the Devil and Satan, who deceives the whole world was cast to the earth, and his angels were cast out with him" (**Revelation**

12). When Satan lost his battle with God's angels, he began to direct his fury at the people of God on earth.

Satan remains a powerful adversary. Satan has been and is still waging war, against Jesus, against the Church, against the Body of Christ. This war is alive and well and growing more intense each day. Jesus did not underestimate His enemy. He referred to Satan as the "ruler of this world" (**John 12:31**). Paul called him the "god of this age" (**2 Corinthians 4:4**). John declared that the whole world is "under the control of the evil one" (**1 John 5:19**). Peter said that the devil prowls around looking for someone to devour (**1 Peter 5:8**). Satan's has continued its all-out war against God's children. In our world today, this war started not only with the secularization process, but also the fascination with "atheism", which essentially is the denial of the existence of God. **Psalms 14 and 53** tells us "The fool has said in his heart there is no God". However, as we all know, atheists are not ignoramuses, but very reflective people who from their perspectives are able to come to certain conclusions, about God and religion. They are always able to defend their positions vehemently. There is of course the perennial struggle between Science and Religion which has become an "either/or" position instead of complementary even as Albert Einstein says, "all religions, arts and sciences are branches of the same tree".

https://www.goalcast.com/2017/03/29/top-30-most-inspiring-albert-einstein-quotes/

The latest of this war is "God bashing". Richard Dawkins the world's best known atheist in his bestselling book "The God Delusion", 2006

https://www.penguin.co.uk/books/102/1028478/the-god-delusion/9781784161927.html said, *"The God of the Old Testament is arguably the most unpleasant character in all fiction: jealous and proud of it; a petty, unjust, unforgiving control-freak; a vindictive, bloodthirsty ethnic cleanser; a misogynistic, homophobic, racist, infanticidal, genocidal, filicidal, pestilential, megalomaniacal, sadomasochistic, capriciously malevolent bully."*

Christopher Hitchen's in his well-acclaimed book says, "God is not great". Ida White says, "Christianity exceeds all other faiths in its power to deform and finally invert the mental process". The war against Jesus is seen in the recreation of the person and nature of Jesus Christ. Movies like "The Last Temptation of Jesus", redefines and reconstructs the person and essence of Jesus. It is bad enough that the war against the Body of Christ is external, coming from outside. The more frightening thing is that the battle is also raging from within the Body, with those who deny the Virgin birth of Jesus, the Resurrection of Christ, the existence of the Holy Spirit, and so on, posing great challenges for the Body.

The war against the Body is also manifest in the emergence of the "New Spirituality Movement", which rejects what it calls the "Old Christian Religion". It claims the OLD religion is bound by rituals, rules and creeds, but which by definitions are necessary components of all religions. The new Spirituality Movement rejects the term "religion" and demands a "relationship". They seem to forget that Christ's entire ministry was relational. The Christian Religion has always been and still is God centered and relational. The New Spirituality Movement has a focus on the self. It talks of individual needs not being met by the "old Christian Religion" that actually says that growth in Christ, is communal, based on interdependence. The Spirituality Movement makes immense references to "spirit", which of course is of unknown origin. The Old Christian Religion teaches us that we are born of the Spirit of God and so God lives in us.

However, in my reflection on this ongoing war, I thought that I do not often hear "loud and clear", the clarion calls to battle by Christians. Are we not supposed to be militants for Christ? **Ephesians 6** reminds us that there is an ongoing war and that we are not at war against flesh and blood but against the rulers of the darkness of this world, against principalities and power and against spiritual wickedness in high places. The Early Christians were aware of this continuous war and so they penned songs like, "Sound the Battle Cry", "Stand up Stand up for Jesus", "Hold the Fort", "Fight the Good fight with all your Might". My favorite is "Onward Christian Soldiers marching as to War". What are we Christians of today required to do? What is our role in this war?

In "The Devil's Advocate", one of my favorite movies, ably performed by Al Pacino and Keanu Reeves, Kevin Lomax lured by the seductiveness of the devil confirms, "Evil surely has its winning ways". This movie takes my thoughts to the emergence of the modern-day band of the "Devil's Advocates" out there. Starting with the power of the pen, Devil's Advocates fight with numerous anti god writings and literature. The anti-god books are quite popular; as soon as they are released, they instantly climb to the "best sellers" list. Subtle or overt, Devil's Advocates are relentless. They are vehement. They fight with all the weapons that they possess. Devil's Advocates are smart, hence they are prolific. Devil's Advocates are loud. They have an appealing fluency for the itchy ears that listen to them. What motives drive the Devil's Advocates? In this the Devil's Advocates are tops. It is not about them, it is about their father, the Devil. Devil's Advocates never miss any opportunity to promote their master. Each day presents with many opportunities. Every medium and every chance is seized. No wonder the Devil's Advocates always seem to have an upper hand.

Then I wonder: Who is on the Lord's side? Where are God's Advocates? Does God need advocates? Some may ask. He is God. He can speak for Himself. However, the Bible contains many Advocates for God, Abraham, Moses, David, and all those prophets of old. Jesus had His Advocates in Paul, Peter, John, James and others. Jesus is the Advocate for those of us whose names are written on the palms of God's hand. **(Isaiah 49: 16).** In return, He wants us to be His Advocates. He wants us to continue to fight the good fight with all our might. He wants us on the highways and the byways. God's Advocates do not necessarily have to come from the pulpit, neither do they have to be to be certified. Thankfully, there are millions of genuine and sincere God's Advocates out there. However, the harvest is ripe and the laborers are still few.

Are you God's Advocate? The choice is an imperative option. The benefits are immense. How often do God's Advocates aim to correct misconceptions about God, about Jesus, about the Bible, and about the Body of Christ? Makers of the movie "God is not Dead" did just that, where a Christian freshman at a college had to defend his faith when challenged by his atheist professor. The movie is well located because the academia in the spirit of Academic Freedom is a fertile ground for analyzing, rationalizing, dissecting and rejecting God. Do God's Advocates take advantage of the many formal and informal situations that present, on the road, in the homes, at work, at play, anywhere and everywhere to advocate for God? How often do God's Advocates attempt to convey God's essence to humanity?

In this ongoing war, renewed zealousness is needed for our Master, Jesus, in a world that is reeling with the adulation of the enemy. While God's Advocates are required to sharpen their weapons, our primary weapon of warfare is still Jesus, the Man of War Himself. Every battle belongs to the Lord. Unfortunately, at times plagued by political correctness and fear, God's Advocates become "dumb" and sit it out. The Bible calls dumbness an affliction (**Mark 9:17**) God's Advocates need the tongue of the ready writer (**Psalm45:1**). We need to have a language that is inspired, authentic, genuine, relevant, meaningful and real. Jesus was a Master communicator. The Bible says when He spoke, the people marvel at His words. God's Advocates need to speak of God's goodness, God's faithfulness and God's loving kindness at all times. Spiritual discernment is needed among those engaged in conducting the enterprises of Christ. Unity is also needed; a house divided against itself cannot stand.

This warfare is a conflict between right and wrong, between the Gospel of Christ and false doctrines. All the talents and gifts that have been received must be stirred up and brought into action. Every ability, each opportunity must be used, for the foes are many. As Soldiers of the Cross, God's Advocates must put on the whole armor of God that they may be able to stand against the wiles of the devil (**Ephesians 6:11**). The nature of the war is such that God's Advocates cannot be neutral or indifferent. In and out of season, like the Reserved Army, God's Advocates must always be ready for battle (**2Timothy 4:2**). Finally, for empowerment, because the battle is on, like David in **Psalm 144**, God's Advocates must always ask the Lord to "train our hands for war and our fingers for battle". Amen.

The Prodigal Son's Brother who Stayed at Home. Luke 15:11-32

In Luke 15:11-32 Jesus talks about lost things, lost sheep, lost coin and lost son. Jesus story of the Prodigal son is about two sons of a wealthy father. One day the younger son asked the father for his inheritance. His father complied, gave him what he wanted, thereafter he took it and left home. He went out of town, squandered what he had taken. Years later, when he had hit rock bottom he returned home. My focus is not on the younger son who went away but on the older son who stayed at home. The story of the prodigal son has been told many times. Preachers and evangelists like to extol the lost son who came back home. They like to tout the story of the prodigal son as a paradigm for lost people who have abandoned their faith, who have gone astray, did all sorts of strange things, some of them have even abandoned God, but who have found the Light and was later restored. No doubt it is a good story!!!.

Many people recount this story over and over again in large congregations to the consternation of listeners. These stories are great, interesting, and above all exotic. They are quaint stories of **redemption**. Meanwhile the stories of those who have stayed in faith, remained in church, been consistent in their religion and devotion are boring. In these days of hyperactive culture, nobody wants that type of story. I personally have been a victim of that. Did you run away from home as a teenager? NO! Have you been sexually abused? NO! Have you been in jail? NO! Are you a recovered drug and alcohol addict? NO. Have you lived on the street before? NO! Have you killed before? NO BOOOOOORING. No one wants to listen to that type of story. It is not exciting. It is plain, dull and monotonous.

Of course, there is justification for that in the Bible. In **Luke 15:4-6** Jesus talked about a man having one hundred sheep and if he loses one will leave the ninety-nine and go after that which is lost until he finds it. When he finds it, he carries it on his shoulders and comes home rejoicing, then he calls his friends and neighbors saying to them "Rejoice with me for I have found my sheep that was lost". I tell you that there is joy in heaven over one sinner who repents than over the ninety-nine who do not need repentance. This is precisely what happened in the story of the Prodigal Son. Deviance was celebrated. The younger son motivated by greed and lust left home, squandered his father's money, got into the wrong crowd, mismanaged his time, rebelled against his father and shamed his family. Then having seen how his choices led to real misery, he came to his senses and returned to his father, who welcomed him very warmly.

Now to the second son, the older brother, the son who stayed at home. The story goes on in **Luke15:25** Now his older son was in the field, as he came near to the house, he heard music and dancing. He called one of the servants and asked what was happening. The servant told him that his brother has come back and his father, being excited is having a big great party for him, with enormous supply of food and drink and immense merriment and rejoicing. The older son got angry and refused to join the party. His father came out to appeal to him. However, he gave a powerful response to his father, which captures and summarizes what he has done while his brother went gallivanting and squandering his father's wealth.

The older son who stayed at home said to his father, all these many years I have been serving you; I have never been uncooperative. I have been committed to whatever you have asked me to do, even the ones you did not ask me to do. I have been innovative. I have been creative. I have looked after business. I have been dependable. I have been responsible. I have been there ensuring the survival of business even when you are not around or have to gone on long trips. I have made profits. I have occupied till you come. I have been loyal. I have never run afoul of your rules at any time; and yet you never celebrated me, you have never rolled out the drums for me. You have never held a sumptuous dinner event in my honor. But as soon as this wayward son of yours returned home there is rejoicing everywhere.

The son who stayed at home believes that he is the victim of an unjust action. He felt that his efforts had been ignored. He felt like an unsung hero. He is the one who had worked in the fields and never complained. He is the one who never gave his father any problems and yet he has never been noticed. The question is "was the older brother right in feeling this way, feeling unappreciated? Should he have just kept quiet and continue to suffer in silence? After all, he was not bound to commitment. Let us remember that He made a choice for commitment. He could have gone the way of his younger brother, but he chose to remain faithful.

There are always many people in the family, in the work place, in religious establishments, churches, mosques, tabernacles, temples, groups, organizations, who are always ready and willing to help. They offer their services without compulsion. They contribute to the effective running of the establishments. They do what they do happily without any murmuring. You call on them anytime, they are available. They do all the right things. They are dutiful, faithful, hardworking, respectable, even respectful, models for good behavior. They can even be described as being "faultless". Unfortunately, they are the ones most taken for granted. More attention is paid to the empty vessels that usually make the most noise. The ones that complain endlessly over everything. The faithful ones are usually passed over. The heads, the leaders, the people in charge usually go after the non-contributing ones because they think that it is their job to pander to them, especially because they paint themselves as vulnerable. Even in some churches, you have pastors who spend most of their time trying to reach the lost while neglecting those committed in the congregation. This unfortunately is pervasive and is a reality in our world. It has always been.

Now let us hear the father's response to the complaint of the son who stayed at home. He said to him, "My Son, you are always with me, and all that I have is yours". Note that the father Calls Him "My son". There are words of endearment**.** Then he added, "You Are Always with Me". Meaning you think that I have not noticed you. You are closer to my heart than you think. You live in my house. You have access to me and I have access to you. You are the heir of my estate. You have at your disposal all that I have. This father manifests kindness and generosity to his son who stayed at home. For him to say those gratifying things to his son means that he has spent some time pondering about his older son's contributions. He has noticed. He has been aware. He has not been unmindful of his son's valuable contributions even though the son had felt neglected.

The father tells him "ALL that I have is yours". Remember the younger son has taken his own share. The fathers claim obviously means that he is not going to share what is left with his younger recalcitrant son. Just because he has come back does NOT mean he is going to claim supremacy over the son who stayed at home. The father was telling older son who stayed at home that he has a lot to gain in the end, even though everything may look lopsided at this point. The son, who stayed at home, has his father's goodwill. He has his father's thoughts and support. His anger and anxiety have been misplaced. His father has noticed his loyalty, his devotion, his commitment. He was going to be rewarded whichever way the father saw fit. The father has not taken his older son who stayed at home for granted.

In this story Jesus is entreating you the son, the daughter, who has stayed at home. He is showing appreciation to you. Jesus is extolling your hard work. Jesus is acknowledging your dependability. Jesus has some endearing words for you. You are the one who cleans and prepares the altar items for worship. You are the one who volunteers to help with the community meals. You are the one who prepares the bulletins each week for service. You are the one who is always available to sort out maintenance issues in the building. You are the one who fills in the gap when no other person is available. You are the one who can be counted upon. You are the one who gave Jesus something to eat when He was hungry. You are the one who gave Jesus something to drink when he was thirsty. You are the one who clothed Jesus when He was naked. You are the one who visited Jesus when He was in prison. There are multitudes of people even in little establishments who do quantum of things that are visible and also invisible.

Jesus is saying, to all of you reading this reflection and you feel you belong to that category "You are always with me, All that I have is yours". You have an inheritance in me, you have a place in my heart, you have a place in my kingdom. When your time is over you will be with me in paradise. Do not be discouraged. Like the letter of John in **Revelation 3:8** to the church in Philadelphia, Jesus is saying, "I know your work, I know your patience. I have set before you an open door, which no man can shut. Amen. May our hearts be encouraged by these words of cheer. Amen.

Children are a heritage from the Lord: Psalm 127:3-5

I was reading an article "The No-Baby Boom" by Brian Frazer, http://childlessbychoiceproject.blogspot.com/2011/04/no-baby-boom.html where he talks about the "zero-child policy" being adopted by many couples which he says seems more stringent than Chinas "one child policy". With the state of global economy, mounting costs of living, housing, transportation, education, daycare, unemployment and underemployment, the ranks of the child-free are exploding. Frazer adds that the empty-nest is no more what happens after the children have left home, many are choosing to take a pass at parenthood and so spend their entire marriages as empty nesters. He also defines the benefits for the child-free thus: "there's less guilt, less worry, less responsibility, more sleep, more free time, more disposable income, no awkward conversations about Teen Mom, no forced relationships with people just because your kids like their kids". In short none of those hassles that come with having children. Brian Frazer also says that one can get a vasectomy at Planned Parenthood for less than the cost of a Boogaboo stroller. Some people do not find this funny, because it is not.

The latest that I read is the **Birth Strike** which is a small but growing movement of young people around the world who are hesitating over whether or not to have children due to worries about climate change.

https://thehill.com/policy/energy-environment/433961-activists-go-on-birth-strike-over-climate-change They say that there is scientific consensus that the lives of children are going to be very difficult as a result of climate change which will significantly worsen the risks of drought, floods, extreme heat and poverty for hundreds of millions of people. Having more children is a demonstration of ignorance, carelessness and indifference to the environment, they say. Although there are heated debates going on for and against the issues. One cannot but wonder about the way society is evolving.

Global birth rates have dropped. Children are increasingly being seen as liability, a burden on families and communities rather than an asset. Many women all over the world end their reproductive years without children, by choice. Male sterilization and the vasectomy business are booming. While many families are counting with delight the number of new additions to their families many are waiting endlessly, longingly, hoping to experience the delight plus of course the inconvenience of grand parenting. Their children have sworn not to be the conduit pipes for bringing some brats into this world. There are enough around, they claim.

The prolife/prochoice debate has persisted with great intensity. Child abuse is on the increase, so does parental abuse for that matter. Instances of female infanticide are still being reported in some parts of the world. In New Zealand the sheep-to-human ratio currently stands at 10 to 1 which means more sheep are being produced than children. Studies are showing that more people than ever prefer the ownership of pets over children. Studies denote that more people see the absence of children in marriages as a factor for marital bliss. Two or three children now make a large family.

In all these I cannot but wonder what is happening to God's injunction in **Genesis 1: 27** be fruitful, multiply and replenish the earth. In all these, the fact that children are needed to replenish the earth seems to be overlooked by many. However thankfully and paradoxically in the "childfree" world, the "childless" continue to struggle to avail themselves of the technological options available. In the "less child world", the "octomoms" (woman who have 14 children and is raising them in the USA) still have a place. Gay parenting though an oxymoron is an increasing phenomenon. Teen parenting is contending fiercely with delayed marriages for spotlight. Millions of people remain devoted and committed to their children is spite of the challenges. While some states are dealing with issues of over population, some are looking for solutions to under and stagnant population by offering incentives for procreation. Quebec is one of such provinces in Canada. Singapore too is looking at ways to encourage young people to get into the procreation business to boost the population that has remained stagnant. Some are realizing that procreation is a vital activity and societal responsibility still is severely needed and necessary for the continuity and survival of societies. It is also something to be considered when we talk of Human Capital, a viable strength of countries like China.

The Bible is not blind to the realities and challenges of raising children. In fact, it records in several places the difficulties inherent in bringing up children. We all know about King David and his numerous challenges with the children of his loins. Ultimately it was David who tells us that children are a heritage from the Lord, that the fruit of the womb is a reward. He also adds that happy is the man who has his quiver full of them (**Psalms 127**). We know that having and claiming this reward does not only happen biologically, neither does it end with one generation. At this point in time, I like to take comfort in the word of God that tells us that our children will be like olives around our tables (**Psalm 128:3**) and that our children and children's children will be taught of the Lord and great shall be their peace and ours also (**Isaiah 54: 13**). Amen

Behold I will kindle a fire in you: Ezekiel 20: 47-48

While reading the Book of Ezekiel, I came across **Ezekiel 20: 47** where God says "Behold I will kindle a fire in you", a significant phrase I thought. It was then, I began to wonder under what circumstances does God kindle a fire is us. Always after a special church event like a Conference, a Revival meeting, a Retreat, a Synod, when there is always a time of euphoria. At that event and after, we all become fired up because we have had a good time with the Lord. We are sure that we have been blessed by the Lord, that the Lord has spoken to us. The good thing is that we always want the feeling to last. But by three months down the line we have at times forgotten all that we have learnt and gained. We are returned to the static place we were before the meeting. I believe it is in one of those times that the Lord can kindle a fire in us. Kindle means to start a fire, to cause flames, to ignite, to light up, to illuminate, to become bright, to arouse, to bring out of lethargy.

The Lord at times knows what we need. He knows the situation we are in more so when we need His fire in us. In the Bible, fire is used to represent the Holy Spirit. On the Day of Pentecost when the Apostles were in the upper room, all as the Bible says were in ONE accord, the Holy Spirit came in form of fire and parted like tongues and rested on each one of them. After the Apostles has had this fire kindled in them, we were told that they all became transformed, they became set on fire for God. With Peters first sermon 3000 people came to the Lord. This fire that was kindled in the Apostles is what Jesus has continued to kindle in His followers every time they present themselves in submission to the Holy Spirit. **Verse 48** adds "it shall devour every green tree and every dry tree in you", How many of us realize that we have things growing in us that should not be there? At times we erroneously think everything that looks green and fresh is good. Green trees are alive and flourishing but not ALL are necessarily good for us. Dry trees are dead, trees that have stopped growing but still occupy some space in us. God is saying that there are some green trees and dry trees should not be in us. These are trees that have been ill planted in us. These trees could be illness, poverty, lack of progress, problems in relationships, children's problem, static positioning, inability to move on, to forge ahead, sin, curses, jinxes, hexes, evil thoughts, etc. The word of God is saying that God is able to ignite a fire that will consume and devour all these green and dry trees.

In the New Testament, **Mathew 15: 13** Jesus now confirms what was stated in Isaiah. He says every plant which my Father has not planted will be uprooted. How significant this connection is, with Jesus affirming that the Fire of God has the ability to consume all the consumables without consuming us. Remember Elijah's contest with the Baal priests on Mount Carmel **1Kings 18:38**. Elijah repaired the altar and set the altar, got everything ready, even poured water on the altar and called upon God to manifest Himself. Elijah had utmost confidence in the God that he serves, that was why he was able to confidently call on Him to demonstrate his power before the enemy. And God did. Another Old Testament story about fires that I love is in **2 kings 1** which tells us a story about King Ahab's son, Ahaziah who became king after his father. He fell from the lattice of his upper room and was injured. Instead of praying and calling on God to heal him, the bible says he sent his messengers to the temple of Beelzebub to ask whether he would recover. This is the same god that the God of Israel had disgraced.

The angel of the Lord appeared to Elijah and told him to ask the people why they go to these other gods, is it because the God of Israel no more exist? Elijah was ordered to go and tell Ahaziah's servants what the angel of the Lord had told him. God told Elijah to tell Ahaziah that he would not recover and that he would die. Some of us will say Wow!!!. is that not harsh. Elijah told the king's people what the angel of the Lord told him. They in turn told the king who in turn asked them who gave them the message. They said it was a hairy man wearing a leather belt around his waist, Ahaziah quickly recognized that it was Elijah the Tishbite. He then sent 50 men to Elijah with a leader. They came to Elijah and addressed Elijah as the man of God. Elijah said if he is truly the man of God as they have said let God confirm it by consuming them with fire. Instantly the 50 men were consumed by fire. WOW!!!! Ahaziah was perplexed. He sent another 50 men to Elijah who again called on his God to confirm His presence by consuming these men. They were instantly consumed again. The king a sent a third group. The leader of this third group was smarter than the first two groups. From afar he started begging Elijah not to not to call on his God to consume him with fire. This man has an understanding heart. By now he has realized that there was a God above all gods, he acknowledged it, he honored that reality. This time God spoke to Elijah and told him go with them to Ahaziah. Ahaziah was persistent he knew that there was something about Elijah's God that he cannot afford to undermine. Elijah went with the people to Ahaziah and told Ahaziah what God said. Maybe he repented of his action we do not know but he died as God has said he would. What remains everlasting is Elijah's God demonstrating His power to the consternation of all standing around.

The second half of **verse 14** says "the blazing flame shall not be quenched and all faces from the South to the North shall see that I the Lord have kindled it and shall not be quenched". All fires lit by man eventually dies. If you lit a fire in your house to warm your house it has to die sometime. If there is a bush fire, it dies when the firefighters go into action. If a house, a car, a building is aflame sooner or later that fire burns itself out or if somebody puts it out. When fire is not continually fueled it dies. But this verse is telling us that fire started by God does not burn out. How consoling!!!. God' s fire burns for aye and forever. The eternal God who is from everlasting to everlasting says that His fire will burn for ever. When God opens a door no man can shut it, the same way when God lights a fire no man can put it out. God's fire does not need external fuel. It is self-generating. It is eternal. It is everlasting. It does not lose its power. It continues to glow as long as we stay connected to the One who lit it, the source and origin, the Holy Spirit. The astounding thing about this fire is that it will not only be lit inside of us, as God promised, it will be around us like a hedge protecting us. While burning off the green and dry trees, it will not consume us. Just like the Burning Bush that Moses saw. The bible says it was burning but not consuming. Wow!!!!!. Just like **Leviticus 6: 12-13** describes the fire on the altar of God. It says, "it shall be burning and it shall not be put out".

The next question is what do we do with this fire in us?. Jesus tells us in **Mathew 5: 16, He** says "let you light shine before men, that they may see your good work and glorify your Father who is in heaven". The fire of God in us will put us in contact with all people of the world who will marvel when they see the fire of God burning in us. When people see this fire they will come near us because we shall be reflecting God's glow, God's beauty. There will be evidences and confirmation that truly God's fire is burning in us. Those who are watching us with curiosity will see, those who are monitoring us with suspicion will know, those who are wondering about us will come to an understanding about us. With the fire of the Holy spirit in us, we will have the fruit of the Spirit. We will also have the gifts of the Holy Spirit, the empowerment, the enablement, that we need, which will be dispensed as the Holy Spirit deems fit for each of us.

You may reading this prophetic word of God which says. "**I will kindle a fire in you**". This is prophesy indeed. There are times when God strategically locates us to for growth, for increase, for restoration for enlarged territories, for immense blessings and for encouragement. It is then God gives us His word which is "a lamp to our feet, a light to our path" (**Psalm 119:105**) strength to our bones and hope for our life. As I write this reflection, I have the inspiration of the Holy Spirit to draw your attention to this unusual Word. The Reflection starts with God's promise to kindle a fire in us. Personally, I want that fire. If you also do, say a silent prayer for yourself and make an affirmation of this well-known song for yourself "I have the light of God in me. I have the Spirit and of the Lord and His ability I have the light of God in me". Amen

Life is a Season: Ecclesiastes 3:1

Ecclesiastes 3: Says to everything there is a season a time for every purpose under the Earth. We all know that each seasons of the Year has its own beauty, and all are established for different purposes, making significant contributions to life. The good thing is that they all work together to achieve God's purposes of life and growth. Seasons are different in each part of the world. But essentially, they all have the same patterns. They all could be divided into four seasons. There is Summer when everything is bright and cheerful. The sun is out. It is a period of warmth, a period of growth with all the beautiful blooms, pretty flowers, a time when people cannot wait to show off their beautiful half naked bodies. It is also a time of bugs and mosquitoes. Soon we come to Autumn or Fall, a time of harvest, with the beautiful shades and hues of red, brown, yellow, red, green leaves that we see around the trees. Many people think it is the most beautiful time of the year. Then the leaves begin to fall and everything looks dreary and dull again.

Then comes Winter, a season of dormancy, a season of closure. Winter is not the most comfortable of the seasons. It is fraught with falls, accidents, crashes, people buried under snow. Some people experience winter Blues, winter Doom, winter Gloom, because it is dark all the time. It's also a time of very bad road conditions and many unhappy situations. But then the flip side is the beauty of the snow and snowflakes. In Sound of Music one of the one of Maria's "Favorite Things" is the Snowflakes on the Window Pane. The white snow settles on the ground, on the roof on the trees which make people wish for white Christmas because it is beautiful, always a remarkable sight. But even in the severe cold, the fire of winter warms up. The glow that comes from the fireplace is pleasant, it is beautiful. After winter comes Spring and everything springs to life again. We start looking forward to Summer. The beginning of another cycle. As we can see God has planned all the seasons that they all work together in perpetuity and continuity

It is an endless cycle. And for sure they come around in predictable cycle. It has been like that and it will be like that till eternity. The season will continue to rotate eternally. It is God's world. It is God's Seasons. He controls them and he enables them. Seasons never fail to show up. **Psalm 74:16** Says "The day is yours the night is also yours. You have set all the borders of the earth. You have made summer and winter". **Genesis 8:22** says "While the Earth remains, seed time and harvest, cold and heat, winter and summer, day and night shall not cease". The rotation of the season is sure. However, as God has planned and ordained the Seasons in nature, God has also planned the Seasons of our lives. We all go through the seasons of life.

Just as the seasons remind us of God's covenant with his people and his faithfulness in all that he does and just as the seasons of nature are predictable, so are the Seasons of Our lives. The Seasons of our Lives also happen for a **purpose**. Just as God's purpose is lived out in all the seasons of the year so is God's purpose in our lives. We all go through the wintertime of our life when our souls are dark and cold and gloomy. When we feel down and out, when it is very cloudy and we still we cannot even see the light at the end of the tunnel. The winter of life is very depressing, could even be sorrowful. A season of winter in our lives may be a time of sickness, heaviness of heart, family issues, death, loss of job, various challenges. The good thing about the Winter of life like the winter season is that it is never permanent. Just as winter season lasts for only awhile, Winter of life ends sometime. No matter how long the winter season lasts, it often comes to an end. No season has ever been skipped. Our lives are designed for a time of up and a time of down. Winter of life may be a time of hardships, but it also signals the end of a particular era.

Whenever we are experiencing a time of Winter in our soul, we must always remember that without Winter there will be no Spring. It does not matter what is going on, there is always a flicker of light somewhere. It could always be worse. There is always a silver lining even in the darkest cloud. Winter season does not always look like a time of excitement, the same way Winter of life. However, in winter of life we look forward to something new, new era, new beginning. God slows us down in Winter so we can later Spring out. We are confident that Spring is coming and summer is around the bend. The seasons never fail. Has Summer failed to show up because of the long winter? Never!!!If you are going through the Winter of life, be rest assured that Springtime of life is around the corner, when new things happen again, when one looks excitedly to the future, when one feels less discouraged. God designs our lives for Rest and Recuperation after a time of intense activity. Without this, there cannot be other periods of refreshing. Just as the Seasons of Nature bring about God's perfect will, the Seasons of Lifework together to bring about God's perfect purpose for us. The farmers are happy in winter because of the provision of water in snow and rain to help the crops. The snow covers the ugliness of the bare trees of Autumn until they grow back in summer.

We know how we all respond to the seasons of nature, how our moods change, how in Summer we feel like Resurrection, we feel like the dawn or beginning of a new day. In summer we work diligently in the heart of the day, we do all the things that God wants us to do. Some people plant in Spring and they begin to harvest in the summer.

The good thing about all the seasons of nature is that none is perfect they are all have their low side, but they still contribute to God's overall agenda. The season of Summer in our lives is a time of Grace, a time of Hope to overcome the cold season of headaches, of anxieties, of grief, of regrets, of complexities, of confusion, of Sorrow. **Psalms 145:14** says the Lord upholds all who fall and raises up all those who are bowed down. It is God who picks us up. It is God who encourages our souls. Just as the seasons of nature **change** the seasons in our lives are bound to change. The seasons have never failed to change because God who controls them never fails. The same way God has ordained seasons of nature for a purpose, the same way he has ordained the seasons of our Lives for a purpose. Things happen for a reason. **Mathew 10: 29** says No Leaf falls from a tree without God knowing about it. Coincidentally the same statement is in the Quran of the Muslims in **Surah 6:59** "And He knows whatever is in the land and the sea. And in no way does a leaf fall down, except that He knows it".

As I said there is good and bad in All Seasons. As much as people find winter gloomy, people say it is time when families bond together. It is a time they see each other more often, it is a time they grow closer, some even say that it is a time when babies are made. (smile) God really knows what He is doing. Let us feel encouraged. After the Flood God made a pledge with human beings that there will always be Wintertime and Summer time. (**Genesis 8:22**) He gave the rainbow with beautiful colors across the sky to seal his promise.

God also made a promise that those who believe in his son Jesus Christ will not be broken. God is always true to his word. In the revolutions of the seasons, the nature of God remains faithful. Let us learn to trust God and to trust His Son Jesus who is a constant source of comfort in time of every trouble, that our troubled situation/season is **not** permanent and that there are always better days ahead. Even in The Doom and Gloom there is always a ray of Sun and Light. Amen.

God's Time and Chance: Ecclesiastes 9:11

I was writing the Reflection on **Ecclesiastes 3:1** which says that life is a season, when I came across **Ecclesiastes 9:11** which tells us that **time** and **chance** happen to us all. I began to reflect on the verse and the connection between the two concepts of time and chance. What is time? The dictionary defines it as all the days that there have been or ever will be in the past, the present, the future. Time is occasion, the moment. How did time come to be? I wondered. From the story of creation in Genesis the first book of the Bible we are told that God created all. He created the day, He created the night, He created the moon, He created the sun, He created the land, He created the water. He created all things and therefore He set forth TIME. By separating day and night so we can count days. If we believe that God created all it stands to reason that He created TIME. And if He created Time it means that Time belongs to Him. God controls time. God is not controlled by time. Which also mean that God is in charge of all. He has always been in charge of all. Whether we recognize that fact and submit to it is a different matter. This brings my thoughts to the Evolutionists. Creationist will easily agree with this fact, the truth that God is ageless, from everlasting to everlasting the Bible tells us that God is God. Genesis did not tell us where He came from. God has always been. He owns, He controls all that He has created including Time.

David in **Psalm 31:14-15** says "O God My times are in your hands". Not only is God a God of Time the implication is that He is also a God of Chance. What is chance? It is opportunity. Time and chance do not just happen. I believe that God make them to happen. He makes them happen for a purpose. He makes them happen for us the creatures that He has created so that we can all seize the opportunity and make the best use of them. In the ultimate scheme of God's plan God has therefore designed the time to be born, to die, to plant, to reap, to kill, to heal, to break down, to build up, to weep, to laugh, to mourn, to dance, to keep, to throw away, to tear, to sew, to cast away, to gather, to keep silent, to speak, to love, to hate, to war to make peace. In all these it is certain that God is not a God of "by chance", meaning accidental, not expected, not planned, coincidental. God is a God of purpose and design. He ordains things. He designs that things would happen.

My question then is do we ALL God's creation, not just Christians, always move, according to God's design, God's time, God's plan, God's purpose? Or do we in our free will are left to our choices and devices? I always wonder. Do we always flow with God's time and chance? Do we always take advantage of God's time and chance? Do we always act promptly in the time and chance that God provides? Or do we always procrastinate, vacillate, oscillate, swaying, moving one way or the other, wavering between two opinions as the Bible calls it, until we miss God's time and chance presented to us. **James 1:6-8** says that "the person that doubts is like a wave of sea driven and tossed by the wind, that man will not receive anything from the Lord because he is double minded and unstable in all his ways". To receive and not miss God's time and chance we have to be stable. If we look closely God always provide the for us the time and chance, but at times we do not seize the opportunity and so we miss the chance. God has a plan for us, that is why He provides structure. When the chance opens, do we go for it or do we not. Many people have missed opportunities then they blame it on bad luck. God is a God of equal opportunities. He provides opportunities for all his creatures. If He has created the world and all the people, then we all are in His hands as the song writer says. Do all His creatures live close to Him to know his mind? Are we always able to discern His time and chance for us. Are we always able to discern His time and chance not only for our own good but also for the good of others around us?

Let us look at a woman in the Bible who availed herself of God's time and chance. It is the story of Esther. We all know the story. It is found in the Book of Esther. Note that in the story God did not directly speak to Esther God used her uncle Mordecai to speak to her. By God's time and chance Mordecai brought Esther to the palace of the king to participate in a beauty contest because the king was sore at his first wife Vashti who refused to be paraded before the king and his drunken friends. But I believe it was God's time and chance that brought Esther to the palace. Esther participated in the contest, won and became the king's wife. When there was a plot to exterminate the Jews. Mordecai told Esther to mention it to the king. She was hesitant because she knew her limitations in that patriarchal culture. She did not have access to the king like in most conjugal relationships where they would share a room and of course the bed every night. She has to be sent for, summoned, and requested for.

When Mordecai noticed that Esther was reluctant, he told **Esther 4:13-14** "do not think in your heart that you will escape the wrath that was coming. If you remain silent, relief and deliverance will arise for the Jews from another place". Mordecai was truly a man of God. He understands that if God gives us a time and chance to something for Him and we refuse to do it or ignore to do it God will give the time and chance to another person. It was then Mordecai added the most quoted verse in that book of Esther. Mordecai said to Esther "Yet who knows whether you have come into the kingdom into the king's palace for such a time like this". God's time and chance. It was time for Vashti to go. She was not a Jew. God needed a Jewish woman to rescue His people. It was at that point that something clicked in Esther's head and she agreed to the assignment. She declared a three-days fast and resolved to seize the time and chance that was presented to her for the good of her people and for her own good too. Esther was saved so was her people. What if Esther had not taken the opportunity of God's time and chance, God of course will replace her and His plan will still be fulfilled. And the story will have a different ending. The time and chance did not come to Esther because she was a woman of skill, or a woman of understanding yes beautiful but she was chosen for the task. Her beauty only paved the way. We never know what God will use in us to place us for His time and chance.

If you are reading this, what is your such a time as this? Have you had your such a time as this? Or maybe you have missed your such a time and chance to do something and you have thrown it away. And you are now regretting, wetting your pillow every night with tears and deeply imploring God for a Second chance. Yes, we have a good and merciful God. He does not close windows on the time and chance that He had offered us and we have rejected. He always provides a second chance, at times another chance because He is a merciful God. Repeatedly in the in the bible we see instances where God gives second time and chance even a third time and chance. See God's relationship with Israel, for instance, God was always giving them opportunities to repent, to turn back to Him but they would always stray and go after another god until He decided to kill off all the disobedient adults and raised a new generation that He took to the promised land.

Our God is also a patient loving God. I remember Gideon and his fleece before God. (**Judges 6**). He was promised victory, but he was not convinced, he had to throw a fleece before God three times. I am sure God was just amused by Gideon's silliness. God however played along with him until he was convinced. We humans do not have that amount of patience with each other. I also look at Jonah, God gave him a specific instruction to go to Nineveh he decided to go his own way until he ended up in the fish belly. **Jonah 3:1** tells us that God came to Jonah a second time. This time he recognized that he had to respond to God's time and chance. Even Elijah told God he wanted to see God, God gave him three opportunities, wind, earthquake, fire, but God was not in them, He was in a still small voice. Even Peter was given a second time and chance after his blatant denial of Jesus. He gave Peter the most significant task of feeding His sheep.

Romans 8:28-30 tells us that for those He foreknew he also predestined, those he predestined these He also called, those He called He also justified, those he justified he also glorified. He has everything in place, planned and so He provides the time and chance for us to walk into his plan. God is a God of Action, a decisive God who plans and execute. He is also a God of providence. Time and chance are part of His provision. Humans like to talk of luck, some people wish each other luck.

Personally, I believe that God is instrumental in anything that happens to anybody. Our responses to the time and chance that He provides result in the experiences that we have. So how do we discern God's time and chance? I think this will be the greatest challenge for all of us. There are many voices out there. How do we not mix up God's voice from the other voices out there? Satan is still dangling time and chance before people just as he did to Jesus. What power do we have to resist him? I think the solution is seeking the Lord's face like King David says in **Psalm 27:8** "Thy face O Lord, will I seek". We need to always commit everything to the Lord. Queen Esther declared three days fasting and prayers before walking to the time and chance presented to her and it yielded positive result. We do not know what Esther experienced in those three days of fast and prayers. All I know is that Fast and prayers have never done anybody any ill. Amen.

Occupy till I Come: Luke 19:13

There has been a lot of talk in the Christian circle about the Second coming of the Lord. Remember all the excitement at the beginning of this millennium, year 2000. Everybody was sure that the end of time had really come. Many people prepared in various ways too numerous to mention for the end of time. Christians equated it with the return of the Lord. Surprisingly nothing happened. Anyway, I thought it was a great reminder of what Jesus said about His coming. Jesus talks extensively about his coming in **Mathew 24:27** he said, "for as the lighting comes from the east and flashes to the west so also will the coming of the Son of Man be". In **Luke 17: 26-31** Jesus said that the day that He will come will be like the days of Noah and also like the days of Lot. Then finally in **Mathew 25:13** He now said, "therefore watch for you know neither the day nor the hour in which the Son of man is coming".

With the amount and level of activities the whole world witnessed, I actually saw it a dress rehearsal for the Great Day. Thinking of the events leading to the beginning of year 2000 and the same amount of gusto that the world saw at that time it occurred to me that the whole world would actually do some good if we are all in a state of preparedness for the return of the Lord. Unfortunately, after all hullabaloo and all the fuss and nothing happened, the whole world became disillusioned and went into a state of inertia about the Second coming. Since then the world has changed and a lot of things, again too numerous to mention have been happening.

However, I shifted my thoughts to Jesus many parables about the end of time. The one that catches my imagination is the one found **Luke 19:13**, a story about a man who went on a business trip. Before he left, he gave money to his servants, he told them "Do business till I come"**.** In another translation He said, "**Occupy till I come".** I think I like this version**.** Three significant issues emanated from the story (1) the master gave minas which is money according to Luke's account. While Mathews says the master gave talents which can be called gifts. The important thing is that the Master gave the servants something to work with, some sort of resource, some sort of leverage. (2) He gave specific instructions as to what they were to do with what he gave them. They were all expected to put these resources to work. (3) When the master returned, he asked for reports about how each person has performed. He asked for accounts because he expected accountability. (4) Then he gave rewards according to the performance of each.

Somehow, I found a lot of correlation with our lives. How do these relate to us? Plenty as we shall see. In each one of us, every human being God has deposited some talents, which we are all required to put to prudent use. We are all expected to put these gifts to proper use until the time Jesus comes. **2Timothy1:6** says "stir up the gift of God that is in you". These are the natural talents that we all have, ability to play musical instruments, too draw, to paint and so on. Some people are just so naturally gifted for some things that come easy to them. **James 1:17** reminds us that every good and perfect gift is from above and comes from the Father of Lights. **Ephesians 4:1-8** says When Jesus ascended on high, he gave gifts unto all men**. 1 Corinthians 12: 4-7** reminds us that there are diversities of gifts, but the same spirit gives them. Our gifts, our talents are for us to use in the Body of Christ and in the world of at large because we are God's Ambassadors.

The next stage looks at how we have been putting these resources to work. In our story, all the servants were given the same number of talents. Equity I would say. The first servant had one talent, he came back with ten more, the second one came back with five more, the next one came back with two more, and the last one came back with just the one that he was given. I wondered what went right, what went wrong. The only reason I can ascribe to the varying degree of performance is **attitude**. At times, our attitude, our sense of responsibility, our availability, our willingness to make an effort, determines what we do with our talents.

Some people know the gifts that they have but they never offer to use the gifts at the disposal of others. They hoard their gifts. Some others use those gifts to oppress, dominate and manipulate people. They deal mischievously and deceitfully with people as Paul says in **2 Corinthians.** In everything said or done by these people, there is a hidden agenda. They use their gifts to selfishly derive benefits for themselves. Thankfully there are those who use their gifts for the benefit of human race, doing everything as unto the Lord. They walk in love, expecting no rewards.

I think for all of us **Occupy till I come** is about accountability and responsibility. **1 Corinthians 4:2** says it is required in stewards that one be found faithful. The employed is accountable to the employer, the married to their spouse and family, the rulers to the citizens and to the society and all of us to God. **Romans 14: 12** says each one of us shall give an account of himself to God. Are we ready? Are we behaving responsibly? Are we keeping our records straight, clean and ready for our Master's return? Our Lives are not our own. We belong to God because, we have been bought with a price. So how are we thinking of our own preparedness for our Lord's return. How are we keeping ourselves "Occupied till he returns"?

In the story in **Luke 19: 15** When the master returned, he commanded the servants to whom he had given money to be called to him that he might know how much everyman has gained by trading. **Matthew 25:19** says after a long time the lord of the servants came and settled accounts with them. That was when they all came to give reports their performance. For sure when Jesus comes, he is not coming for the Jamboree that the world is preparing for Him. He is going to ask us to give an account of all we have done in the body **Romans 14:12** says each of us will give an account of himself to God. **2 Corinthians 5:10** says We will each receive whatever we deserve for the good or evil we have done in this earthly body. This means that there is stewardship. There is day of accountability, there is a day of reckoning. It is clear and obvious that we are expected to live out our lives and in fact our everyday temporal lives with her eyes towards our Master's return. The second part was when the servants reported their performances, their activities to the master, they were rewarded. The one who did nothing with what he had been given, was driven out from the presence of the master and called wicked and lazy servant.

In the field of Education, we talk of **evaluation and assessment**. This is what is done at the end of a course, a program, a project. Our evaluation is not just based on our last minutes performances. It is based on what is called Cumulative records. How we have been performing from the beginning to the end. Our cumulative records consist of three stages of evaluation and assessment. The first one is **formative** evaluation, this is what is done at the beginning of the project or program or course. It is also called **Baseline Assessment**, that is what is on the ground, what we started with, all of the resources and leverages that we have, the requisites for the program that we want to embark on. For us what we started with are our abilities, our talents, our gifts, our money or resources in various degrees, and various measures. God knows what we all started with, what we have all been given. All these are in our cumulative record file.

The second stage of the assessment is called **Continuous Assessment** which is also called **Monitoring** or at times called **Midterm Assessment**. This is to measure how we are doing. If we are not on point, we have the time and opportunity to correct it before the end and Final Assessment. For us whether we believe it or not Jesus has continuously and continually been monitoring us. He has been checking us out and he's been giving as rewards as we go along. The beauty of continuous assessment is that it gives us opportunity to check ourselves, to remedy things that need to be rectified, and to make efforts to improve. The beautiful thing is that as God increases our responsibilities, He increases our abilities, our potential, our capabilities, our empowerment, and our strength. That is why with some people as the Lord gives them more assignments, the Lord elevates them. The more strength they develop the more power they have. The more their coast becomes enlarged, the more their scope is increased. God gives all of us enough ability to cope with any responsibility that we have.

So how are we ALL doing? What are our scores? Are they looking good? If they are we are encouraged to go on, if not this is the time to make amends. Jesus is saying Occupy, Do business, Improve your chances, Prepare and get ready for the final stage of the assessment which is the **Summative Assessment** or **Evaluation**. This comes at the end of the project. It completes the cumulative records. The Bible says after death there is Judgment. How are we preparing for judgment? As we approach and await the Lord's Day what are we doing to improve our performances?

I believe we should watch out in **three** areas. The first one is our **Talents**, our gifts. Let us resolve today to begin to put to maximum use our talents. Let us set our priorities right, let us make the right choices at every turn. Let us do only that which will improve our grades. Let us start using and sharing our talents if we not have not been doing that. Let us use them to edify each other and to glorify God. If you have been doing that, there is still room at the top. The best is yet to come. The second area is **Time**. This is very important as we do not have much time. Remember it can happen anytime as Jesus said. The Bible says we should also ask God to teach us to number our days so we can apply our hearts to wisdom. Let us learn to redeem our time. Let us stop wasting time on useless pursuits and invest our time wisely on things that will qualify us for eternity. The third area is **Money**. Why money? The Bible says "Money answers all things" (**Ecclesiastes 10:19).** I have another Reflection on Money so I will be very brief here. Avoid waste, maximize returns, buy up your treasure in heaven, ensure that your investment is pleasing to God, spend money carefully, avoid consumerism, wanting everything that is in sight that you can lay your hands on. **1 Corinthian 9: 25** says in all things exercise self-control. Avoid debts. **Romans 13:8** says "owe no one anything" **Psalm 37: 21** says the wicked borrows and does not repay.

Finally, 1 Peter 4:10 says to each one of us that has received the gifts, minister to one another as good stewards of the manifold grace of God. **Romans 12:6-11** says God has given each of us the ability to do certain things well. God has given some people the ability to prophesy, to speak out when we have faith that God is speaking through you, if your gift is serving others, served him well. If you are a teacher do a good job of teaching, if your gift is to encourage others do it, if your gift is to give and if you have money share it generously. If God has given you leadership ability take the responsibilities seriously. Do not allow yourself to be intimidated by anyone, you are only responsible to God. And if you have gifts for showing kindness to others do it gladly. Don't pretend that you love others, really love them. Hate is wrong, stand on the side of good. Love each other with genuine affection, take delight in honoring one another, never be lazy at your work but serve the Lord enthusiastically.

The question is not whether we are working at all but whether we are working to the best of our ability. That is what responsibility is about. Are you a Workman that need not be ashamed? (**2 Timothy 2:15**) Are we doing all that needs to be done? If the Lord comes today can we say that we have attained, can we honestly say that we have run the race? Can we say we have increased the talents that we have been given at the beginning? The Lord is telling us today to buckle up to use a Jamaican parlance. Jesus said, "not everyone who calls me Lord, Lord shall enter into my kingdom". Doesn't that frighten you? Today is self-assessment day. For me I know that I am not at my best. I thank God for the opportunity and strength to do what I do but I also know that the best is yet to come. There is still a lot of room for improvement. I don't want to rest of my oars. I am willing, ready and desire to sit more at the feet of Jesus and learn more so as to be able to do more. What is the Holy Spirit telling you right now? Unto whom much has been given much is expected. Are you ready to Occupy till Jesus comes? Only you can answer the question. Let us pray for strength. Amen

Money Answers All Things. Ecclesiastes 10:19

There seems to be a lot of talk about money these days, those who have it, those who do not have it; those who spend it, those who watch others spend it; those who take it illegally, those who earn it legally. Then there were those who Occupied Wall Street to remind us of the social/economic inequality, greed, and corruption in the world. The Bible has a realistic perspective about money, **Ecclesiastes10:19** says, "Money answers all things". Of course, money is important. It is our time, our toil, our sweat, our food, our shelter, our clothing, our agent of exchange and bargaining. It is the material power that enables us to live, move, and do as we please in this world. We also know that God is not averse to our having money because we learn that from several passages of the Bible. **Psalm 35:27** tells us that God has pleasure in the prosperity of His people. According to **3 John1:2** God wants us to prosper in all things and be in health even as our souls prosper. **Deuteronomy 8:18** tells us that it is God who gives power to make wealth. We also read that there are people in the Bible that God has blessed with extreme riches.

King Solomon comes to mind. Abraham, also a favored one of God had immense wealth and was financially prosperous. While on earth Jesus knew about money, talked a lot about money and spent money. He had a treasurer among His Twelve who kept and managed the money. Jesus even paid tax. He gave Caesar his due.

What then is the problem with money? The problem is that there seems to be too much money in the hands of a few people and much less in the hands of many others, resulting in gross inequities. It is also how we acquire money and what we do with it that makes a difference with God who wants us to use money according to His principles. The Bible highlights some negative aspects of money. **1Timothy 6:9-10** says, "The love of money is the root of all evil, those who desire to be rich fall into temptation and many foolish and harmful lusts which drown men in destruction and perdition". **Proverbs 28:20** tells us "a faithful man will abound with plenty but those who hasten to be rich will not go unpunished". **Proverbs 11:28** condemns those who trust in their riches and add that they will fall while the righteous will flourish like the foliage. This means that abounding in righteousness is wealth in itself. **Proverbs 22:16** also tells us that whosoever oppresses the poor to increase his own wealth, or gives to the rich, will only come to poverty. This is a strong condemnation of secular leaders who exploit the people, oppress and marginalize the poor to increase their riches. It is also a condemnation of religious leaders who manipulate their congregation to make money out of their vulnerabilities. Their life style belies their calling. **Psalm 62:10** gives a stark warning that if riches increase, those who have it should not set their hearts on their wealth.

The Bible establishes a line between contentment and covetousness, greed and need. **Ecclesiastes10:12** says that those who love money never have enough, those who love wealth are never satisfied with their income. It adds that godliness and contentment is great gain, if we have food and clothing, we should be content. In today's world, this may not be ideal for some, who like Oliver Twist continue to want more, and more and more. **Luke 12:15** reminds us that life does not consist in the abundance of things possessed. **1Timothy6:7** tells us that we come to this world with nothing and we shall all leave with nothing. It is then surprising to see the spirit of greed and consumerism so pervasive. It is equally amazing what people will do for money. **Micah 3:11** talks of prophets who divine for money. All these alert us to God's laid down rules about the use of money both in the secular world and in the so call religious circles.

In the Christian world, people are fed with various positions and perspectives about money. There are the **Prosperity preachers** who believe that wealth comes through godliness, the consequence of religious piety, a sign of God's blessing to those who are faithful to Him. The implication is that those who are not rich do not have God's favor. **1Timothy 6:5** tells us to distance ourselves from people "who suppose that godliness is a means of gain". In their numerous money-centered messages, the prosperity preachers measure their spirituality by their wealth. They boast about how much they have and how God has blessed them. They tout their opulent life styles as success and evidence of God's love. However, they promise instant results and overnight success to those who give to God. They also add that large donations would result in windfall from God. They tell the people to give money to their leaders so that they can become rich like them. They also promise that God would grant healing to people's numerous ailments if they donate immensely to their preachers. Nonetheless, they add that if their followers do not get a breakthrough, it is because they did not give enough money in the offering. In short, they blame the poor by saying it is their fault and lack of faith that cause them to be poor. In spite of the Biblical guidelines on tithes, prosperity preachers always urge Church members to continually sow more financial seeds to reap bigger and bigger rewards. They actually do not care about societal poverty neither do they contribute anything to help the poor. All they care about is the enrichment of their pockets and their pleasure. Unfortunately, the prosperity preachers have become a threat to faith, when money does not drop from the sky as promised by them, some followers become disillusioned and drop out of church.

Then you have the **Poverty preachers** who believe that poverty is a virtue. They quote Jesus as saying that it is hard for a rich man to enter into the kingdom of God. They also say that Jesus was poor and so true followers should be poor. Actually, the Bible says that Christ was rich, but for our sakes, He became poor that we might be made rich. On the other hand, some Poverty preachers do not talk at all about money. They do not tell their congregation what the Bible says about money. They indirectly deny their congregations the blessings that come with prudent and godly giving. For example **Malachi 3:10** says, "Bring the whole tithe into the storehouse, so that there may be food in My house, and test Me now in this," says the Lord of hosts, "if I will not open for you the windows of heaven and pour out for you a blessing until it overflows". This essentially means that those who give to the kingdom to address the needs of the church should expect to reap from what they have sown. However, this does not mean that the more money they give the more money God will give them.

So how does God want us to use money? To start with, Jesus talks about the poor who will always be with us. We live in an imperfect world with a huge imbalance of wealth and power. God is a God of justice and wants his people to make a difference in the world, standing up for those who cannot stand up for themselves and sharing what we have with those who have nothing. As Christians living in an unequal world, we cannot continue to ignore the pervasive inequities that surround us. Above all, we cannot choose to do nothing about it, undermining what we can contribute both in major and minor ways. After all **James 1:20**, tells us that pure religion is to look after the orphans and the widows, who by all categorization would fall into the group of the poor. Some people have no conscience about flaunting their wealth around the people whom they have milked dry to create wealth for themselves. The Bible has given the rich some responsibilities. The rich should cheerfully seek to help those in need as God gives them opportunity. They should show pity to the poor, they should be sensitive to their needs and they should be open handed towards them. In **James 2:2-4**, the Apostle Paul rebukes those who show favoritism to the wealthy and treat the poor as if they are not as worthy of respect and honor. They treat the rich extremely well by giving them the best seats in the church but shaming the poor by making them sit on the floor.

However, **Proverbs 17:5** says, "Whoever mocks the poor reproaches his Maker" They also forget that **Proverbs 22:2** reminds us that the poor and the rich are made by God. **1Samuel 2:7** tells us that the Lord makes poor, and makes rich, he brings low and lifts up. Therefore, if we are going to extol the rich, we must also not condemn the poor. **James 2:15-16** says suppose a brother or a sister is without clothes and daily food and if one of you say to them, "Go in peace; keep warm and be well fed," but does nothing about their physical needs, what good is it? **1John 3:17** says, "But whoever has the world's goods, and sees his brother in need and closes his heart against him, how does the love of God abide in him?" The love of God and giving to those in need go hand in hand. Paul in **2Corinthians 8:13-15** indicates that the church is a place where those who have much are able to supply the needs of those who lack what they need. He says that in the name of equality those who have should supply the needs of those who do not have. **2Corinthians 9:7b** also tells us that we should give "not grudgingly or under compulsion, for God loves a cheerful giver."

Secondly in **Matthew 6:19-21** Jesus told the people not to lay not up for themselves treasures upon earth, but to lay them up in heaven because where their treasures are is where their hearts will be. This means that people should not set their hearts and focus on their wealth or else they will become desensitized to the things of God. Consumerism and accumulative instincts deprive people of the right focus about what Paul says in **1Timothy 6:7-12** for we brought nothing into this world, and it is certain we can carry nothing out and having food and raiment let us be content. Certainly, the sum total of life is not as Solomon and Paul put it "eat drink and be merry for tomorrow we die". There is a lot more to our existence than that.

Interestingly, the social world is also entrenched in the discourse about money. Some people say that money cannot buy happiness. We all know that is not very true. I think of all the people living in abject poverty that the World Bank classifies as living on less than a dollar a day. They will experience happiness when their basic needs, food, shelter and clothing are met. ABBA in one of their songs says, "Money must be funny in a rich man's world". Extravaganza is the game of the rich. Extreme poverty, homelessness, victimization, inequities, marginalization, lack of basic needs and the perennial widening gap cannot be funny in a poor man or poor woman's world. The poor man and woman lament about all the things they could do if they just have a little money. Money may not be able to buy love, as the Beatles said in one of their songs, but money can show God's love to the poor. However according to Bible there is hope for the poor. **Psalm 113:7** says God raises up the poor out of the dust and lifts the needy out of ash heap.

Finally, the truth is we all have responsibility to make and use God's money according to His guidance. **Proverbs 10:22** says the blessing of the Lord, makes rich, and He adds no sorrow with it. Thankfully, there are still many generous people in the world today. However, one cannot continue to ignore the spirit of greed and consumerism that is pervasive in our times and in the global culture today. In the haze of self-gratification, self-indulgence and accumulative instinct people still sidetrack and ignore the poor. Everyone pays lip service to the plight of the poor while aggravated stealing and aggressive accumulative instincts go on unabated in a world where Mahatma Gandhi says that there is enough for the need of the world but not enough for its greed. To deal with the lopsidedness, in our world, can the rich desire, take and consume less for the poor to have some relief from the pain of insufficiency in their lives? Just wondering! The temptations to ignore are rife. Paul in **1Timothy 6:6** linking contentment and godliness tells us "godliness actually is a means of great gain when accompanied by contentment". Can our collective prayer therefore be Agur's prayer found in **Proverbs 30: 7-9**, "*Lord, deprive me not, give me neither poverty* *nor riches, feed me with the food allotted to me lest I be full and deny you or lest I be poor and steal and profane the name of my God*". Amen.

Go forward. Leave the gate. Cross over Exodus14:13-15. 2 Kings7:3-8. Luke 8:22

This reflection is based on three separate readings. I was reflecting on what to share at an event that I have been invited to speak, and it came to me that I need to talk against stagnation: "Go forward, Leave the gate, Cross over" were the concepts that came to me. With the help of the Holy Spirit I was able to pull them together to form a continuum. The first one is found in **Exodus 14: 15**, We know the story, God has just used Moses to effect the deliverance of these Israelites from the hands of the Egyptians. They had just been set free after God has handed ten strange plagues on the Egyptians. The Israelites left, but as soon as they left, Pharaoh changed his mind and he pursued them with his well-qualified army. In **verse 1** of that chapter The Lord told them to camp by the Red Sea. As soon as they camped, they saw Pharaoh and his army coming after them and of course they were frightened. They were between the rock and a hard place, Pharaoh behind, the sea before. Where would they go? What would they do? The Egyptians represent a place where they no more want to be, the Egyptians were the enemies, they represent oppression, slavery, wickedness, domination, lack of freedom, a place of unhappiness, a place of problems. But then walking in front they saw a vast sea. This appeared as hopelessness. There was no way through, but then God gave Moses a strange command, **Go Forward**!!!Go forward to where? To the sea? To perish? Even if they could swim, they had all their luggage with them. Whoever goes into the sea with vast luggage on their back but then came this strange command to go forward. Essentially march into the sea, into the unknown, into what appeared to be a place of potential danger. Go forward and they did. We will see what happened later.

The second story is an interesting one found in **2 kings 7: 3-8** Four leprous men were sitting at the gate of a city. At a point they said to each other "Why are we sitting here at the gate until we die". The gate, the door, on the mantle of a building is usually a place of inactivity. If you stand at the gate, you are neither in nor out. Not much happens at the gate, standing at the gate does not yield any result. You cannot do much at the gate. The gate is a place of dryness, it is a place where there is no fruitfulness, and it is a place of no production, at the gate one is just rooted to one spot. In fact, the gate is a very narrow spot. You cannot install anything at the gate. It is an entrance, it is a place that leads to someplace else. It is a transitional place. To have anything done you either go back to where you are coming from or you go in to enter into a much bigger space behind the door, behind the gate, so that you can achieve something. These lepers looked at their situation, they were stuck at the gate. They knew it was not a good place to be, they knew they needed to move, they needed to leave the place of inactivity. They evaluated the risks that existed. If they went through the gate which led to the city, inside the city was famine, inside the city was the Syrian army, which meant death, inside the city was uncertainty; nonetheless they knew that remaining at the gate was no option. So they decided to **leave the gate**. We shall see what happened when they left the gate and moved into the city; with all the potential risks and danger.

The third story is from the New Testament and is found in **Luke 8:**[22-25]. Jesus has been preaching and bringing the glad tidings of the kingdom to the people. Jesus had told the people some parables, even explained the meaning of these parables. He has even responded to His mother's and brothers' visit. At a point Jesus decided that something else needed to happen. He needed to do other things. You cannot be doing the same thing over and over again. It becomes routine, you lose creativity. That was when in **Vs 22** He made a move, he gave a new directive to his disciples, who did not question him. "Let us **cross over** to the other side of the lake". The disciples followed him. There are some lessons to be learnt from these three stories.

The first one is that at times and usually, a time comes in our lives when we need to move to the next stage, when we need to get away from inactivity, when we need to get away from routine, when we need to get away from fretting, worrying, anxiety and take a bold step of faith, and move into the unknown. The Israelites did, the Lepers did, the disciples did with Jesus. The second consideration is what motivates us to move, at times the Lord gives commands, instructions that look outrageous or just undoable. What do we do with that instruction, do we obey or not? In the first story the Israelites were told to "Go forward" into the sea. Although not very willingly but with a lot of murmuring against Moses their leader, they did anyway. In the second story the Lepers after a lot of reflection and evaluation took a decision to leave the gate and move into the city with all its attending problems. In the third story, Jesus virtually commands the disciples to come along with him to the other side even with all the potential danger of the sea. They did not argue, they did not question, they followed.

Third consideration is that at times there are surprises ahead even in the unknown, even in the face of potential danger. In the first story the sea parted, the Israelites walked through, but as soon as the Egyptians attempted to follow them, the sea closed in on them and they perished. They saw God's hands at work. The sea did not part until they moved closer. In the second story when the lepers got inside the city, in a land where there was famine, they discovered that food was waiting for them. They had enough to eat, even had other supplies, in addition to food, they had silver and gold and their decision to move was also crowned with success. In the third story, Jesus simply gave a command and they conformed. Jesus' disciples did not claim fatigue, they did not ask for a break. They jumped into the boat and followed Him. But as soon as the boat set sail, there was a storm. Of course, the Apostles were frightened, remember some of them were fishermen, and so they have seen storms before, but I think this must be a big storm that left them frightened. But then what came out of it? They had the opportunity to witness Jesus perform a great miracle of stilling the storm, exercising his power and control over the elements. In these experiences, the Apostles came to have a new understanding of their Master, to see him demonstrate his supremacy over the elements, over diseases, in the healing of the woman, with the issue of blood, even over death in the raising of Jairus daughter and over demons in the deliverance of the demon possessed man in Gerasene.

The fourth consideration is that things happen when we take that step of faith, when we obey. When people go forward, when they leave the gate, when they cross over, things happen. How do all these apply to us, you and me? I believe at times God is saying to us all, that there are times when we need to go forward, to cross over, to leave the gate. There is always uncertainty about what lies on the other side but every move requires a step of faith. Most times we may not know what is on the other side, but from the stories we have read, success always awaited, surprises awaite, the Lord's guiding light also awaits on the other side.

Job 33[14] tells us that God may speak in one way or another. Yet man does not perceive it. We worship a versatile God. He speaks in many ways if we sit in one spot and we do not open ourselves to his versatility we will miss what He has to say to us. In this reflection God has used three stories to prove a point. God is a God of diverse ways. We cannot say to ourselves that we know how God moves, that we can predict what he will do at every point. God said His ways are not our ways and His thoughts are not our thoughts. (**Isaiah 55: 8-9**) Have you been too long at the gate? Have you been too long at this side? It is time to cross over, to go forward, to leave the gate.

I believe that calls like these are at times calling us to spiritual growth, in our corporate lives and in our individual lives. Spiritual growth is a continuous and continued process. Spiritual growth is becoming more mature in Christ. We cannot experience growth if we keep doing the same things over and over again without exploring new ways and new options. Spiritual growth is an act of discipline. It is an activity in holiness. God today is calling all of us to a higher level of devotion, higher level of commitment. Go forward, Leave the gate,

Cross over, in your engagement with the word of God. The Bible calls it lamp to our feet, a light to our path. God teaches us through His word. The more we need it, the more we study it the more we find in it Pearl of Great Price. Faith comes by hearing and hearing by the word. We all grow through our interaction with the Word. **Isaiah 40:8** says "The grass withers, the flower fades, but the word of our God will stand forever".

The Word of God is new each day. God's revelation unfolds each day just like his mercy. The Holy Spirit gives us divine revelation each day. God's Word is anointed. David in **Psalm 119** says "Teach me O Lord the way of your statutes and I shall keep it to the end". There are benefits in reading and studying the word God. **Romans 10[14]** says "how shall they call on him in when they have not believed, believed when they have not heard, hear without a preacher". God has given us preachers and teachers we all grow through personal study and hearing from others who preach and teach. Surprises await us when move from our comfort zone and cross over. Just as the Apostles saw Jesus in a new light, we too will be surprised by a shining light.

What about our prayer life, go forward, leave the gate, cross over. In our prayer life all of us may say we pray, but there are deeper depths to prayer, higher heights to achieve, prayer helps us to have a deeper desire to seek God's face and build our future on a firmer foundation. If you have always prayed individually, cross over to corporate prayer. Personal prayer and devotion are essential and good, so also is designated corporate prayers. It is like pieces of wood in the fireplace. When they are together, they give each other glow; remove one, it soon begins to die. Have a prayer partner, Join prayer sessions if there is any near you. "Effective fervent prayer avails much", so says the Bible.

God is always calling us to go forward in how we communicate with him. Our prayers should not only be for ourselves, "God bless me, bless my mother, bless my father, bless my sister, bless my brother, so they can all bless me". Pray for people you know and those you don't know, pray one for another, the Bible tells us to pray for parts of the world that are distressed. Don't say "I am okay and they are not and that is okay by me". Cross over to the other side with how you pray. If you know someone who is struggling tell them like Peter said to the cripple at the gate, "Gold and Silver have I not, but I will say a prayer for you". Pray for your pastors, pray for your priests, pray for your leaders, pray for the leaders of your country of your community, your workplace, **1Timothy 2:2** says we should pray for those who have dominion over us so that it may be well with us. If it is well with them, it will be well with us. Leave the gate in your prayer life, do something else otherwise we will shrivel like the Lepers said: "If we stay, we will die"

What about keeping fellowship with and loving others. We are not only required to love God and worship Him, but we are also required to love our neighbors. What is our relationship with others around us? How much of each other do we know? The Bible tells us not to shun the assembly of each other. We come to church to fellowship not only with God but also with one another. David in **Psalm 122** says I was glad when they said unto me let us go into the house of the Lord. In God's presence there is fullness of joy and pleasures forever more. Not only do we come to appear before God, we also come to affirm our love for each other. The church is a community where we love and support each. The church is a place where fellowship starts and other things follow. If you have been sitting at the gate in terms of loving your neighbors, the Lord is calling you to leave the gate. Your neighbors are not only your church people, they are people in your neighborhood, in your workplace. Do you love all people with the love of the Lord or do you simply stay cocooned in your own little world? Jesus is telling us to cross over to the other side. Reach out to people, show others you love them, we are Christians imitating Christ. Jesus did not sit on one large throne and expected people to come to him. He was itinerant, he was always on the go, visiting people in their homes, interacting with them at all points. Why, because he cares for people.

Lastly, note that when God told Moses to Go Forward, it was a collective move, the entire band was required to move. They all crossed the waters together. The same with the four lepers, it was a collectivist *we*. They supported one another; they moved *en masse* and worked together in consonance. The lesson here is that No man is an island. We all need each other for support. As for me, I have resolved to to go forward, leave the gate, to cross over to the other side, more so as Jesus himself is coming along with me. I am also enlisting my friends, my family, my neighbors to come along so we can all journey together. What about you? Will you come with us? Be blessed as you do. Amen.

Understanding the Presence of God

Psalm 95:2 says let us come before His Presence with Thanksgiving. **Acts 3:19** says repent therefore and be converted that your sins may be blotted out so that the times of refreshing may come from the Presence of God. All these passages and more talk about the Presence of God. I constantly hear about the Presence of God so I decided to explore this in my own reflection. What exactly is the Presence of God? Exactly what does presence mean? A presence is an appearance, a condition of being in one place, being in the sight of? We all know that God is a Spirit. He is unseen. He is not concrete. We cannot hold him so we think, we cannot also touch him. If this is so, can someone or something that is not tangible, that is not concrete, that has no physical form have a presence? If God is an unseen Spirit not concrete not tangible how can we continue to talk about the Presence of God. The Bible says no one has seen God and yet we have a quantum of instances where God has manifested His Presence to various people in various forms. "Does God really have a Presence" is what I want to explore.

The primary question will be how does God show up? How does God make his appearances? How do we know God is around and how do we recognize his presence? Starting from the Book of Genesis we hear about the Presence of God. Genesis says that the Spirit of God was hovering over an unformed earth. Then the Presence of God later became manifest in a voice that spoke the world into existence: "Let there be light and there was light". (**Genesis 1:3**) Everything else was commanded into existence. the Sun, the moon the stars the planets etc. The Presence of God then became physical. It translated in two hands that molded Adam and fashioned him into God's image. Thus, we know that God has a form.

Subsequently God also fashioned Eve into existence which affirms the Duality of God; male/female. The Presence of God became more concrete. Genesis says that in the beautiful garden of abode, a dwelling place that God has prepared for Adam and Eve, God would come in the cool of the evening when the sun was not high. The Sovereign God, the Supreme God, the Creator of heaven and earth would make an appearance, would manifest His Presence and spend time with Adam and Eve. Wow! God would interact with them, be in fellowship with them. Some theologians call this anthropomorphism, ascribing human attributes to God. For me they are good enough for our illustrations.

Then we come to Cain and Abel, children of Adam and Eve who both offered sacrifices to God from the fruit of their labor. When Cain out of jealousy killed his brother Abel, we are told that God appeared to Cain and demanded of him his brother. We all know about his belligerent response to God, "Am I my brother's keeper?" We read that when Cain could no longer bear his guilt he walked out away from the Presence of God. Then came Noah who God told to build an Ark because he was going to destroy the Earth that he had created. The Bible says that God gave Noah some instructions about the ark and what would be placed in it. We do not know whether it was a face-to-face interaction or whether it was a dream, or a vision but the Presence of God was so real to Noah that he recognized that the instructions came from God and he responded in spite of being mocked by the people around him.

Then we come to Abraham who is described as God's friend. Abraham experienced the Presence of God in various ways. The Presence of God was a voice that told him to relocate from Ur. The Presence of God was a command that ordered him to sacrifice his son to God. At another time the Lord appeared to Abraham in the form of three men, who came to his house. After being entertained by Sarah his wife, they conveyed to him and his wife their impeding fatherhood and motherhood. The Bible says these Three Angels spoke as ONE. Abraham saw them, bowed down to them and then addressed the three of them as ONE. He says my Lord Do not pass me by. I think the concept of the Triune God was introduced to us. Another strange thing about this appearance of God in the form of three men was that after they left the Bible says Abraham recognize that even though God has left Abraham was still in the Presence of God and he knew it. Jacob experienced the Presence of God as a Wrestler who fought with him in a dream. Jacob later said in **Genesis 32: 30** I've seen God face to face.

Then we come to Moses, God's friend who also saw the Presence of God in various manifestations: as a Burning Bush, as a Pillar of Cloud by day and as a Pillar of Fire by night. The Bible also says God spoke to Moses face to face as a friend. Moses desired the Presence of God, asked for it and got it. He said to God, "we will not go if your Presence will not go with us". God did that for 40 years. God's Presence moved along with Moses and the children of Israel while on their very long journey. The Presence of God as a cloud was not only experienced by Moses as an individual. God manifested himself to the whole congregation at the Tabernacle.

Then we come to Balaam the sinner? Not really a good man, one who was hired by Balak because of his evil propensity. He was asked to curse the children of Israel. God appeared to Balaam and told him not to curse but to bless the children of Israel. To Balaam God Presence was so real that he conformed to the voice that he heard not to curse. The Presence of God was in a wooden symbol The Ark of God. Can God be anywhere He wants to be, even in a Box. How did we know God was truly present in this wooden box? When Uriah tried to stabilize this box by touching it, he was instantly struck dead. Some elements become holy when God's presence is in them. However, David danced before this same Ark and God was pleased with him.

Deborah a woman ruler of Israel a prophetess of God, a warrior, a wife, a mother in Israel experienced the Presence of God as a voice that relayed instructions to her concerning going to war with her Chief of staff Barak (not Obama). She responded with obedience and the war was won. The Presence of God is not gender related. God manifests His Presence to both men and women. God is equitable, He does not favor one gender over the other. Deborah ruled the people of Israel for exactly 40 years just like David. She was described as a worshipper like David. She was a successful Warrior like David and the Bible describes her reign a successful as David's. God favors and empowers men and women equally to respond to his Presence.

The Presence of God does not only hover around, does not only come forth as in a voice, the Presence of God penetrates the individual and possesses them. We come to Gideon who experienced the Presence of God as Spirit coming upon him. When Gideon became overwhelmed by the Presence of God, he did strange things. The Bible says he began to blow the trumpet which he has not learn to play. (**Judges 6:34**) Then we come to Samuel, a mere child who experienced the Presence of God at a very early age. He heard God call his name and through the guidance of the elders he responded appropriately: "Lord speak for your servant is listening". God's presence is not only for adults but also for children. God will not only manifest himself to mature people like Abraham but also to young people who are ready and willing to cooperate. Samuel submitted to God at a very early age. Samuel did not rebel against his parents for dumping him in the house of God at such a young age. He did not express anger at being deprived of his youth. while his mates were going to school and playing as children. He was growing up in the House of God. Try that in today's world it would be called Child abandonment or even Child abuse or violation of Child's rights

Now to David a man after God's own heart. David was the one who told us that there is joy in the Presence of God (**Psalm 16:11**) God's presence was so real to David that he had the habit of inquiring of the Lord we are told. (**1 Samuel 30:8**) David will not do anything without first asking God. What a relationship!!. Should I go? Should I stay? Should I pursue? Should I fight? Should I strike? David had to be sure he was always doing the will of God. David understood the Presence of God. God did not limit the manifestation of his presence to David in one pattern. It was diverse and David recognized them all. Solomon, David's son, God's favorite child who God gave a pet name Jedidah also experienced God's Presence in a dream where he received wisdom and riches. Job experienced God's Presence in the form of a whirlwind, a very powerful encounter for Job. Isaiah experienced God's presence in a vision. He saw God in full Majesty seated on a throne. Daniel experienced the Presence of God as the Ancient of Days, an old man with a Long White Beard with a head full of white hair.

In the New Testament Jesus himself, the Son of God, experienced the Presence of God at his Baptism in a voice that says "This is my Beloved Son". After Jesus death and His resurrection, before his Ascension to Heaven, Jesus Presence was seen in various places. Jesus Presence has become physical yet not concrete. Mary saw Him at his burial site, but she was not allowed to touch Him. Jesus came through the walls to appear to his disciples. Jesus manifested his Presence to those two disciples on the road to Emmaus, walking along with them, but did not recognize Him until he shared food with them. After Jesus Ascension, Paul experienced the Presence of Jesus in the form of very bright blinding light on the road to Damascus that knocked him out. The apostles experienced the Presence of God on the day of Pentecost in the form of Tongues of Fire that rested on each of them. After that they became empowered to go and do the work that Jesus has prepared them for. In the Book of **Revelation 1:10** John experienced the Presence of the Lord when he was in the Spirit of the Lord, on the Lord's Day, as a loud voice saying "I am the Alpha and Omega, the First and the Last". We have seen the various manifestations of the Presence of God as documented in the Bible from Genesis to Revelation.

Now from all these line by line accounts, as the Bible calls them of the various and numerous manifestations of the Presence of God there are some conclusions that we can draw about the Presence of God. *God's Presence is multidimensional.* God's presence is not a single manifestation. It is not in a mono pattern. It is not expressed in one unique way. Rather the manifestations of God's presence are manifold, varied and numerous. *God's Presence is ubiquitous,* a big word that means everywhere. God's presence is not restricted to a single location. God's presence is omnipresent. *God's Presence is real both physical and non-physical.* He is invisible yet visible. He is a voice. He is a hand. The Presence of God is dynamic. The presence of God is real because God is real. The Presence of God is tangible even though He is a spirit. The Presence of God defies description. He is around us as well as inside of us.

God's Presence is not predictable. Remember Elijah when he was running away from Jezebel and he went to hide? God told him to stand on the mountain so that he would behold the Presence of God as God passes by. A great strong wind tore the mountains, broke the Rocks but God was not in it. There was an earthquake, but God was not in it. There was a fire and God was not in it. Remember God has manifested His presence in all these forms before to Job in a whirlwind, to Moses in a fire and I am sure Elijah was expecting God to manifest himself again in any of these forms. Did he? No! God chose to manifest his Presence in a still small voice. We cannot say because his manifest himself one way yesterday, he will do it the same way today. We cannot predict God. We cannot put God in a box. We have to learn to move with his dynamism, we have to go along with his various and mysterious ways, otherwise we will miss him.

God's Presence is active not static, not passive. God's presence is always on the move and so must we. This means the Presence of God is Interactive. The Presence of God is mobile. There is always some forward and backward movement. God is always giving some instructions, having conversations with us, if we are listening. God is always touching us if we are feeling and open to him. God is always communicating. He is always listening and he's always responding to what He hears. Remember, **Psalm 94:9** says "does He who plants the ear, can He not hear, does He who forms the eye shall He not see".

The Presence of God is compelling. It usually elicits a response from us. Even though we think He appears and disappears, that he comes and goes, God's presence is a constant fixture. The Presence of God is manifest to individuals and is also revealed to the corporate body like to the children of Israel under the tent. This means the Presence of God is not limited to good and perfect people. The Presence of God is not to be trivialized or toyed with. God takes His Presence very seriously. God's Presence is awesome in power. God's Presence is significant. May God help us to understand this. Amen.

In Faith Join Hands, Inspire Hope: PWRDF Slogan

In Faith Join Hands, Inspire Hope is PWRDF slogan. On one of our PWRDF Days I chose to delve deeply into the concepts and explorer how they relate to the work of PWRDF. To start with Faith is the fundamental principle of Christianity. It is not mere belief, but trust. It is faith that gives Christianity its whole name, character, and nature. It is faith that gives us a new relationship to God. Faith makes us sons and daughters of God and joint-heirs with Christ. Paul in **Romans 4** cites Abraham as the greatest example of faith. Abraham believed God that he was going to be the father of many nations, even though he was 99 years old and his wife was 80.

Hope is the consequence of faith. Hope is the anticipation of something better. It is the anchor that sustains the Christian in all the storms of time. Hope is not only a privilege and a blessing; it is part of a Christian's duty. Hope is a feeling of expectation and desire for a particular thing to happen. We are not sure if something is going to happen, but we hope it does. In itself there is no surety about the word. However, with God in the picture we have confidence. Paul in **Ephesians 2:12** says without God there is no hope. Hope that comes from God is the kind that holds on even when events would suggest that there is no way that our promise can come true. **Hebrews 11**, cites many examples of those who are beacons of hope, those who held on to Gods promise through all situations and sufferings. What would life be without hope? The person who becomes despondent loses hope.

Faith and Hope are joined together. They cannot and do not exist apart from each other. We need faith to believe and hope to endure. We must have the faith to believe and hope that God's grace is sufficient. On a day-to-day basis, we need to demonstrate faith in our lives, which will teach us to rely on God and hope for all things. Our faith in God affirms our trust that He is able to take care of things for us. Hope is something that we all know about, but until it becomes a reality in our lives; we keep wondering and worrying if those things promised will ever come to be.

The Bible links Faith and Hope to Love. **1 Corinthians 13:13** says that faith, hope and love endures or abides. Love is at the center of God's creation. The Bible makes it clear that love is both an act and a gift from God. Love is not just something we have for one another. It is also something we have for God. The Bible says that we cannot claim to love God if we hate each other. Loving God and loving others are intertwined. Joining the three concepts a theologian says that they all constitute a tree. "Faith is the root and trunk, hope is the branches, love is the fruit." Another one describes the three thus: "Faith is the inward union of the soul with Christ. Hope is the support that gives us strength to battle with the present. Love is the outward manifestation of what we feel within." I like both analogies.

However, PWRDF the Anglican organization involved in Disaster Relief puts it all differently. PWRDF urges us In Faith, In Hope to Join Hands. What does it mean to Join hands? Joining hands is an expression of Faith. Joining hands is a demonstration of Hope. Joining hands is a symbol of Love. Joining hands is fulfilling Jesus injunction: Love God. Love your neighbor. Joining hands is collaborating with the Holy Spirit to fulfill the purpose of God. Joining hands is demonstrating unity. Joining hands is giving. Joining hands is being there for each other. Joining hands is being loyal to all, *being* supportive and engaging in fair play because it is the right thing to do. Joining hands is loving without hypocrisy. Joining hands is being kind and affectionate to one another with brotherly love". Joining hands is genuinely caring one for another and upholding each other. Joining hands is being a Good Samaritan to others. All these we see PWRDF do time after time, through all disasters all over the world, the latest we see is at the occurrence of fires at Fort McMurry.

In our world today, the evidence of "not joining hands" is quite stark and rampant. It is manifest in man's inhumanity to man. Not Joining hands, is also manifest in the struggles between the rich and the poor, the oppressive systems of the world, injustice, inequities, deprivation, marginalization, recklessness, misappropriation of public funds, embezzlement, organized crime, thefts, racism, domination, politicized religion, erosion of accepted values, exploitation of the masses by secular and religious leaders, political correctness, decline of family systems, intimidation, manipulation, aggression, violence, kidnappings, children's recalcitrance, permissiveness, pervasive poverty, greed, in a world that Mahatma Gandhi says has enough for everybody's need but not for everybody's greed.

Joining hands is doing unto others what we want others to do to us. Joining hands is loving our enemies, blessing those who curse us, doing good to those who hate us, and praying for those who spitefully use us and persecute us. Joining hands is loving each other in familial relationships, husband/wife, father/mother, children/siblings, honoring each other and not provoking each other to anger. Joining hands is having the mind of Christ and affirming each other as sons and daughters of God. Joining hands is being noble, sensitive, thoughtful, unselfish, sincere, cheerful, loyal, warm, not puffed up, not behaving rudely, not envious, not arrogant, and not spiteful.

Joining hands is allowing God to make something beautiful and harmonious out of the discordance of our lives. Joining hands is delightful as we walk along together. Joining hands does not love in words alone but in actions. Joining hands requires commitment. Today I ask "Are you in on PWDF's position of Joining hands? It starts with us joining hands with one another. Joining hands is not a solo endeavor but a collective commitment. You hold my hands. I hold your hands and we all hold hands with PWRDF. If you are in, Hold the hands of the person sitting next to you or around you and say to him or her. "I will Join Hands with you to do all that is required of me." Let the other person also respond by saying the same thing. "I will Join Hands with you to do all that is required of me" God bless you all. Amen.

And Peace for All: United Nations World Peace Day: September 21st

The United Nations International Day of Peace also known as **World Peace Day** is celebrated each year on September 21st, which coincidentally is my father's birthday, Cornelius Adeoye Banjo, a man known to be a man of Peace, to recognize the efforts of those who have worked hard to end conflict and promote peace. Peace Day is also a day of ceasefire, personal or political. On the International Day of Peace, people around the world take part in various activities and organize events centered on the theme of "peace." The day is also dedicated to World Peace.' The word "*peace*" usually evokes many images, issues, concerns, and strategies, which vary from person to person, group to group and even from nation to nation. Individuals tend to relate what they regard as "peaceful" conditions and events to their own circumstances, needs, and aspirations. Yet despite this diversity, there are often common expectations about peace shared by many people worldwide. Whatever cultural, ethnic, or geographical identification, a majority of people share similar yearning for inner peace (personal peace) as well as the desire for a wider peaceful society (societal peace). That the world is extremely violent and turbulent is not in doubt. That there is need for peace is a basic assumption.

Peace is a goal, an ideal, which cannot be, contested by anyone even the most belligerent people. The wars, conflicts, aggression, all over the world have jolted many to the issue of escalated violence, which has become a reality of life. Peace then as antithesis to violence has also become an option. In the wake of increased violence in the world, UNESCO declared year 2000 as the Year of Peace and the following ten years a Decade of Peace. Peace is of interest to all of us. In this reflection I celebrate peace with all the fellow citizens of the world. I also continue to raise awareness about personal and societal peace in all facets of our lives more so, on the spiritual level. King David in his innumerable problems, a people to rule, wars to fight, Saul's hatred, his sons' open rebellion and so on, did not fret, instead in **Psalm 4:8** he says, "I will lie down in peace and sleep for you O lord make me dwell in safety". David thus being at one with certain reality and with confidence in God demonstrates an internal equilibrium, an essence of personal peace.

It is of interest to note that there is Negative peace, which is mere absence of tension, conflict, and war. However, negative peace is depicted in personal conflict, which is a state of peacelessness or the absence of personal peace. Peacelessness can be marked by poor health, mental exhaustion, anxieties, depression, sadness, worry, stress. Pain, guilt, fears, loneliness, loss, injustice, and personal tragedy, are also barriers to personal peace. All these can bring about a state of internal disequilibrium. Men and women now find it harder to live within the framework of twenty-four hours. The excessive pressure of modern living, have brought mental stress to many. The "rat race", excessive materialism and consumerism resulting in neurosis and various addictions. These days people also face frustrations, from low pay, lack of fulfilment on the job, over work, and long hours of work with minimum pay. From these come mental fatigue, worry, nervousness, anxieties, and the like. All these exert pressure on people's internal equilibrium; resulting in lack of personal peace and ability to remain focused.

Sometimes it is said that unless an individual has first attained personal peace, it is meaningless to work towards **societal peace.** The connection between the two is established. Without personal peace, people cannot contribute to societal peace. Without societal peace, people cannot experience personal peace. Search for societal peace therefore depends upon the creation of peace-loving individuals who will have both the cognitive and affective drives to work for a peaceful world. As individual's personal peace is vital to the attainment of societal peace, Cox (1986) said "the building of a peaceful world requires that we first work on ourselves and cultivate a strong sense of personal peace". This can be attained through the satisfaction of basic human necessities, including not only material needs but also political, social, cultural, economic, and psychological.

Societal peace is peaceful secure existence of people within their boundaries and communities. In some rich nations, the symptoms of inner peacelessness are manifested, for example, in rising rates of addiction and psychological illness. Unable to find or maintain personal peace, many people resort to chemicals and drugs to keep themselves calm. Societal conflict today has reached such massive proportions that human survival itself is at stake. Societal conflict looks at violence in the media, violence in schools, and even in sports fields. Wars, kidnappings, senseless drive by shootings, police brutality and other various forms of attacks are the tragic consequences of societal violence.

The attainment of societal peace must therefore address demilitarization at micro level, reckless possession of guns, investments on arms, which should be converted to meeting basic human needs like food, housing, health care, jobs, and education. Societal peace should include discouraging war toys and games for children, violent television shows and movies, and all those things that heighten violence in the society. In heterogeneous societies, the search for societal peace must focus on developing intercultural sensitivity, which promotes tolerance, acceptance, and respect, for the cultural identity of all people. Societal peace would also create the awareness that there are universal values that unite people of different cultures and social systems and emphasize respect for each other's rights.

Personal peace seeks to develop personal and spiritual growth to cope with the pressures of life. Among faiths and religions, there has been a quest to attain peace of mind, through the practice of religion and spirituality. Meditation, visualization, yoga, are also practices that people have engaged in to help attain this equilibrium. Unfortunately, symptoms of societal disequilibrium include a steady erosion of spirituality and the practice of religion with the attending secularization processes. Religion and Spirituality play strong role in search for personal peace. Religion is a system of beliefs, symbols, practices and rituals based the conception of the sacred or the supernatural realm that guides human behavior. As a social institution, religion gives meaning to life and unifies believers in a community. In the practice of religion, many people claim awareness of the supernatural or a feeling of coming in contact with God or gods, resulting in what they describe as the "ultimate religious experience" which results in internal peace. Religion shapes behavior, attitudes and creates identity. It is deeply personal, yet communal.

However, some people have said that religion as a social institution has not addressed their spiritual needs. Hence, they have migrated to the New Spirituality Movement. It is not uncommon to hear people say that they are spiritual but not religious. Carol Ochs makes a distinction between the two. She says, "Religion is an insight into the common experiences of mankind, while spirituality is mankind's personal experience." Some have said that it is difficult to define "spirituality" or even "religiosity" because they mean different things to different people. For some it is the belief in God, the Supreme Deity, for some it is the Goddess, for some it is the focus on "self", for some it is the acknowledgement and connection to some "Force" or "Power" out there. For some it is the rejection of formal religious institutions like Judaism, Christianity, and Islam. For some it is the attachment to the less formal New Age and Traditional religions or even cults with charismatic leadership. Nevertheless, religion and spirituality both encompass people's relationships to the Ultimate, based on their conception. Both are expressed in everything that people do. Both support and affirm what people accept, or deny and both provide meanings for people and answer their deepest questions of Where do I come from? What is the meaning of life? What happens afterlife, if there is any?

Peace is universal in application. The whole world celebrates peace in one form or the other and at different times. Christmas, Holidays, Hanukkah, Sallah, Kwanza, Summer and Winter Solstice, etc, are all seasons of goodwill, love, and peace. Although some religions have been portrayed as either peaceful or violent, they all have one fundamental concept that we treat others as we would expect to be treated ourselves hence that Universal Golden Rule. All religions and faiths have teachings, ethics, and values that address humanity and the need for peace and harmony. Throughout the ages, religious founders and leaders have talked peace, preached peace, and tried to practice peace. Yet we are confronted with the reality that many conflicts have emerged and wars fought on grounds of religious claims. It is a sad fact that religion has been used to justify wars, engineer social conflicts, cause societal violence, justify persecution, and sanction slavery. It has been used as a means of oppression by people in power to justify the status quo through the claim of divine privilege and authority. We still see everywhere evidence of intolerance, bigotry, hatred, among the religious peoples of the world. How then are we to reconcile the two tendencies?

All religions greet using peaceful terms. All religions have notions of peace in their scriptures. I seek to remind us of some. In Judaism, the Hebrew word "Shalom" means peace. The Song of Peace "Sam Shalom" in the Sabbath liturgy asks God "Grant us peace, Thy most precious gift, O Thou Eternal source of peace." In Christianity Isaiah calls the Messiah "The Prince of Peace" Christianity began with angels singing "Peace on earth and goodwill among all people." **Psalms 34:14** states "Seek peace and pursue it." The name Islam is derived from "silm" the Arabic word for peace. The common form of greeting among Muslims and to all people "Salaam alaikum" means "Peace be upon you." The response "Alaikum es-Salaam" means "Peace be on you too." Buddha says, "There is no happiness greater than peace." Hinduism says, "Without meditation, where is peace? Without peace, where is happiness?" Hinduism echoes "Shanti, Shanti, Shanti" meaning "Peace, Peace, Peace." Confucius says, "Seek to be in harmony with all your neighbor, live in peace with all your brethren". Jainism says "All men should live in peace with their fellows; this is the Lord's desire." Sikhism injunction is "Only in the name of the Lord do we find our peace." Zoroasterism deposes "Nature only is good when it shall not do unto another whatever is not good for its own self" Shinto affirms "Let the earth be free from trouble and men live at peace under the protection of the Divine". Taoism says, "Weapons at best are tools of bad omen, loathed and avoided by those of the Way." The WICCA Reed says "Bide within the Law you must, in perfect love and perfect trust, Live you must and let to live, fairly take and fairly give. Be true in love an ye harm none".

Christians are urged to contribute to things that ensure peace in the home and peace in the communities. We are required to imbibe God's injunctions that form the basis of peace in our lives and in our communities. All of us must learn to trust God for inner peace in the midst of difficult life situation. We are enjoined to be kind, compassionate to one another, forgiving each other, just as God forgave us. In **Isaiah 57:21** God says, "there is no peace for the wicked'. Pope John Paul's in his message of World Peace Day 2005 connects peace with "doing good." He refers to Saint Paul's letter to the **Romans 12:9** that says, "Flee what is evil and hold fast to what is good." **Verse 21**: says, "Do not be overcome by evil, but overcome evil with good". Pope John Paul like Saint Paul affirms that peace is attained when evil is defeated by good, when we acknowledge that violence is an unacceptable evil and proclaim peace as an option for good.

Jesus in **Matthew 5:9** says "Happy are those who work for peace; God will call them His children". An Oriental spiritual sage rounds it all up by saying that The Sermon on the Mount, Buddha's Compassion, Hindu's Ahimsa, Obedience to the Will of Allah and Confucius Analects can ALL combine as to be the most potent influence for Justice and Peace for All. The Prayer of Peace by Saint Francis of Assisi 1226 A.D captures this essence of working for peace. "*Lord, make me an instrument of your peace. Where there is hatred, let me sow love. Where there is injury, pardon, Where there is doubt, faith. Where there is despair, hope, Where there is darkness, light. Where there is sadness, joy. O Divine Master, Grant that I may not so much seek to be consoled, as to console; to be understood, as to understand, to be loved, as to love. For it is in giving that we receive. It is in pardoning that we are pardoned, and it is in dying that we are born to Eternal Life*". Amen. https://en.wikisource.org/wiki/A prayer of St. Francis of Assisi

PWRDF 60th Anniversary. The Valley of Dry Bones: Ezekiel 37:1-14

Albert Einstein tells us "Only a life lived for others is a life worthwhile". Sixty years ago, the Anglican Church of Canada, through a resolution at its 1959 General Synod in Ste. Anne-de-Bellevue, Québec, voted to formally take up Jesus' call that we always hear in the gospel: "*I was hungry and you gave me food, I was thirsty and you gave me something to drink, I was a stranger and you welcomed me, I was naked and you gave me clothing, I was sick and you took care of me, I was in prison and you visited me".* (**Matthew 25: 35-36**). That resolution created Primate's World Relief Fund and for its first decade it responded to emergency and refugee situations throughout the world. Today, PWRDF supports development partners involved in a wide range of projects and programs all over the world, some of which we have just seen in the PowerPoint Presentation. Throughout its sixty years of ministry, PWRDF work has been about changing the lives of others.

Jesus also offered a road map for those who follow him. He said: "feed the hungry, give drink to the thirsty, welcome the stranger, clothe the naked, care for the sick and visit the prisoner". All of us followers of Christ are called to do that in our parishes, in our various churches, in our communities, and in our larger world. Specifically, as Canadians Anglicans we are called to do that in partnership with PWRDF to help others around the world. Jesus also called on his followers to continue the ministry He began when He said, "Truly I tell you, just as you did it to one of the least of these who are members of my family, you did it to me". To continue Jesus' ministry therefore, is to respond to Jesus call for each of us to love the other. Loving the other means doing something to help the other as Jesus would want us to. PWRDF has offered for 60 years a means to help others in places where you and I cannot be. And so, the 60 years journey has indeed been a partnership of Blessings. Interestingly the journey has not only been about helping others, it is also about changing our own lives. In the process we become reactants, while changing others we also change. So, I want to briefly focus on how we can continue to be not only change agents but also changed beings.

For this reflection I have chosen to focus on an Old Testament reading **Ezekiel 37: 1-14** which is literarily a Prophetic message for all of us. Prophet Ezekiel lived in an era when there was a lot of movement of people. That time some people were in exile as it was known. There was dislocation, migration and settlement issues for people. It was in that era that Ezekiel was called by God to address the serious issues that are pervasive in those days. In the reading, God by Ezekiel's account took him in the spirit to a valley of dry bones. Only God knows how many centuries or years that those bones have been there. Dried, withered, disjointed bones, that have been disconnected from each other, not functional in any way. Obviously, they were human bones. It seems that God has been watching these human bones in the valley for years until God decided to do something about them. He then chose Ezekiel to be His change agent. God asked Ezekiel to look at those bones and asked him a very poignant, significant and piercing question. **Ezekiel 37:3** "Son of man, can these bones live?" I can imagine Ezekiel with a tense reaction wondering what all that was about, bones that have been lying there for possibly centuries. They could even be the bones of the Israelites that had died on that 40-year wilderness journey.

Ezekiel was perplexed. The possibility of a change to those bones in their situation was so dire and remote. He knew that there was No answer to the question that God was asking him. Ezekiel had no clue what to say or what was expected of him. How can these bones come alive? He must have been wondering if this was God's sense of humour. Dry bones coming alive!!!. As far as Ezekiel was concerned the God who asked that question must have an answer for it. But being a prophet that he was, he acknowledged God's supremacy in all things and so He threw it all back at God and said, "Lord I have no idea". He looked again and the smart guy that he was responded in **37:3**) "O LORD God, You know.". Then came the strangest instruction that has ever been given. God now told Ezekiel to prophesy to the bones. (**Ezekiel 37:4**) "Prophesy to these bones". I think Ezekiel must have been so transfixed that he had no time to ask questions. God gave him the words to say and he just said them. Remember Moses. He was always having discussions with God. If it were Moses, He would have sought explanation from God. Ezekiel was not Moses, who the Bible says talked face to face with God. Moses was God's friend. But Ezekiel was God's prophet. Prophets hear from God and say or do what God tells them. God told Ezekiel what to say to the bones, without time for any reflection, he did exactly what he was told to do and something remarkable and strange happened.

Ezekiel 37:7-8 says suddenly there was a noise, a rattling. The bones that had been scattered, disjointed all over started coming together, bone to bone. Not only were the bones restored to their rightful places, the flesh and the sinews were restored, their skin was restored, and the structures were made whole again. I can imagine Ezekiel's reaction to this phenomenon. Right under his eyes the bones were restored to human form. However, there was something missing as God showed Ezekiel. God now gave Ezekiel a second instruction. He told Ezekiel to "prophesy life into the bones". Again, Ezekiel did what he was told to do and the dead and dry bones, all came alive. They became humans in motion, an army and a "vast multitude" as the bible calls them. Can we imagine how many bones were restored?

After reading the story I asked myself What can I learn from Prophet Ezekiel's story and experience? To start with, the lived reality of today's world is not much different from what Ezekiel saw in that valley of bones. There are many dry bones in the world today, bones of different shapes and sizes, all disconnected and disjointed from each other. Dry bones are the extremely poor people who cannot afford their basic human needs of food, shelter and clothing. Dry bones are the underclass, the outcasts, the untouchables, who do not fit into any of the known class structure: the upper class, the middle class not even the lower class and so they fall into the underclass by their very low status in life. Dry bones are the very sick, like the lepers of those days, who are without hope of restoration, without the opportunity of accessing the system whereby they can be treated and cured. Hence, they were sentenced and ostracized, living lonely lives, where they remain dormant. Dry bones are the imprisoned ones, some there due to no fault of their own, but without hope of ever getting justice. Some are there for life because of some recalcitrance and violations and so without hope of mercy and grace. Dry bones are the marginalized, the powerless ones who are variously exploited by the unjust systems of the world. Dry bones are the refugees who have to suffer the effect of unjust dislocations and unfair settlement and integration issues. Dry bones are slaves of various forms of addiction: drugs, alcohol, gambling, sex, pornography, that they have become so incapacitated that the possibility of restoration seems unattainable. Dry bones are the people of this world who have been disenfranchised by the various wicked governments of the world, who do not serve the interests of the people, but their own.

Also, I thought God must love all those dry bones. God has been monitoring those dry bones for a while and when it was time, God who makes all things beautiful in His own time, moved to do something about those dry bones. God loves those dry bones and so He moved to rescue them. God has a plan even for dead dry bones. He wanted them to live. So, He enlisted Prophet Ezekiel to be His change agent. God would always do what He wants to do. Our God is also a God of completion. He would always finish what He had started. That is the privilege of His Sovereignty. If God wants many dry bones to live, they will. If God wants dry bones to be restored to life, He will do it.

However, I also realize that not only do dry bones exist in the world around us, in fact many people are directly or indirectly faced with the reality of dry bones in their own lives. They could be victims of broken homes, victims of dysfunctional poor relationships, victims of societal violence, victims of kidnapping and human trafficking, victims of random shootings in places of worship, victims of people who celebrate what is evil and condemn what is good. Dry bones in peoples lives could be severe children's problems of varying dimensions, stagnated life, workplace challenges, unemployment, underemployment, poor finances riddled with debt of various magnitude, unfulfilled dreams, undesired state of singlehood, loneliness, health issues, loss of Faith in Spiritual Journey, frustrations arising from many things, disappointments etc. It could be anything.

Sadly enough, there may also be dry bones in the lives of people we know, in people close to us, in family members, in friends, in coworkers, in people in our communities, all those people we pray for every Sunday in our Intercessory Prayers because they have some dry bones in their lives. The big question then is What does God want us to do about the dry bones. Remember God told Ezekiel to pray, to pronounce His word in a prophetic fashion over all those dry bones. I know that God is always asking all of us the same question that He asked Ezekiel. "Can this large expanse of waste, this revulsion, this injustice, be reversed"? Can all these dry bones in these hopeless situation, victims of the world they live in, be restored?

The good thing is that God knows that the answer does not rest with us. Just as it did not lie with Ezekiel. God came to the rescue. When Ezekiel pronounced God's Word over the situation, there was an instant reaction as we have heard. God gave Ezekiel the empowerment to do something about the dry bones, God is always telling us that all of us can do something about those dry bones around us. Doing something about dry bones is not just the responsibilities of prophets, and priests. It is the responsibility of the entire Body of Christ. There are many people who are living in a comfort zone. They do not have sensitivity to the dry bones that we are talking about. God is always looking for people that He will use to make many dry bones come alive.

We do not know why God chose Ezekiel. There were numerous prophets around in those day, but He chose Ezekiel to do the job. Maybe it was his willing heart, with a vibrant faith that does not question God's purpose. As you are reading this reflection, I am sure I am sure some of you are wondering about the many dry bones out there. Can they come alive? We wonder. It may look foolish to some of us to pray God's word as Ezekiel's did. But Ezekiel as a prophet knew that with God Nothing is Impossible. What about us? Can we be God's hand extended to rescue and restore the dry bones of the world? Can we resolve to be part of God's plan to bring alive many dry bones. It is God's world. He is aware of the anomalies. After all He was the one who drew Prophet Ezekiel's attention to those dry bones in the valley.

God loves not just all of us going around in our daily business as we are always told, He also he loves those dry bones out in the valley.

For 60 years, with Faith, PWRDF has been going out into many valleys with dry bones. PWRDF has not only been praying as God commanded, they have also been acting as God's change agents. God has been restoring many dry bones through PWRDF from the many happy faces that that we saw in our Power point presentation today. For 60 years, PWRDF has been giving manna to people in the wilderness. PWRDF has been able to do all that because people have worked together with them in all their endeavors. Today God is asking us to renew our pledge to continue to support PWRDF more than we have done in the past. Are we ready and willing to continue to be part of God's plan to continue to bring dry bones alive through PWRDF? Are we ready to continue to be God's change agent? Can we make that commitment? I am sure that we can. Amen.

The second part of this reflection is that is that God also wants to address the dry bones in our own lives. It is nice to hear that God loves us. There are times when God does more than just tell us that He loves us. He acts. Just as God did not ignore those bones in the valley, God wants to do something about the dry bones in our own personal lives. God gave the Word. God sent forth His Word and healed them and delivered them from their destruction so says **Psalm 107: 20**. Dry bones can be so endemic that people can lose hope. Can dry bones live? God is saying that dry bones can come to life for us and for people around us. I know that some of us may be saying to ourselves. "Yes, I have had this dry bone for so long in my life, I have even learnt to live with them". Some may say "I have surrendered it all to God. I have stopped asking God to do something about these dry bones. I will just leave it to Him". Yes, that is good but remember those bones in the valley have been there for years, they have even been forgotten. Then One Day God showed up with Prophet Ezekiel and a Prophetic Word.

Are you ready to trust God to give life to the dry bones in your life? Everything may look far-fetched. Prophet Ezekiel did not question, neither did he doubt. He simply did what God told him to do, then he then left everything to God. Not only is God addressing our own dry bones, God is also enlisting all of us to get on board and start doing this restoration work in our vicinity and in the lives of people around us. What do we do? Let us all bring to mind all the dry bones in our own life, also think about the dry bones in the lives of people that you know. There are dry bones everywhere. Try and identify these dry bones, give the dry bones a name, unemployment, addiction, children's problems, relationships problems, financial issues, imposed singlehood, loneliness, health issues etc whatever it is. Bring all these identified dry bones to God. What happens after the Prayers is not up to us. It is up to God. Your dry bones will be different from mine. Only you can name your dry bones. I cannot name them for you, just as you cannot name mine.

At this point I want you to say this edited version of the prayer that God gave Ezekiel in Chapter14. After that leave it all to God. "Dry bones in my life, dry bones in the lives of all that I love, dry bones in my family, dry bones in my children's lives, dry bones in my friends' lives, dry bones in my community members lives, dry bones in my neighbors lives, dry bones in the lives of people at large: *Dry bones, hear the Word of God. Come O breath of God, from the Four winds, breathe into all these dry bones so that they may live again*". Amen

The Pursuit of Happiness: Happy are those whose hope is in the Lord: Psalm 1:1

We have just stepped into the New Year. It is always a time of mixed emotions, a time when some people are joyfully evaluating the achievements of the previous year and are happy with themselves. Happiness is defined as a state, a condition of being pleased, delighted, favored, joyous, merry, gay, blissful, satisfied, felicitous, the absence of flutter or anxiety, experiencing an inner peace. We know that there are times when some of these words do not describe our internal state. There are myriads of things in this world that can create a state of happiness and even of unhappiness. The beginning of the year is also a time when some people are disappointed with how the past year has been for them. When people have not achieved what they expected, they may be unhappy. They may have trepidations about the New Year, anxieties about unfulfilled dreams, uncertainties about what lies ahead, and little hope about what is to come.

Challenges, problems may create a state of unhappiness for some. People can also be unhappy about their personal, family, spiritual and financial situations. Ill health, death of a loved one, professional and career hardship, educational problems, joblessness can also cause disequilibrium in the lives of many. Or worse still, being like Chris Gardner, in the Movie "The Pursuit of Happyness" ably performed by Will Smith, without money, without a job, without a wife, without a home, but with a young son on hand who needs to be cared for can be an unhappy situation for some. Unhappiness is also caused by Fear: fear of the unknown, fear of unexpected outcome, fear of failure, fear of ridicule, fear of being alone without anyone to help. There is also the fear that God has abandoned one, wondering whether God still cares, fear that they may have to face the battles by themselves, fear that God is going to allow them to stew in it for so long that they might actually go under.

The truth is everyone has had to face some harsh realities of life at one time or the other. Another truth is that unhappiness is not a permanent fixture in anybody's lives. To use Shakespeare's expression, "they have their exits and their entrances"; they come and go. Naturally, we all want everything around us to run smoothly at all times. We all want the engine of our lives to keep moving without any impediment or interruptions. However, while happiness is not jumping up, laughing out loud or dancing uncontrollably to Pharell William's "Happy Song" just to cover the turmoil that may be going on inside, unhappiness is a reality in the lives of many. However, another truth is that happiness is relative. What will make me happy is not what will make you happy. However, the Bible paints a different picture of happiness. The Word of God tells us that our happiness is not dependent on the events and the circumstances that surround us. It is actually dependent on things far more substantial, other great realities. In my reflection, I choose to focus on what the Bible says about happiness.

Deuteronomy 33:29 says Happy are we, who is like us, a people saved by the Lord. Saved means redeemed, restored, rescued. If we have been brought out, of the miry clay and our feet are set upon a rock and our steps are established (**Psalm 40)** we should be happy. If we have been brought out from darkness into God's marvelous light, if we are sanctified, justified with righteousness imputed to us we should be happy. If we have been redeemed by the precious Blood of the Lamb and headed for eternal life, we should be happy. **Psalm 144:15** says Happy are the people whose God is the Lord. There are different gods out there, zillions of gods that are worshipped in this world. Hinduism alone has over 3 thousand gods. All traditional religions practiced all over the world have thousands of gods that are worshipped every day. There was the time in the Middle East before Islam was founded; the people in that area worshipped 365 gods a year, each god for each day.

David in **Psalm 115** describes such gods as work of human hands, created by the people for themselves. He adds that these gods have mouths, but they do not speak. They have eyes but they do not see. They have ears but they do hear. They have noses but they do not smell. They have hands but they do not handle. They have feet but they do not walk. In short, they are not functional, they are not effective. David however reminds us that our God is in heaven doing whatever He pleases. Our God is Supreme, Sovereign, a God above all Gods. He has dominion over all things. Some people boast of connection in high places; they know the right people in the right places. They know everyone of importance in the political or social hierarchy. If we know our God, we should be happy because our God is the Most High One.

Psalm 146:5 says "Happy is the one who has the God of Jacob for His help". Help is assistance. It is support. Help is someone providing for us what we lack. Where does our help come from? The bible says it comes from the Lord who made heaven and earth. A songwriter describes God as "Our help in ages past our hope for years to come, our Shelter from the stormy past and our eternal home". Help is the Rock upon which we stand and lean on. Our help is in the Lord who is always ready to assist us in time of trouble when we call upon Him. God helped Jacob, when he cried to him. God protected him on his journey. God even changed his name and blessed him. Our God is an unchanging God, the same yesterday, today and the same tomorrow. Since we have a God who is always ready, willing and able to help in times of need, we should be happy.

In **Proverbs 16:20** Solomon says, "Happy is he who trusts in the Lord". Trust is to have faith in someone. We usually have faith in people because they have proved themselves faithful and trustworthy. Our God says He is faithful even if we are not. Has our God proved Himself faithful to us before? Has he come to our aid before? Do we have a reason to trust our God? Has he ever let us down before? Do we agree that we have a God who is dependable, who is reliable? Is "God the Faithful One, so Unchanging" as the songwriter says? If we do, we should be happy.

The one that I like most is **Psalm 94:12** which says; happy is the man whom God chastens. **Proverbs 3:11** adds my son do not despise the chastening of the Lord. Do not detest His correction for whom the Lord loves He corrects, just as a father corrects the son in whom He delights. **Hebrews 12:6-8** adds for whom the Lord loves He chastens, for what sons or daughter is there whom a father does not chastise. Which of us as children of earthly parents have not been chastised before? Which of us as parents do not chastise our children? We discipline them. We correct them so that they can learn from their mistakes. The same way if we are God's children, He has a right to discipline us. If we agree that God should chastise us we should be happy. Some people may not like that idea of God chastising us. However, Job says something solid about God's chastisement. He says "Happy is the man whom God corrects therefore do not despise the chastening of the Almighty, for even though He bruises us, He binds up. He wounds but His hands make whole". (**Job 5:17-18**). Job even adds, even though He slays me yet will I trust in Him. God chastises whom He loves, even through the discipline, He does not abandon. The Bible says Weeping may endure for the night, but joy comes in the morning. This means that even if our state of discomfort is a result of chastisement from the Lord God, we should not be despondent. When God bruises, He binds. When He wounds, He mends. His hands put us back together. God's chastisement often provides opportunities for us to learn in our dire situations. **Romans 5:4** tells us that tribulation brings out patience, patience brings out experience and experience brings out hope. Wow!!!.

So now, you are feeling unhappy and miserable because of the failings of the past year. David in **Psalm 70** sent an S.O.S to God in his desperate situation. He says: "Make haste oh God". Are you going to call on God in your moments of distress, or are you going to sit and moan endlessly about how unjust the world is, and thus allow your situation to overwhelm you? If we allow ourselves to reflect, we will remember that we have been there before, when everything was "doom and gloom" and how God has picked us up, came to our rescue and made a way where there was no way. In His own time, He makes all things beautiful. God did not promise that we would not have challenges; He says He will not give us more than we can bear and He will be with us in those times.

James 5:11 says Happy are those who endure. Endurance means the ability to sustain, the strength to go on, and the fortitude to survive. Tough times do not last but tough people do. Can you see light at the end of the tunnel? Do we realize that tomorrow is always a new day and that the sun will still come shining through? At the beginning of this New Year God is speaking to us through **Nehemiah 8: 10.** He says, "Do not sorrow, for the joy of the Lord is our strength". In addition, as the songwriter has urged us, "Rejoice in the Lord, Rejoice again I say Rejoice". Be Happy! For the Lord our God is our Strength and our Shield (**Psalm 28:7**). Amen.

Lord, Teach Me to Number My Days: Personal. Psalm 90

I was born in the blessed month of April. While thankfully reflecting on the fact that God gave me and many other April babies out there another year to celebrate life, my thoughts went to **Psalm 90** usually identified as the Psalm of Moses. With birthdays in line I thought this Psalm provides an opportunity for introspection. Moses started this Psalm with an acknowledgement of the omnipotence of God with the word "Lord" which means the Supreme One. He then talked of His strength in providing a place of refuge for him and by implication for all of us. It is significant that Moses did not say that God provided a dwelling place. He says that God Himself is the dwelling place, which is an astounding claim. It reminds me of **Psalm 91:1** which says "He who dwells in the secret place of the Most High shall abide under the shadows of the Almighty". Dwelling in God guarantees our protection.

In Verse 2 Moses then gave a panoramic view of how God has existed before the mountains were formed, and even before the earth and the world were created and ended with a breathtaking affirmation of God, "from everlasting to everlasting You are God" In short saying God you are eternal, immutable and you are unchanging. God your nature is permanent. To Moses God is awesome in nature and surpasses all limits. In **Verses 4 to 6** Moses talks about how Time with God is endless "a thousand years in God's sight are like one day". With God time flies, it goes so quick, so fast that at times we do not notice. Moses then talks about how nurturing, God is. God tends us, God looks after us, nonetheless before Him we are all like grass which grows up and flourishes in the morning. But unfortunately, in the evening when it is cut down, it withers and dies. Moses affirms that we are here today gone tomorrow, no notion of permanence!!!!!!A great reminder.

In verse 7-9 Moses affirms what we all know, that we have a forgiving God who "sets out our iniquities before Him". He knows we are struggling with our journey of sanctification, nonetheless he does not deal with us according to our sins. What a profound view of God's generosity to us. Moses then swung to Verse 10 where he now contrasts the impermanence of our own lives with the permanence of God. He says that our life is transient with limited life span. He says the days of our lives are 70 years and if by reason of strength they are 80 years, which however are soon cut off and we fly away. Just a small reminder there that nobody lives forever. In verse 12 in the light of all that Moses knew about God, he then prayed a significant, deep, intense and outstanding prayer "So teach us to number our days, that we may gain a heart of wisdom", a prayer as poignant as David's own in Psalm 25:4. "Show me your ways O Lord, teach me your path".

From all these I could not help wondering where Moses description and the affirmation of God with that sharp summary came from. Obviously, it must have come from his deep and personal knowledge of God. Moses is described as a prophet whom "God knew face to face" (**Deuteronomy 34: 10**). The Bible also says that the Lord would speak to Moses as one speaks to a friend (**Exodus 33:11**). Moses relationship with God was intimate, up close and personal. Moses days were God filled and God centered.

Moses expression "number our days" caught my attention. I then began to reflect on what Moses meant exactly by this numbering of days, what would be the dynamics of numbering of days and also the implication from Moses perspectives. Does it mean merely taking note of our days, like keeping a diary? When we human beings number our days we do the chronological thing, counting and recounting our achievements in days, months and years. We say things like, I was born in year so and so, started school five years later, finished school in year so and so, went to college in year so and so, got my first job in year so and so, fell in love in on day so and so, got married in year so and so, had a baby on day so and so, had another one in year following year, bought my first car in year so and so, followed by my first home in month so and so. Thus we continue to number our days.

There is nothing wrong with taking note of our life's achievements. It gives us the opportunity to thank God and praise Him for the land marks of life, for the appreciation of the blessings that have come our way, and for looking into the future. However, Moses prayer was not teach us to number our "months and years" but to number our "days". If numbering of days, months and years is as easy as keeping a diary of life's event which many people routinely do, I don't think Moses would need to pray about that. But I believe Moses had something else in mind. Moses was thinking more about "daily" interaction with God.

If Moses were to "number his days" he would talk about being pulled from a stream as a baby in a basket. He would talk about being raised as a privileged prince in the court of Pharaoh. He would talk about how he eventually discovered that he was not an Egyptian but Hebrew. He would talk about the events that led to his killing an Egyptian. He would talk about his escape from Egypt and finding himself a worker in the house of Jethro. He would talk about marrying Jethro's daughter. He would certainly talk about his call by God from the Burning Bush. He would talk about his 40 days experience with God on the Mount without food and water. He would talk about collecting from God what has become the blue print for God's children, The Ten Commandments.

He would talk about God's command that he returns to Egypt to rescue the Israelites from the hand of Pharaoh and also about the plagues that God unleashed on Egypt that led to their release by the hard-hearted Pharaoh. He would certainly talk about the great phenomenon, the parting of the Red Sea and the part he played in it. He would add to it the 40 years journey in the wilderness, and how God fed them with manna and even how the people's clothes were not torn, their feet not swollen and their shoes not worn (**Deuteronomy 8:4).** Moses would even talk about his experience with these hard-headed people that left him frustrated to the point that he disobeyed God's simple instruction at Meribah. He would definitely talk about God's anger with him which led to God's decision that he would not enter into the Promised Land. As an aside to get the full story of Moses life, I suggest you watch the movie: The Prince of Egypt or The Ten Commandments which I actually prefer. It is quite interesting. It captures the long life of Moses. From all the accounts in the Bible, Moses life led from one thing, to another and another and another all towards one goal, to achieve some purpose, God's purpose for Moses and God's purpose for His people. Moses numbered days made sense to God, to Moses and even to all of us reading about it in the scriptures today.

The key aspect of Moses numbering of his days was that each day, Moses walked with God. He walked in that "pillar of cloud" by day and the "pillar of fire" by night. He delighted in God's presence each day to the point that he told God that he would not go anywhere if God's Presence did not go with him (**Exodus 13:15**). Moses certainly lived his days for God. On a daily basis, Moses consulted with God and submitted at every turn to God's plan and intention. He responded to God's agenda. He agreed to God's purpose and in wisdom he changed course whenever he was asked to. Moses was able to achieve all that he did in his 120 years of existence because he daily numbered and monitored his days with God's benchmark. I am sure that his daily reflection, his daily consultation with God and his daily evaluation of events helped him to stay on course till the end.

Of course, Moses made some mistakes, like all of us he was human. He had a very tough task, he knew it and so he stayed close to God on a daily basis to acquire a heart of wisdom to do the job. When Moses life's assignment was over and God told him he would not be crossing over to the Promised Land, Moses in wisdom accepted God's decision and prepared the next person to carry the torch by laying hands on him (**Deuteronomy 34:9**). He readily wound up and gave Joshua his handing over notes. I believe that for all these God rewarded Moses with a very long life that his eyes were not dim and his strength not diminished (**Deuteronomy. 34:7**). The Bible also said that when Moses died God buried him in a place that up till today no one knows where his grave is, not even the modern archeologists. What a significant end to a significant relationship!!!

Overall, Moses did not undermine the challenges of each day of his long life; neither did he take his relationship with God for granted. Moses established a solid relationship with God because he knew that "numbering of days" would not be easy for anyone and so God's help would be needed. Hence to receive God's help everyday Moses devised and put together that prayer for assistance: "Teach me to number my days". I believe that the significance of "numbering of our days", as the Bible tells us, is that God daily loads us with benefits (**Psalm 68:19**). Each day, we receive goodness from Him. Each day we receive provision from Him. In addition, Jesus, God's Son carries our burdens day after day. For all these, the expectation is that we should be accountable to God on a daily basis, should we also ensure that we return something to Him on a daily basis.

I thought to myself what about all of us, me, you, my co-April babies out there and many others who will read this, how do we number our days? What would numbering our days mean for all of us, for me, for you, and for everybody? It is bad enough numbering our years in birthdays. It is a tedious task. At times we forget. We forget friends' birthdays, couples at times forget each other's birthdays, parents forget children's birthdays, children forget parents' birthdays, siblings too forget. Monitoring each day of our lives is therefore a greater challenge.

At personal level, I then ask myself, how do I make each day of my life memorable so that like Moses the overall layer of my life will be a profound life lived for God? I believe that Moses "numbering of days" involves some four concepts that I have identified: meaningful, fulfilling, worthwhile and purposeful. As I celebrate my birthday this month, I thought I could make it not only to be a time of rejoicing, but also a time of self-introspection and reflection on these concepts as I could apply them to see how they can contribute to the overall numbering of my days. Firstly, on a daily basis I need to ask myself has the day been meaningful to me, **meaningful** to the people around me, and above all meaningful to God. I need to know what meaning God would ascribe to how I have spent each day that He gives me? Can I at the end of each day truthfully say yes that I have lived the day for God, for humanity and for the good of all? I need to know if each day satisfies some predetermined requirement which is what **fulfillment** is about? **1Corinthians 15:32** says that Our life is more than "eat and drink for tomorrow we die" What are the set goals for my life? What do I want to achieve? Have I at the end of each day inched closer to the fulfillment of those set goals. At the end of each day, I want to reflect on if the day has been **worthwhile.** Has the day been worth the time and worth the effort? Has the day been worthy of God's attention? Does the day have a merit? Has the day been worth numbering? Is my numbered day **purposeful**? To what purpose do I live each day? Purpose is something that one intends to get, do or plan. I know that my life is not created by accident but for a specific reason to achieve a specific intention. The question then will be What is the ultimate purpose of each day of my life? I can only work towards it if I know it, otherwise I will just be like the wave of the sea that is driven and tossed about by the wind (**James 1:6**). And how do I know this purpose? I believe it is by walking closely with God like Moses did on a "day to day" basis to know, to understand and to fulfill that purpose. Also to pray "Day by day oh dear lord three things I pray, to see you more clearly, love you more dearly, follow you more nearly, Day by Day".

The second part of Moses prayer has to do with "wisdom". He says teach us to number our days that we may gain a heart of wisdom. Wisdom is not some advanced form of knowledge or learning. It is not a rare sense of deep understanding; neither is it something mystical or mysterious only possessed by some Oriental sage. Wisdom in Greek is "*chokmah*". It simply means skills of living. Wisdom is commonsense, it is understanding the way of the world. It is not what one knows intellectually, but what one does practically with what one knows. It is truth applied. **James 3:15** says that wisdom comes from God therefore wisdom is divine. It is knowing how God works.

What then is the connection between numbering our days and having a heart of wisdom? I believe that I need wisdom that comes from God to navigate my life each day. I need wisdom to move me from one point of my life to the next, so that I can be who I need to be in Christ Jesus. As I number my days, I am expected to reflect on the unique opportunities that have been granted to me each day and how I have made use of them. I know that I am not required to be perfect, but I am required to make the effort. Thankfully, I am given each day to improve as I go along. Having a heart of wisdom is "critically" giving thoughts to and analyzing the events of each day If I do not *achieve* what I set out to do one day, I should restructure to strive again and again looking for opportunities to make amends and look for ways where I can improve. I believe that God in His scrutiny found Moses days, meaningful, fulfilling, worthwhile and purposeful. Of course, there is ample evidence of wisdom in Moses' life. I believe the overall GOAL is to live a profound life for God and to live it in consonance with His will in my life each day. I like the chorus of a favorite song that captures the essence of our numbering our days "One day at a time Sweet Jesus that's all I am asking from you, just give me the strength to do everyday what I have to do. Yesterday's gone Sweet Jesus and tomorrow may never be mine, Lord help me today, show me the way, one day at a time". So knowing fully well that I cannot do this by my individual strength and that I need help from above with the attending "wisdom", I pray to walk in Moses footsteps, applying his prayer as my own daily supplication, "Lord, teach me to number my days, that I may gain a heart of wisdom". Amen.

SECTION FOUR

Women Centered Reflections

As a **Feminist Theologian** interested in Women's issues especially role of Women in Religion, I have included in this Section some Women related /Women centered Reflections. Enjoy.

Contents

Women: The Apple of God's Eye: Psalm 17:8

Each year on March 8th, the whole world celebrates the International Women's Day (IWD), a global celebration of the economic, political and social achievements of women past, present and future. IWD is the story of women's attempt to participate on equal footing with men, an occasion for women from diverse ethnic, racial, and cultural background to come together and look at decades of struggles for equality, justice, peace and development. It is also a time of appreciation, love and respect for all women. Since the first celebration of International Women Day in 1911 over 100 years ago, the world has seen women, more active and more involved in all areas of human endeavors. Women are participating more and excelling in science, in politics, in formal and non-formal religion, in education, in technology, in oil industry, in the Military, in the Police Force, in the workplace as managers and directors, in their own businesses, in the world financial and economic systems, above all as heads of their own households. Women have come a very long way. Overall, things have become much better for women but not altogether. In some parts of the world, there is still a high-level systemic discrimination against women. Women still earn much less, than men do; hence, they rank as the poorest of the poor. Women are still denied some basic rights. Women still work very hard but do not get the rewards that they deserve. Above all, despite the fact that women are generally known to be peacemakers they are still victims of wars, of aggression and of all forms of violence in the home and in the society at-large.

While celebrating, I wondered where all these inequities came from. When men want to oppress or subdue women, they quote the Scriptures. They talk of Paul's injunction that women should not be heard. They blame the fall of Adam and Eve on the woman, as the one who brought sin into the world, forgetting, according to a friend of mine, that it was the weakness of the stronger sex for the weaker sex that brought sin into the world. After all, God's instructions not to touch the apple went directly to Adam not Eve. Therefore, not taking responsibility for his own act of disobedience and recalcitrance, he blamed the woman whom God had given him. Even prominent Christian theologians like St. Augustine have said strange things about women, like "But separately as helpmate, the woman herself alone is not the image of God: whereas the man alone is the image of God." This was said in spite of the fact that the Bible in **Genesis 1:27** says God created man in His own image, male and female He created them. Tertullian, a Christian philosopher spoke of women as "devil's gateway". Thomas Aquinas another prominent Christian theologian described woman as "misbegotten men". There is a Judaism Prayer which says "Blessed art thou O God, King of the Universe, that I was not born a woman". (Not in the Bible)

However, knowing that all these do not represent God's mind about women, I decided to share with you some of what the Bible says about women and what God's thoughts are about women. We have heard that women are weaker than men are, yes physically, but that is about all. The Creator who made man and woman did not create one inferior to the other. He created them equal but different. Starting with creation **Genesis 2:7** tells us that God formed a man from the dust of the ground, verse 19 says out of the dust of the ground God formed every beast of the field and every bird of the air. However, when it came to the creation of the woman, verse 22 says that God made a woman from the rib that He had taken out of the man. In short, the woman was the only creature not formed from the dust of the earth. It is significant that God's special creation was brought into being through a special process.

God's word indicates to us that God cares for women in a very special way. God's option is always for women. God loves women the most. Women are dear to God's heart. He has a special place in His heart for them. Women always touch God's heart. Women Are the Apple of God's Eye, (**Psalm 17:8**). The Bible says we are fearfully and wonderfully created by Him, this our souls know very well. (**Psalm 139:14**). The Scriptures take women seriously. The Bible is full of accounts of women, who are role models for other women. A substantial portion is devoted to women issues, women's achievements to be celebrated and even women's failures to serve as lessons for others. God did not include these accounts for literature's sake. They are there to illustrate God's thoughts about women. I will mention just a few of these citations.

In the book of Genesis, we have the story of Sarah, Abraham's wife. She appears as God's paragon of a married woman. Sarah stands to teach women the characteristics of godly womanhood and humble submission and affection to husband in marriage. She calls her husband "lord", the Bible says. I am aware of Feminist Theologians reaction to this. I also know about the controversy that surrounds the concept of "submission" in marriage. However, this is God's word. We have the story of Miriam, Moses and Aaron's sister in **Exodus 15:20-21.** She burst out and organized women into a spontaneous worship of God with tumbrels and dances after the crossing of the Red Sea. Miriam knows the value of thanking God and praising Him for His goodness and for His wonderful works to the children of men.

This same Miriam was stricken with leprosy by God, when she challenged her brother Moses who had married a dark-skinned Ethiopian woman. God is intolerant of racism in any form, even from His own. In the book of Exodus, we have the story of Shiphrah and Puah the midwives who refused to kill babies when the king commanded them to do so, a tough assignment. Through this singular action the life of the eventual deliverer of Israel, Moses was saved. We have the story of Jochebed, Moses mother, (**Exodus 2:1-10**) who was determined to save her son, Moses, from being killed by Pharaoh. She displayed bold faith by putting him in the river, was rescued by Pharaoh's sister, and raised in Pharaoh's palace until it was time for him to save the Israelites from bondage. We read of Deborah, (**Judges 4: 1-9**) who was not only a wife but also a prophetess and a judge. In a war against an aggressive neighboring country, she led Israel with her Chief of Army staff, Barak to victory. She was a ruler for 40 years, the same number of years that David and Solomon ruled.

The Bible devoted a whole book to Ruth, a widow, who showed loyal love to her mother in law, after her husband died. She said, "Wherever you go I will go". Her love and devotion was rewarded, when God gave her another husband who was the great grandfather of David, from whose line Jesus eventually came. There was also Abigail (**1 Samuel 25:1-44**) described as the woman of dignity, the wife of a wealthy foolish man Nabal, who acted foolishly by denying to give some food to King David who was coming from a war and was hungry. A woman of peace she quickly went to appease the king on behalf of her husband to avert a catastrophe. There was Esther a beautiful woman, a praying woman who ordered a fast and prayer to save her people from death. Esther knows that a woman who fears the Lord shall be saved.

We have the story of Leah trapped in a loveless marriage because she was not as beautiful as her younger sister Rachael who has captured her husband's heart. **Genesis 29: 16** says Leah's eyes were delicate but Rachael was beautiful of form and appearance. She stayed committed and faithful to her husband Jacob until God's purpose was fulfilled in her. God was not insensitive to Leah's plight. Verse 31 says when God saw that Leah was unloved he opened her womb and but Rachael was barren. Leah went on to have six sons and a daughter for Jacob. One of them was her fourth son Judah, from whom Jesus in Christian tradition got the title "The Lion of Judah" (**Revelation 5:5**) representing the Triumphant Jesus. Rachael eventually had two sons. There is a lot more to that story that can be read in another reflection. We also have the story of Mary the young mother of Jesus who allowed herself to be used of God to bring to the world the Son of God for the redemption of humankind.

However, the Bible is not partial in the account of women. We have stories of women who are not role models for us, women who disobeyed God and got condemnation from God. The Scriptures gave extensive coverage to the lives of these women for a balanced view. We read about Lot's wife who through lack of faith displayed stark obedience to God's instruction and was duly punished. We have the story of Delilah

(**Judges 16: 15-17**) the one who betrayed her lover Samson's and sold his secret for money, which eventually destroyed Samson. We know of Saphira, Ananias wife who allowed Satan to fill her heart, lied to the Holy Spirit, and received instantaneous judgement. We know of Herodias who had John the Baptist beheaded because he drew Herod's attention to the evil that he and Herodias were engaged in. We know of Job's wife (**Job 2:9**), who told her husband to curse God and die. She had no appreciation for the goodness of God in their lives. No wonder her husband dismissed her as a "foolish woman". We also have the story of Jezebel the wife of King Ahab who introduced paganism into the Israel. In the Book of Revelation, she was described as that woman who seduced the servants of God to commit fornication and eat things sacrificed to idols.

In several places in the Bible, God affirms the equality of men and women, and sets the rules for gender equity. To start with, in **Joel 2:28,** God promised to pour out His Spirit upon all men and women. Sons and daughters will also have the gift of prophesy. God enacted several protective laws for women. Here are some of them. In **Numbers 27:1-10**, God affirms the rule of inheritance for women. There was a man Zelophedad who died and left behind five daughters. He had no son. As was the custom only men would inherit the property. However, these daughters went to Moses, and demanded to be given their father's property for their possession. This was a sensitive issue, even Moses could not culturally solve it and had to take the case to God who changed the rules and said that the daughters were right in making that demand. They should instantly be given their father's inheritance as if they were sons. Today in some cultures, women are still not able to inherit their father's properties. Obviously, they have not received that memo from God. In **Deuteronomy 24:1-4** God said that when a woman marries, divorces and marries another man, she must not go back to the first husband to prevent her being exploited by him. God has envisaged the mental harassment the woman would be subjected to in that type of remarriage. The evidence abounds in our social world today.

Regarding the newly married woman, in **Deuteronomy 24:5** God also says that when a man is newly married, he must not be drafted into the military service, he must be excused from duty for one year so that he can stay at home and make his wife "happy". These days, we know how many men take off immediately after marriage, for work, for business or to go to war, leaving the newly wedded wife at home bewildered, frustrated, pregnant, and scared. God cares about many little things that concern women. In **Deuteronomy. 21:10-14** God dealt with issues of women who have been captured as victims of war. We all know how women are routinely raped and misused in war situations. God says they shall not be sold for money nor be treated brutally. Obviously, in today's world, some warlords did not also receive this memo from God. He then gave regulations and guides that will serve to protect the human worth of such captive women and lead them to restoration. What tenderness and sympathetic understanding from God!

The Bible also did not overlook the Rape of women. The Old Testament dealt extensively with the issues of rape, sexual assault, sexual harassment, sexual abuse and trafficking of women. All these are still happening in today's world. The punishment prescribed by God may appear severe, but with the trauma and emotional scar experienced by women victims, no punishment is too much for the perpetrators of these vicious acts. Widows' plights are also quite important to God that they are mentioned 84 times in the Bible. **Psalm 68:5** says God's providence is special over them. In **Isaiah 1:17** God asks people to plead for the widows. In **Isaiah 10:2** God says woe to those who rob the needy of justice, and who let widows become prey. In **James 1:27** God considers it pure religion to take care of widows and provide for them under the law. In **Exodus 22**, God orders that no one should afflict the widows and orphans else if they cry to Him, He will surely hear them and avenge. This is much needed today considering victimization of women that leads to the prevalence of poverty among them.

In **Malachi 2:15** God protects the rights of the wife. God was explicit about men attitudes to their wives. God says husband should not break the marital promise to their wives. He says none shall deal treacherously with the wife of his youth. Today, many marriages end in divorce, because the men do not keep their marital vows. God also says that he hates divorce because He wants people to work at their marriage. He knows that women who go through divorce suffer emotionally and psychologically and suffer even more from the events that lead to divorce. God is also very sensitive to the issue of barrenness in women. In **Exodus 22:26** God says none shall be barren in His house. God demonstrated His compassion for many barren women in the Bible, Sarah who became pregnant at 80 years old, Rebecca wife of Isaac, Rachael, Samson's mother, Hannah Samuel's mother, John the Baptist's mother, Ruth after her first husband died. Etc. Some societies today are still very hostile to women who do not have children in a marriage.

From all the aforementioned, it is very clear that God has been very mindful of women. So how should women respond to God's love for women? To start with, Jesus said we should love God, love our neighbors as we love ourselves. If God Almighty loves women so much, we too should love Him and love others as we love ourselves. Of course, many women in this world do not love themselves. They quote many reasons. Some say it is difficult being a woman. Therefore, they would rather be a man, as they assume that men do not have the type of problems that woman have. Loving ourselves as women involves belief in ourselves as women. It involves having a positive awareness of ourselves as women. It involves understanding ourselves as women. It means appreciating ourselves as women. It means working hard to achieve all that God wants for us as women. Unfortunately, some women still place limitations on themselves. They say things like "I am just a woman and I can only do so much". Some hardly strive to be all that they can be because they probably do not love themselves enough to try.

Are you glad that you are a woman? Are you comfortable with yourself as a woman? Every woman should feel good about herself. Every woman should shout from the rooftops, to borrow James Brown expression. "I am a Woman and I am Proud". Why? God is passionate about women. Every woman who has ever screamed "God why did you make me a woman" should ask for forgiveness. God has His reasons for creating you a woman. Every woman should at all times express appreciation for God's stake in women, because no matter the problems that we have, we know that in God's own time, He always makes all things beautiful for all women. Let all continue to support one another and stride along together towards fulfilling God's purpose for our lives as women. Amen.

Naomi, A Woman of Faith, Hope and Resilience: The book of Ruth

There are two books in the Bible named after women Ruth and Esther. These women were so significant that their stories made a way into the Bible. I decided to look at the book of Ruth. I have always had an issue with that Book. Some people say the Book is predominantly about Ruth that is why the book is named after her. However, I see it differently, the book of Ruth is the story of two women, Naomi and Ruth whose lives were intertwined. Over the years, I have heard preachers and Bible studies focus on Ruth but not always on Naomi. Personally, I think Naomi is the Star of the Book of Ruth. Why the Book is not named after her I do not know. But from my studies of Naomi, I think she is a Woman of Faith, Hope and Resilience. That is why I have chosen to talk about her. There is a lot that we can learn from Naomi.

Let us take a look at this not always mentioned woman. The book of Ruth starts with the story of a man called Elimelech. He was married to this woman named "Naomi" which means "Pleasantness" They had two sons Mahlon and Kilion. We might say that they were upper middle-class people because we later knew that they were landowners. They lived in Judah, which was quite fertile and conducive. Suddenly there was famine, which as we all know is hard on people. Rather than continue to scrounge and suffer Elimelech took his wife and two sons and moved to a place called Moab, which was a greener grass for them. They prospered for a while. Elimelech and his wife raised their sons to adulthood. Unfortunately, during their stay in this new place Naomi's husband, Elimelech died leaving Naomi behind with their two sons. Naomi became a single mother left to raise two sons on her own. We can imagine how hard that must have been for her especially far away from home. Naomi raised the two boys to adulthood, and they eventually married two women from among the Moabites. One married a young woman called Orpah and the other a young woman called Ruth. At this point, we did not know if Naomi had a primary objection to her sons getting married to women of a different culture. Inter cultural marriages were not quite acceptable at that time. After all Abraham told his servant to find a wife for Isaac among his own people. From all evidence, Naomi accepted the two young women into her family and they were all supposed to live happily together forever.

Unfortunately, tragedy struck again this time in double dose. The Bible says about ten years later possibly one after the other, before the young men became parents, Naomi's two sons died. What a catastrophe!!! This left Naomi without her husband and without her two sons. However, she was left with two daughters-in-law. A blessing in disguise!!!!. At times we humans always allow disappointments to overwhelm us to the point that we do not see any benefits in any situation. Yet the Bible tells us that All things, which means the good, the bad and the ugly to borrow from Clint Eastwood movies work together for those who put their trust in God.

This was definitely was not a glorious time for Naomi, with the pain and sorrow of loss. This is when we begin to see Naomi's resilience. This is when we begin to see Naomi's strength in adversity.

Naomi plodded on with her two young daughters in law. Definitely, it could not have been easy for them without any men in the family at least to help with the hard chores. Somewhere along the line, Naomi heard that Judah her hometown had become prosperous again. The famine had ended. We then wonder how she knew. She must have stayed in touch with her roots. She did not abandon her connection to place of birth as some would do to their detriment. It was then she decided to relocate back home, as many immigrants do after they have lived in another land for some time. Some do it for emotional connection to their roots. Some do it because they have people back home who still mean a lot to them.

She informed her daughters in law of her decision to go back to her homeland. This must have been strange for the daughters in law wondering why that decision after so many years abroad. I believe if we build dependence on God, He guides our decisions. However, in a strange twist of event the daughters-in-law resolved to go back with her. Remember that they are not even from her place. Naomi probably wanted to go back to her own people so she would grow old and die in her own land. She did not anticipate this reaction expressed by her daughters in law. Naturally she was not open to their decision. But they insisted. She saw their gesture as an act of kindness, thoughtfulness for an old lady. She gave in and agreed that they should come along with her.

They set out on the journey. However, they had Not gone far on the road when it occurred to her that it was an unfair expectation to have of these two young women follow her home. Right in the middle of the road, this practical woman of action, stopped and explained to her daughters-in-law that they should Not proceed with her on the journey. She demanded that they go back to their families. She thanked them for their kindness to her and to her sons who were their husbands. She also thanked them for choosing to come along with her. She then prayed for them. In **Ruth 1:9** She said among other things: “May the Lord bless you with the security of another marriage” Of all the things that she could wish for them, all she asked for was the blessings of husbands for them. I can imagine the reaction of these two young women. They chose to go with their mother in law, Naomi, and right in the middle of the journey they were being sent back. I wonder what would be the reaction of you and I to Naomi's refusal for them to continue the journey with her? As I said God's purpose is always unfolding.

What is the significance of Naomi's prayer for her daughters in law? This was an era when women depended solely of the provision of their husband. Naomi had known life with a husband, and also without one. She was also aware of the struggles and the challenges of being a Single woman. She did not want her daughters-in-law to go through what she went through. In her love and kindness, she entreated them to go back to their land where they would likely get other husbands who will provide for their needs. This is the act of a considerate woman. Her thoughts were not for herself. She would definitely need those women to help her out in her old age. But she shifted focus on their needs rather than on her own. How many of us are like that? Some of us would have a sense of entitlement. After all they are her sons' wives and they should serve her for life.

Not only was Naomi a considerate woman, she was also a woman of faith. Naomi has built a life of dependence on God. Her belief in God's providence was unshakeable. "May the Lord bless you with the security of another marriage" she said. Naomi believes that "All things, all good and perfect gifts come of God", even husbands. Many young people do not consider spouses as gifts from God. They think that their charms, their beauty, their education should get them a partner. How many have faith that God is an Ultimate Provider, that He is able to give us precisely what we need at the right time. Remember the songwriter that says that in His time he makes all things beautiful. **Habakkuk 2:3** says "For the vision is yet for an appointed time, but at the end it shall speak, and not lie: though it tarry, wait for it; because it will surely come, it will not tarry". Naomi believes with all her heart that God will provide husbands for these young women. Just as I believe in my own heart that God is able to provide companions mete for those of you who are seeking His face for partners. Wait it will come to pass. Naomi kissed the young women and bade them goodbye and all of them broke down in tears on the road as it happens when partings are hard.

However suddenly, the young women changed their minds, they would Not go back. They said, "We want to go with you to your people". Wow! what devotion and commitment to their mother in law. But Naomi the practical one said to the, why should you go with me? For what reasons? She analyzed for them how unrealistic and unfair that would be. She asked, "Can I still give birth to sons who will become your husbands?" Of course, age was a factor. She insisted on their return to the land of Moab, their own homeland where they have lived all their lives. Naomi and the young women were genuine in all these expressions. Is that not what God expects of us all the time? Sincerity.

However, at this stage Naomi said something strange. She said, "Things are far more bitter for me than for you. The Lord Himself has caused me to suffer." For the first time Naomi expressed her thoughts about all the tragedies that had befallen her. Naomi even acknowledged the hands of God in all her tragedies. There are times God allows tragedies in our lives for His purpose to be achieved. Naomi the woman of faith understands that. However, she insisted again that the young women return to their land. It was at this stage that Orpah the other daughter in law chose to go back to Moab. We do not know what led her to accept Naomi's suggestion. We no more heard of her again in the Bible. But God knows. There are times when certain things need to give way so that other things can happen in. At times some decisions are hard. Some decisions are spirit inspired and some decisions are actually brought about as a way of opening doors for other things.

Orpah going back allowed Ruth to insist on going to Judah with her mother-in-law in spite of further resistance from Naomi. Ruth said what became a classic statement of the Book of Ruth, "Do not ask me to leave you and turn back. I will go wherever you go and live wherever you live. Your people shall become my people and your God will be my God". So Naomi in her graciousness seeing that the young woman was adamant and determined, allowed her to proceed on the journey with her. This is the point where most preachers give Ruth the "thumbs up" for her commitment to her mother in law. However, I give my "thumbs up" to Naomi. For me, Ruth's statement speaks more about the type of person Naomi is than about who Ruth is. Naomi had not obviously been the typical mother-in-law, the wicked mother in law, the one who tolerates her sons' wives, the one who is always quick to find faults with daughters-in-law, the one with a sense of entitlements. Ruth's statement is an affirmation of who Naomi had been to her. "I will not leave you" is an expression of solid attachment that people express when someone has been good to us. This also affirms the strong bond that had developed over the years between these two women.

Naomi seemed to have genuinely accepted Ruth and Orpah as her own daughters, in spite of their being foreigners. She did not tolerate them as some would. She clearly loved them. She had stuck with them and they had stuck with her developing a special affinity towards each other. This type of attachment is rare. Naomi would always think of these women before she thought of herself. Even in a critical moment, of decision, Naomi put their interest first. She knew that living alone would be a challenge, but she was willing to release these young women to start new lives of their own. I think it was this thoughtful demonstration of love and consideration, that made Ruth insist on going away with Naomi to a foreign land, a place quite alien to her. Naomi did not abandon the young women when their husbands died. Ruth did not see any reason why she would abandon the older woman. In these days of divorce, deaths of spouses, speed dating, and remarriages, these young women would have left long before now especially in an individualistic culture like the one we live in.

Ruth went back to Judah with Naomi. On arrival, another strange thing happened. The women of the city were excited to see Naomi and were calling her by name. Instead of responding to the excitement of the moment, Naomi said this: "why do you call me Naomi, which of course means Pleasantness. She said "call me Mara" which means bitterness for the Lord has made life very bitter for me. I went away full but the Lord has brought me back empty. The Lord has caused me to suffer and the Almighty has sent such tragedy". For the second time and in one sentence Naomi made reference to her tragic situation, called the name of God about four times and ascribed her past tragedies as coming from God. This reminds us of Job's statement: "The Lord Gives and the Lord Takes".

This has very serious implications for all of us. We have all been taught that the Lord is good. Jesus said Only God is Good If He is so good why does He allow awful things to happen to us, deaths of loved ones, illnesses, loss of jobs, loss of homes etc. etc. Does God really allow all these unwelcome things in our lives? The discussions are still on. Even if He does, would there not be some implications? When we talk about the journey of faith, we also talk about religious experiences. I am sure that in spite of the many challenges, that some of us may have experienced in our lives, I am sure that all of us can still testify to the goodness of God in our lives. Like David, in **Psalm 124**, we can all say: "If the Lord had not been on our side, all the raging waters would have swallowed us alive"

Even if God had allowed severe things to happen to us would we not say as one of our Hymns tell us: "God is working His purpose out". Even in tragedies, God's purpose is always unfolding. We remember Joseph being sold into slavery by his brothers. We remember the same Joseph being sent to prison for a crime he did not commit only to become interpreter of dreams which catapulted him to a position of power. From many tragedies of life have come some good things. It is definitely not easy to be in a dark place. The question is how do we handle being in a dark place?. Do we see a dark place as a precursor to some light at the end? Alternatively, do we submit to the darkness?

Let us see how Naomi handled her dark place. Naomi and Ruth returned to Naomi's place of birth with no husband, no two sons, no money, she returned worse than she went. She had choices. She could "lay down and die". She could allow depression to get a hold of her or she could pick herself up and decide to carry on knowing that there is life after life and that God is still in the midst of it all. On arrival back home Naomi and Ruth went to look for jobs. Since they had returned at harvest season, Ruth got a job working as a gleaner on a farm owned by a man named Boaz who was related to Elimelech, Naomi's dead husband.

It was a hard work, and due to age factor, Naomi had to stayed at home while Ruth went out daily to work to sustain both herself and her mother in law. However, Naomi was not just lying idle at home. She was not going to take Ruth for granted. She was not only preparing food for Ruth when she goes out to work, she was thinking and planning. Her situation was not going to be the end of the story. **Ruth 3:1** says, One day Naomi said to Ruth, "My daughter, It is time that I found a permanent home for you so that you will be provided for". Note her words of endearment Ruth has become her "daughter", no more her daughter in law. The ever-considerate Naomi was constantly thinking about the future of this young woman. She knew that she could not allow Ruth to continue in this hard life.

So she conceived of a plan to get Boaz to marry Ruth. Boaz was a man of integrity and was greatly respected by everyone. He was a prominent man of noble character. He was known for his kindness and as a boss knew how to treat his employees. And he was not married. Naomi's plan was for Ruth, this beautiful young woman, to make herself pretty and perfumed up, and go down to where old man Boaz is sleeping after work, uncover his feet and cuddle up next to him. Then just wait for him to tell Ruth what to do next. The interesting thing here was that Naomi's plan was not well thought out. She would throw Ruth and Boaz and wait for something to happen. It looked a desperate plan, even obscene if you ask me. Nonetheless, it was a plan. **Proverbs 19:21** says, "We can make many plans, but the Lord's purpose will prevail".

Some people have asked why we need to plan if God's will is going to prevail. You are looking for a job. God is not going to write application for you. You are looking for a life partner and you have turned yourself into a hermit refusing to interact with people. You are looking for some promotion at work you are not working hard at the one you have. Even when we believe that God is involved in our lives guiding and directing all things, does that mean we should DO NOTHING? On the contrary, it means we make plans and wait for God's hand to move. Of course, there are times when God initiate things on our behalf. There are also times when He wants us to move first. Naomi did just that. She had no clue where her plans would take her but she trusted in God. In the end, her plans paid off.

Boaz was not exactly a Hollywood star. He was not the hunk. He did not have a six abs pack. He was rugged and older than Ruth. However, he was a good man who would be a good husband to Ruth. This is a lesson for young people looking for life partners. They usually build a mold and start looking for someone who would fit into that mold. He must be tall and handsome. He must be rich etc. That way they miss good opportunities. The world is full of surprises. We cannot put people in a box. Naomi did not. She was on a mission, she was very practical about it, and it brought desired results.

As the story goes, Ruth went ahead with Naomi's plan, co-operated with her mother in law. In the end, Boaz took notice of Ruth. He went through the required process of marriage and eventually married Ruth. Not only did Ruth get a good man to look after her, Naomi got back her family's inheritance, because Boaz redeemed her family's property. Naomi had a very difficult beginning. At times, it looked like everything was dark for her. However, after all the tragedy light came on for her. In it all Naomi was unshaken in her belief that God exists and God is sovereign. God the Almighty reigns in all the affairs of men. Not only does God reign in all the affairs of men, and though sometimes we get the hard end of the stick, one thing is sure God's works, and purposes are for the good and happiness of His people. In **Jeremiah 29: 11** God said, "For I know the plans I have for your, thoughts of peace and not of evil, to give you a future and a hope". Whether the Lord gave or the Lord took away, Naomi never doubted that God was involved in every aspect of her life. God was always on her lips. There were times when obviously she did not like how God had dealt with her. Overall many people would admire her for her unshaken belief in the Presence of God in all her situations.

How did things turn out for Naomi? Ruth married Boaz and God gave them a son named Obed. Naomi then became the focus of all things. To start with, the community rejoiced with her after they watched her come to town bitter and broken. They rejoice to see her fully restored and overflowing with joy. The women of the town said, "Now Naomi has a son again." They saw Ruth's child as a gift for Naomi. What a blessing. The women also said to Naomi: "Praise the Lord who has given you a family redeemer. May this child restore your youth and care for you in old age." What an insight from the women. The Bible said that Naomi looked after the boy as if is he is her own. Of course, he is her own. He is the son of her daughter-in-law who had become her daughter. Guess what, Obed became the father of Jesse, who was the father of King David, a prominent lineage. Naomi thus became the grandmother of Obed the great-grandmother of Jesse and the great-great-grandmother of King David from whose line Jesus came. What a great inheritance for Naomi. Remember Jesus is described as the Son of David. This is where it all came from. What an Amazing end to the story of Naomi.

Are you struggling with issues? Are you suffering in many ways? Many Christians are suffering from different forms of adversity and affliction. Belief in Jesus does not take away every tragedy. If our life is at all like Christ's, we will face pain and hardship. Jesus even said this to His Apostles and to Paul. However, what sustains us all is this unshaken belief that God is not unmindful of what we are going through. There is nothing wrong with being angry, even brutally honest with God about our situation. There is nothing also wrong in our expressing our frustration to people around us as Naomi did. The most important thing is not to forget God's faithfulness and love. Faith in God's providence does not mean we do nothing. Sometimes it means we Think, Plan, Act. This is what Naomi did. Sometimes it means we

Wait. Like Naomi urged Ruth at many times to just WAIT and see what the Lord will do. Naomi went from a woman to be forgotten to a woman to be remembered and mentioned in the Scriptures. Truly, there is always light at the end of the tunnel. May God give us all enough strength to build resilience to sustain us in this journey. Amen.

Leah, the Other Woman: Genesis 28&29

I wanted to start this year with a woman centered reflection. The Bible is full of stories of women who can be models of encouragement for us women. There are times when we as women feel that we have the most challenges in the world and at times we do not know what to do about them ourselves. However, the bible is full of stories of men and women whose situations are not perfect but who learn to deal with their situations and come out victorious. My story is found in the book of **Genesis: 28 and 29.** Find time to read the story in full later. The story starts with two brothers Jacob and Esau, both sons of Isaac and Rebekah. Jacob stole his brother's blessings from their father with the connivance and support of their mother Rebekah. Esau became angry and sought to kill Jacob. Jacob fled from his brother's anger. Now they have both grown up. They both had specific instructions from their father not to marry Canaanite women who were not of the same tribe as they are. At the time of this story they were both of marriageable age. Esau, the older brother married from Ishmael's descendant. Ishmael was Abraham's first son born by Hagai, his wife Sarah's maid.

Jacob went eastward, the story tells us where he had a dream at Bethel when he saw angels climbing up and down a ladder. In that dream God blessed Jacob and they named the place Bethel which means "God is here". God is always where His children gather, because God is an Ever-Present God. Later Jacob went on his journey soon after he saw a beautiful woman feeding some cattle. Actually, he was on his way to see his uncle Laban. This beautiful woman called Rachael was a shepherdess and she was coming to fetch water for the sheep. Jacob quickly swung into helping her like what any gentleman would do when they see a damsel in distress. Jacob introduced himself to her and actually told her that he was looking for a man named Laban. It happened that Mr. Laban was Rachael's father. That was exciting for Jacob! His search was over and soon the beautiful lady took him home to her father.

Mr. Laban was quite excited to see his nephew, the son of his brother Isaac. So he welcomed him and made him comfortable. Now the Bible describes Rachael as a "beautiful woman". When Jacob saw her on the road, it was instant attraction. He was quickly drawn to her and her beauty. He fell in love with Rachael the moment he set eyes on her. Jacob settled into his uncle's house and got to helping him out. As we know, there is always much to do when people live on farms and extra help would always be welcome. After living with and working for his uncle for one month, the man asked him what he wanted for his reward. Jacob did not equivocate, he did not think twice and so he asked his uncle if he could marry Rachael even though they were related. In some cultures, that is allowed as long as they are not blood brothers or sisters.

Mr. Laban was taken aback. Actually, in **Genesis 29:16**, we were told that Laban had two daughters Leah and Rachael. The Bible says that Racheal was beautiful in every way with a "lovely face and a shapely figure". Jacob was a very smart man. He did not just tell Laban to give me your beautiful daughter to marry. That would be foolish and presumptuous of him. So he made a good proposal to Laban **Vs 18**- he said "I will work for you seven years if you will give me your younger daughter". He was specific. Laban thought this was a realistic offer so he agreed to it. In **Verse 19** he told Jacob "I would rather give her to you than to anyone else". So the seal of agreement was made. Jacob set off to work his head off for seven years. He worked. He was in love. At the end of seven years, he went to his uncle **Vs 21** and said, "I have fulfilled my contract, now give me my wife so we can be married". Laban said sure. He set a day for marriage and invited everybody. Jacob was excited he would at last get his trophy wife that he had worked for.

Everything was set. The guests were all there and as is the custom during the ceremonies his wife was brought to him but usually veiled with her face covered. In this culture, not like in the church when the husband would unveil the wife at the altar to ensure that he has his right woman in front of him. In this culture the woman's face would be covered throughout the ceremony. At the end of the day after the guests were departed, the husband would take his wife to the bridal chamber, where he would presumably consummate the marriage. The Bible says in the night the bride was brought to Jacob and in his excitement, he slept with her. It was later in the morning when he took a good look at his wife that he discovered that his uncle had played a trick on him. Lo and behold, the woman he had slept with, the covered-up woman he had married was not Rachael but her older sister Leah. The man was furious. The woman he was given was not the woman he had worked for. I can imagine him storming to his uncle demanding an explanation for this switch. Vs 5 he asked, "What sort of trick is this?" He felt betrayed and cheated. He confronted his uncle who calmly told him; "You see, I cannot marry away the youngest daughter when the older sister is still unmarried. She would become an old maid and nobody would have her". Laban now said Vs 27, wait until the bridal week is over, that is the honeymoon week, then you can have Rachael if you agree to work another seven years.

Jacob did not refuse the offer, he had no choice. He really loved Rachael and she was what his heart was yearning for. Without any hesitation, Jacob agreed to this "buy one get one free offer". He worked another seven years so he could get the woman he really loved. Talk about commitment, devotion. At the end of the second set of seven years he got his original bargain. But what happened was that without it being his original intention, Jacob became a confirmed polygamist, married to two sisters. This is where the story begins.

Genesis 29: 31 says "When the Lord saw that Leah was unloved, He opened her womb but Rachael was barren" Leah was the first wife but not the first love, neither was she her husband's first choice. Leah was unloved. You think you have marital problem? Talk about a loveless marriage where the husband was just going through the motions. There was no spark in him for his wife. His heart was somewhere else. Leah was experiencing rejection by the man she was married to. She knew her limitations, she knew her challenges. She knew what she was up to. To start with she was not as beautiful as her sister so there was no competition there. She was not the preferred one. She was the older maid. She was not a spring chicken. She was not even a second choice. She was no choice at all. She was imposed on the man. Rachael had it all. Rachael's name means "a female sheep", "ewe", gendered, soft, elegant, feminine and delicate. Leah's name means "mild cow". Cow is an animal that produces milk, large and clumsy, awkward, all they are good for is to produce milk. However, the Bible says, "she has eyes like a gazelle, soft lustrous eyes, a redeeming factor". She was nonetheless the underdog. But you know what? Leah was not bitter. She quietly accepted her lot. She did not try and compete with her sister or edge her out, claiming to be the senior wife. She just accepted her lot.

But remember what we heard in the verse we just read. God had compassion on her and favored her. God made her fertile. **Verse 32** now says Leah conceived and bore a son and she named him **Reuben** for she said the Lord has looked upon my affliction. The Lord has seen my pain and so the Lord has given me a son. Although this man does not love me, hopefully he will begin to love me. Can anybody relate to Leah? It's not just in relationships that people feel rejected. In the workplace, your boss, your supervisor, the Director is always comparing you to your colleague to your disadvantage, for reasons that are not clear. You try to do your best but you are still side tracked. Your best is never good enough. When promotion time comes, they give it to someone else.

At home your parents played favoritism, always preferring your sibling, always saying your sibling is better than you, always running you down. Some parents at times do tell their children that they will not amount to anything. Telling them they would end up like their good for nothing father. At play when you were younger, one friend dumped you and moved on to form alliance with another friend, leaving you deserted and unwanted. In intimate relationships, your boyfriend, your partner, your husband, your finance, your significant other dumps you for another one after cheating on you. We can all imagine what that would feel like. Even at school, you were never the teachers favorite, you have been snubbed by the teacher just trying to show that you are smart and the teacher only pays attention to just a handful of students in the class. You know how this feels. In church, maybe not everywhere but there is still favoritism. Pastors, Reverends, Priests, demonstrate that they prefer some people more than others. This evokes feelings of anger, low self-esteem, in people, feeling a disadvantage.

But do you know the good side of the story? It is always in our lowly estate that God cares for us, that he shows compassion for us. David in one of the psalms says, "When my father and my mother reject me, the lord will take care of me" Psalm 27:10. It is when we are at our lowest ebb that God rises up on our behalf and helps us. When we are down and out, when we feel alienated, when we feel rejected, devalued, the Lord rises up to help us just like he did for Leah. God came to Leah's rescue and gave her something to be joyful about. Has God ever come to your rescue when it looks like everyone is against you? If you think hard you will know that He has! He always does. When the whole world seems to be on attack, when it seems that there is no one to help, God always shows up. Our God is always faithful. He sends help from the sanctuary when we least expect it. He did for Leah what she could not do for herself.

Let's take a look at Leah's responses to the goodness of God and God's intervention in her situation. Verse 33 says again Leah conceived and bore a second son she said because the Lord has heard that I am unloved He has therefore given me this son also. She called his name **Simeon.** Good thought. Leah recognized and appreciated God's favor, God's mercy and God's intervention and acknowledged the good that God has done for her. Vs 34-Leah conceived again, this time she bore her third son. And said now this time my husband will become attached to me because I have borne him three sons. Therefore, she named him **Levi**. In a patriarchal society, where boys are valued more than girls, that should have enhanced her position with her husband. Or rather, she expects that it should. Sons are for fathers, daughters for mothers. That is how most people think. Unfortunately, the three sons did not do the trick. Men like sons. She was hoping that after three sons her husband would no more treat her like a milking cow but would actually show some genuine affection for her. But it did not happen. The man was absolutely sold on Rachael.

One thing I found interesting was that Leah was the one naming the children. Usually in that culture it is the man that gives the children names, especially as they are sons. And I thought of why Leah was the one naming the babies. Remember Rachael the loved wife was still barren. I figure Jacob was not quite excited about the sons that were being reeled out by Leah. I can image Leah asking him what he would like to call his son and he would say something like "Call him whatever you like" Wow!!!. However, there was something wrong in Leah's constant response. Although she appreciated God's gifts, ascribing the birth of the boys to God, she would always relate them to her husband's missing love for her. Her thoughts were focused on her husband. She always assumed that God's blessing was to buy her husband's love. In the names she gave the boys, there was that grieving pain, a biting desire for the love of her husband. Yes, she deserved the man's love. After all she was fulfilling her own wifely responsibilities. She continued to make herself available for the man. She did not deny him the rights to her like some would do in this, our modern world. Feeling unloved is a ground for divorce. She kept at her commitment to the marriage and the man. While she continued to hope that God's gifts for her would change her husband's stance toward her, she did not know that God had other plans for her.

Vs 35- However, Leah conceived again. The fourth time and something different, something phenomenal happened to her I don't know what, but suddenly in a flinch she changed focus. She bore a son and called that son **Judah** meaning **"Now I will praise my God**." Then she stopped bearing. Leah at the birth of her fourth son shifted focus to God. She no more related her sons to the love of her husband. What a remarkable turn-around. A significant thing happened to Leah. There is a song that says, "Put your eyes upon Jesus". This was exactly what Leah did fourth time around. Leah decided she would no longer pursue a hopeless cause. She will just shift gaze to God and allow God to fix everything for her. After all the frantic search for her husband's love, Leah finally came to her own, finally accepted her situation and finally placed everything in God's hands. "I will now praise the Lord", Leah said. Leah finally surrendered herself to God. She devoted her last son to God. She suddenly recognized that God has not been blessing her so that she can use them as an act of barter to trade for her husband's love. It took **four** sons to realize this. She said to herself even though I am still unloved after three sons, with this fourth one I will shift focus to God. I will praise him. It was at that time that God's purpose began to be fulfilled in Leah's life.

Jesus the Messiah, your Lord and mine came through the lineage of Leah. Her last son, whom she finally dedicated to God, whom she named Judah is the one through whom Jesus came to earth! Wow!!! What a blessing for Leah! In **Revelations 5-5**. Jesus is called the Lion of the tribe of Judah. Jesus came through the lineage of an unloved woman. As if that was not enough, the finest priests of God came through her third son **Levi**-called Levites Priests. Jesus both the son of God and Priest derived descendancy from this hated woman.

We have read the story of Leah, an unloved woman who in spite of challenges persevered. Is there anyone feeling like Leah, rejected, alone, cut-off, alienated, despondent, not preferred, side tracked. The point is that at times we do not understand why things certain happen to us. But in it, all God always use it to bring something good. Leah finally decided to praise God for All she has received. The keyword in her final reaction was **Praise**. The Bible says God inhabits the praises of his people. (**Psalm 22: 3).** The Bible says when the praises go up the blessing will come down. Praise turns mourning into dancing. Praise turn ashes into oil of rejoicing. Praise brings surprises, revelation and clarity to things. Praise is what David uses to defeat the forces of evil. Praise is uplifting. Praise takes us to higher level, higher grounds. Praise lifts our spirits up when we are down. Praise is a force that changes us and our situation. Praise, Praise, Praise! The greatest lesson from Leah is the Importance of Praise. Praise changed everything for Leah. Praise of God earned Leah a place in history.

However, let us note that praise is not an uncontrolled disruptive emotionalism that we see in some churches. Praise is pure, heartful devotion and connection to God Almighty. Praise is lifting up your heart and voice unto the King eternal in ultimate adoration. Praise is absolute surrender to the One who breaks the darkness with a liberating light. Hallelujah, praise the One who set me free. When we are immersed in the thought of who God is and what He has done for us, it is in our deep reflection of the goodness of God that praise erupts. Like king David in **Psalm 34** let us make a resolve "I will bless the Lord at all times. His praise shall continually be in my mouth". Let us give our praises and adoration to Jesus the Lion of Judah. Let us pledge our allegiance to the Lamb. Let us praise Him ever in joyful song. Amen.

Your Maker is your Husband: Isaiah 54:5
Your Desire shall be for your Husband: Genesis 3:16

Once I was going through the scriptures and I came across **Isaiah 54: 5** says which "For Your Maker is your **Husband**. The Lord of Hosts (Jehovah Sabaoth) is His Name and your Redeemer is the Holy One of Israel. He is called the God of the whole earth". I was arrested by this superlative description of God. However, what I found most interesting is the reference to God as Husband. **Genesis 1: 27** affirms that God as the Creator as our Maker. If God is the Maker of both men and women, the implication is that He is also the Husband of both of them. In **Isaiah 54: 6** God calls us both male and female His youthful wife.

Revelation 19: 6-8 says "Let us be glad and rejoice and give Him glory for the marriage of the Lamb has come and His wife (meaning those who have given their lives to Him) has made herself ready".

If the bible says God is a Husband, what qualifies God to be a Husband? In my line of work, we talk about the status that people occupy and the roles attached to those statuses. If we are husbands, wives, daughters, sons, sisters, brothers, friends, grandparents etc, we all occupy a status and we all have corresponding roles to play or perform. A husband is more than someone who has married a wife, someone who has consummated a relationship, a husband continually fulfils his responsibilities. **Isaiah 54:6-14** tells us the things that God says He will do as a Husband. God says out of compassion, He will call us and take us out of our grief like a young woman who has been abandoned by her husband. As a forgiving husband, God says he will no more be angry at us His wife. He says He will remain loyal to us and his covenant of blessings for us will never be broken. As a generous husband says He will give us precious stones rubies, sapphires, jade, emeralds, crystals and jewelry, he will even build our place of abode with these stones. He says that our prosperity will be great. As a caring and considerate Husband, God says He says He will make us live under a government that is "just and fair" for our comfort. As a protective Husband he will keep our enemies far away from us and we will live in peace and no terror, dangers and threats will come near us. In verse 13 God even says that He will personally teach our children. God says our enemies will constantly be defeated because He is always on our side. In verse 17, God says no weapon formed against us shall prosper and every tongue that rises in judgement against us will be defeated because He will raise an army to destroy their plans. Wow!!!!. God's relationship with His wife is that of committed love.

Does anyone know of any husband like that? Hello!!!!! All women will tell you that there is no perfect husband. Most men only try. God has provided this model for a good husband which looks absolutely impossible. But we all know that God is not a slave driver. He understands that earthly husbands are human, therefore they need His grace to fulfil all these expectations. If all earthly husbands make 50% effort women will have less to complain about and there will be fewer divorces and breakups. How much does God love us men and women His wife? His Divine love for us is all love excelling. It is Agape love, a strong, yet tender, ardent, compassionate devotion to us as His being, as His creature, as His children and as His wife. Our well-being is close to His heart. His love is benevolent affection. His love is everlasting love. His love for us is a living stream from His heart. It is inexhaustible. His love translates into giving. He created us out of love and provides for us out of love. His provision is unparalleled.

If God is the Husband of all, He has certain expectations of all of us as His wife. How are we required to respond to God's Love as our Husband? I was looking for that answer in the Scriptures and I think I found it in what God told Eve. He said in **Genesis 3:16b:** "Your desire shall be for your husband and He shall rule over you". Wow!!!As a wife we must desire God as our Husband and we must allow God as our Husband to rule over us. This is a great challenge. How easy is this for us? I had such fun, analyzing how both men and women treat God as a Husband. Both men and women actually treat God as they treat their earthly Husband and earthly Wife.

I will start with the women. For sure at times we women treat God the same way we treat our earthly husbands. To start with, that "submission and rule over" thing is a problem for some of us. We think it is some form of domination and control. Actually, it is one thing that feminist theologians complain about in all the religions. Women are required to submit. The Scriptures give too much power to the men. However, with us the women, when we first meet a man, we fall in love, our "head is over our heels" as they say, that is we are turned upside down. We dote upon the man, giving him all his heart's desire, gifts, food, and everything else that he needs. We are just walking on the moon, floating in the skies. We are in cloud nine. In short, the love is very "hot" as they say. We are always in conversation with the man.

Then we marry the man and all hell breaks loose. When we have to do the dishes, clean the house, go to work, do all the dirty stuff, get pregnant, start having and raising children, even clean up after him. After some time, the glamour gradually begins to fade away, the excitement is reduced and all temperature cools down. But then when we decide we want something from the man, a car, new furniture, new wardrobe, we warm up to the man. We become coil. Of course, the man falls for it, as soon as we get what we want, we fall into the routine again. Frankly one cannot spend All the time mooning over one's husband. The assumption is that he is loved and in any case, we have other responsibilities, work, children, parents, extended family etc. But at times men demand and want 100% attention. If the man feels neglected we embark on an elaborate show of affection to reassure him. Who can blame us? In short, the show of affection is like a yoyo, up and down, which could be alright in secular relationships.

However, the problem at times is we unconsciously transfer this to our relationship with God. When we have just become new Christians, we are on fire for God. We are excited. We are eager, we are hungry for His word, and we have passion. We are constantly in prayers and reading the Word. We are ready to share Jesus with anybody who cares to listen. We are ready to tell our friends about our new-found love. But when the cares and the toils of this world come upon us, prayer becomes tedium, church attendance becomes drudgery. We have excuses, we are tired. We cannot come to church on some Sundays because we have other things to do. We cannot come on Wednesday night for Bible study. We cannot come on Saturday night for prayer meeting. We slept late so we cannot wake up to come to church on Sunday or even Saturday if we are Adventists. We have a long day ahead of us so we cannot participate in anything. Excuses! Excuses!! Excuses!!!

But when we need something from God a new job, money, a house, a car, a fruit of the womb, His healing touch on our ailment, spiritual growth, a turnaround in our children's lives, an amend to our relationships, we rush back to Him. We start coming to church again.

We are the first to get to church the last to go home. We wake up at 3 am to talk to God. We pray and fast, we fast and pray. We go through the Bible for all God's promises and we appropriate the relevant ones to us at that particular time of our need. Yes, we need God so it is time to bribe Him with our attention.

But as soon as we have received the blessing we so fervently prayed for. It is time to relax. The Lord has blessed us. He is good all the time we tell ourselves. He is gracious. Maybe we have been promoted to an executive position. All our official engagements take precedence over God. We have now been installed in a new comfort zone. We are now basking in this new favor. That is when we think a tenth of our income is too much for the church All that money for the church!!! When our income was low, we paid tithes, a 10% but now a ten percent of our heavy income is too much for God, so we pay 5% of it forgetting that He requests of us 10%. But if another trial comes on the scene or if God decides to use a circumstance to draw us back to Him. We cry to the Pastor or the Priest please pray with us. We scream "God, where are you?" God says I have been here all along, but you have ignored me because you are excited about the previous blessings that I have given you. God, I need you. God says no problem. He is a good God. Like your husband whom you have ignored all the while He takes you back and like a Gracious God that He is, He blesses you again and again. While our love for God remains stable, our time for God waxes and wanes like a yoyo, while God's love and commitment to us as a Husband remains constant and unchanging.

What about the men? Men have a peculiar problem here. Men are used to being the husband, the head of the household, the master, domineering, dominating, in charge, in control, the boss, the provider. Men are "natural" husbands. They know how to play that role very effectively by instinct and by practice. But now men are required to navigate a new territory, they are now required to engage in role reversal. Men are now required to be the wife, all submitting and being in subjection to their husband, God Almighty. At the beginning of all relationships, the man is usually more in love with his woman. The passion is usually more intense on his side. The woman, the object of his affection, is the apple of his eye, the sugar in his tea, the butter on his bread, the jam in his toast, the collar on his shirt, the button in his sleeves. He is very attentive to her, to her needs, spending time with her, spending his money and affection on her in all ways imaginable. The man can be very lavish and very expressive both privately and in public at times. He is very exuberant about his wife. He is generous to a fault, not only physically but emotionally as well. The sun rises and sets on the face on his woman. The woman is riding high

Unfortunately, studies after studies have shown that men's love dies out much faster than women's love. Like sudden death in soccer the fire blows out quickly, the game is over, the man is out of love, the woman is out of favor. The woman is no more looking as divine as she used to, she is no more as dazzling as she was at the onset. Household chores and age have taken their toll on her; working two or three jobs for the family's survival have depleted her energy. She has got some bulges around the waist; the lines have started to show on the face, the knees have begun to buckle. She is now fat and clumsy. Every quality that was admired in the woman now becomes her weakness. She is strong becomes is headstrong. She is sharp-minded becomes she is pushful. She is accommodating becomes she is uncooperative. She is smart becomes she thinks she knows everything.

What does he do? He grows cold and withdraws into himself. At times he begins to look for a substitute. If he is in the Lord and under God's grace, He is able to resist the temptation. As the wife grows older the desire for her is more of duty than of passion. His devotion and affection for his wife waxes and wanes and at times it dies completely. Men are usually able to compartmentalize themselves into different segments, with the same person they can be a friend, a husband, a brother, a partner, a whatever they choose to be at that very hour or time. The man's relationship with his woman is controlled by the man. He determines the direction and pace that it will go and he expects the woman to abide by it which usually results in conflict and we know what can happen.

However now God is saying to the men, as my wife your desire shall be for me your Husband and I your Husband shall rule over you. Wow!!!Men playing the role of a wife with all that submission. At times it gets complicated. Men know how to be a husband, but do they know how to be a wife? Actually, without knowing that they are wife to God, men at times treat God as if they are the husband of God. Men's love for God is usually very intense at conversion. They bring all the macho to God's work. The intensity, the adrenalin flows, the devotion, the commitment, the faithfulness is unparallel. But as soon as the man rises in position of power, rises in importance in his community, rises in hierarchy on his job, rises in his political quest, Pastors/Priests will tell you that is when they cannot get the men to do much in the church. They come to church with their appointment book. If the Pastor/Priest wants the men to do something in the church, it is Oh pastor I think I have a meeting on that day. I will check my appointment book and get back to you. I know that does not happen everywhere. uh!

But when he was not in a big position, he was always available. Studies have also shown that as men rise in position of power and status God and God's affairs becomes less important in their lives. Again, maybe not the men everywhere but men somewhere. The man because of his hyper masculinity and macho stance ascribes his success to his power, he pats himself on the back for his hard work, he ascribes his success to himself and to what he calls self-motivation and hard work. There is a survey which says only 5% of the world's successful men have time for God. It is even worse if he is scientific. He wants everything proven. He wants it scientifically proven that God exists. He does not believe in this faith thing, "evidence of things not seen and evidence of things hope for". While the Bible says you believe before you see, He wants to see before he believes, like the doubting Thomas. Did you know that there was not a single female doubter in the Bible. The women just believed. Uh!!! Men who are now used to playing the role of the husbands are now required to learn to be a wife who must desire her husband, God, and who must allow God his husband to rule over him in all his ways, in all his thoughts and in all his decisions. Men now have dual responsibilities, they are required to be androgynous, that is they have to play the role of both genders, being a husband and being a wife. This is a great task and that is why ALL men need our prayers constantly.

The first half of the text says Your desire shall be for your husband. So how much desire should we both men and women have for our Maker our Husband. What is desire? It is our passion, our love, our intent burning, our craving, our want, our wish. How much should we want God? How much passion should we have for God? David was a man of passion who demonstrated his intense desire for God. In many of his Psalms he demonstrates his overwhelming love for God. He says I will sing to the Lord as; long as I live. I will sing praises to my God while I have my being. His praise shall continually be in my mouth. David adds I will trust in God. In all my ways I will acknowledge Him. I will tell of His marvelous works, I will be glad and I will rejoice in Him. I will delight to do the will of my God. I will sing of the mercies of the Lord my God for who in heaven can be compared to Him. I will proclaim His goodness. Wow!!!! all that adulation, all that intensity. David surely knows how to adore his God.

A perfect Husband deserves a perfect wife. A perfect groom deserves a perfect bride. Let me ask the men how much effort do they put into being God's perfect wife, God's perfect bride. In God's view, David was a perfect role model even with all his imperfections that God calls him "a man after His own heart". How we all envy David. David was not only a role model for the men he was also for the women. So for all of us, how much desire do we have for our Perfect Husband. Is our desire, our passion for Him and Him alone? How much do we revel like David in God our Maker, our Husband? Only you can answer that question.

The second part of the text says, He shall rule over you. Everybody has a Lord whether you believe it or not. Someone or something will always be Lord of your life. Something will always control your life. Something will always be the focus of your existence? If you do not allow God to rule over you, something or someone else will motivate your actions, your impulses, your thoughts, your utterances? It can be your job, your earthly husband, your earthly wife, your children, the love or quest for money, the desire for success, the pleasures of the flesh, your emotions, your finances, your relationships. It could be the desire to please, the desire to be better than everybody else, the desire to always have people's approval, the desire to win over someone. It could even be the desire to please yourself, because you believe charity begins at home and you should love yourself more than anybody else? Who or what rules over you? Check your motive. Only you can answer that question. Does God your Creator, Your Husband rule over you? This passage demands that He does. God demands the total control and Lordship of our lives. Jesus says we cannot serve two masters, we will love one and hate the other. This means when someone or something else is in control of our life, when someone else rules our lives, GOD has been pushed out. God says He will not share us with anyone. In **Exodus 20:5** God says "you shall not worship other gods for I, the Lord your god, I am a jealous God". Indeed our God is a jealous God, who deserves all our attention. At this point I ask all of us both male and female reading this reflection to pledge our allegiance to God our Husband, to make a solemn promise to be faithful and remain in our submission to Him. Amen

When the Woman is a Minister: My Favorite Reflection

In the Body of Christ for a long time there has been this prevailing attitude about the Ordained Ministers, those ones that are called and ordained in the church to fulfill certain roles. While the ordained person is aware of his/her role as a worker for God, most of the others step back expecting the ordained to do all the work. The truth is ALL are called. Jesus injunction to go to the highways and byways was not meant for just a selected group. It is for All people be they women or men. All are called to service. Jesus gifts to the Church is for all, both Men and Women, the Ordained and the Laity. Hence if All are called to service, where do women fall?

In the body of Christ, we talk about "minister". Who is a Minister? Who ministers? One meaning of minister is diplomatic representative of one government to another, an envoy, an ambassador. In the religious institution, there are Ministers who perform religious functions. As Minister of God they are authorized to conduct religious worship and administer sacrament at Mass. They are also members of the House of Clergy, Bishops, Pastors, Priests, Deacons etc. They are also required to give service, to give care, to aid, to attend to wants and needs and to provide comfort. The Bible says when we become Christians, we become God's ambassadors, we become His royal Priests and Priestesses, we become His peculiar people. A Minister of God is one who walks with God, who lives the Word, who contributes to the work of God through a ministry and makes an impact in his/her contact with the people in his/her environment.

Overall the Christian Ministry is not about being ordained, which creates elitism within the Body, a class of specially privileged people that are at times disconnected from the people that they are supposed to serve. There is an increasing gap between the Laity and the Ordained. Most ordained ministers cannot be reached at home or during critical times, or in time of need for spiritual emergency cases. Most churches have grown so large that many like the woman with the issue of blood cannot get near enough to touch the hem of the priest/pastors' garment for prayer, for counselling and for healing. Mystery is attached to the ordained person. Ordination evokes an attitude in the ordained because they are deemed to have a special status. Christian Ministry is about Serving. It is about commitment. It is about sacrificial living. It is about making an Impact on Contact. Jesus worked. He was anointed but not ordained. I am not undermining the position of the ordained person. I am saying that ministry is not only for the ordained person. The church is meant to be participatory. The importance of other believers must be acknowledged. The church is a community of believers in communion with God and with one another. Since people matter to God, they must matter to each other. Our service, our ministry, must therefore be to one another.

As a woman centered person, my call has always been to see more "Women in Ministry", to see more women ordained or not, play more significant roles in the ecclesia What is Women in Ministry? It is Women empowering Women. It is Sisterhood of Women. It is Women's daily service by Women for Women. It is pursuing the concerns of Women both inside and outside the church and in various communities. It is increasing the participation of Women in the service of God and in the affairs of the Church. It is Women using the gifts that God has given them for the good of the Body. It is Women having a strong voice, and a strong presence in the Body. It is Women sharing their experiences with one another, sharing our love, our will, our reason. It is being a living sacrifice which will be totally acceptable to God, because of Christ's work in us. Amen.

How do Women minister? **1Timothy 4:1** says Do not neglect the spiritual gift within you. The Ministry of women pervades the entire church, because women pervade the whole church. Throughout the Bible women were not spectators. They played active vibrant and vital role in the day to day function of the Church. There is a ministry for each and every woman. There are various ministries for women in the Bible, we shall explore some of them.

The Single Women Ministry: 1 Cor. 7:34 "And the woman who is unmarried cares about the things of the Lord that she may be holy both in body and in spirit". Many women do not appreciate their state of singleness. They do not realize it is a unique opportunity to serve God. Singleness is a permanent state in life for some and a temporary state in life for most. Many women experience periods of aloneness. The response is to see singleness as a call to a committed life, not a lonely life. The single woman should live in a covenant relationship with God and is called upon to develop her gifts, human and spiritual to offer comfort and solace to other members of the body, and thereby to contribute to the building of the church. The single woman is called to develop a deep love relationship with the Lord and to channel her love in pure productive and generous ways to the service of others. Responding to God's call to holiness can be a source of great strength and consolation to the single woman.

Spiritual strength that comes from knowing Jesus enables the single women to do the work in the world and be happy in her single state. The promise of God's Word is that we will experience fullness of His presence in our lives as we seek to know the Lord, love the Lord, and follow the Lord. We may be single, but we are never alone. The spirit filled single woman responds to loneliness by focusing her devotion upon Jesus and by drawing near to the community of faith for support and wisdom. You may be alone, bereft of human companion but you never stand without God, who is the constant companion and an ever-present guide for every believer. The single woman can experience great freedom to devote herself to work, friendship and service, all of which can contribute greatly to the church and the extension of God's kingdom on earth. A generous willingness to assist others can lead to happiness and fulfillment for the single woman. A single woman can always say **Psalm 62:1** "My souls waits in silence for God only from Him is my salvation. He is only my Rock and my salvation, my stronghold, I shall not be greatly shaken". In the single woman's ministry the women would encourage each other, strengthen each other, bring in other single women, who are prone to depression. Single women are not necessarily young unmarried women, but divorced and separated women, women who have never married, widows, all women in a single state. The purpose is to minister to each other, to share each other's problems, help each other grow in the Lord. When women are strong at individual levels, they bring in that strength to the larger body of the Church and that is how the church becomes stronger.

The Mentoring Women Ministry: Titus 2:1-8 says that they admonish the young women to love their husbands and to love their children. **Proverbs 27:9**-Ointment and perfume rejoices the heart: and the sweetness of a woman's friend gives delight by hearty counsel. **Proverbs 13:20***:* He who walks with wise women shall be wise, but the companion of fools will be destroyed. One of the largest and most vital areas of ministry for women is that of mentoring. The word "aged "in **Titus 2** simply means the older woman not necessarily in age but the mature experienced woman. The injunction to teach the younger women is not necessarily in reference to youth but freshness. Those to be mentored are not just young wives but those who are still young in the Lord. These need to be nurtured. Jesus Christ commanded His disciples to make disciples of all others. Spiritually mature women have the responsibility to mentor those women who are still at the milk stage. They would disciple other women and bring them to the meat stage and maturity in Christ. They would teach the younger women reverent behavior, godly conduct, good lifestyle to give the young women the opportunity for spiritual growth and that the Word of God may not be blasphemed. They will also teach them how to love their husbands, love their children, be sexually pure, to be good home makers, and to guard the sanctity of the home. **Proverbs. 31: 10-31** describes the virtuous woman who is a paragon of virtue, trustworthy, industrious, organized and loving. Her husband totally trusted her, her children praise her and her home is a model of efficiency. She still finds time to reach out to the community to help the poor and to increase her family's resources through wise investments and productive management of all placed in her care. Moreover, she was as outwardly beautiful as she was inwardly wise. The virtuous woman described here is more valuable than rare jewels. Because of her wisdom she has the ability to live life in a responsible productive and prosperous way. The woman earns her place in the gates of the city i.e. the most public place, the city hall and market place. She is woman whose hand work brings material reward. This woman pursues traditional female jobs such as making clothes farming, merchandising. Her energies are not only directed towards providing for her family but also towards meeting the needs of people in the community. She is a role model. The older women can guide the younger women in fulfilling these roles. Surely there are many young women out there to be helped. This is an outreach ministry that could curb the rate of teenage pregnancy, in our community, could resolve other youth problems, could help bring many young people into the fold. Mentoring is about encouraging, exhorting and persuading. It is the divine ability to inspire, to reassure, to strengthen, and affirm those who are discouraged and are wavering in their faith. It is to provide support, usually moral and psychological to women not necessarily younger women but even fellow older women who may be going through difficult periods, experiencing conflict, or even low self-esteem and need to be encouraged to let them know that they are appreciated. It is also about giving some kind of personal counselling.

The Women Evangelists Ministry: Acts 1:8 "You will receive power when the Holy Spirit has come upon you and you will be my witnesses in Jerusalem in all Judea and Samaria and to the ends of the earth". Evangelism is the divine enablement to effectively communicate the message of Christ to unbelievers so that they can respond in faith and move towards discipleship. Jesus affirmed the Ministry of Women in Evangelism. The most evident is His interaction with the Samaritan woman at the well of Sychar. **John 4:1-30** Culturally Jews and Samaritans do not associate with each other. Moreover, for a Rabbi to speak in public to a woman was considered improper. Jesus regard for this woman was truly revolutionary. After their meeting she returned to her city and presented her witness. The Bible says Many believed in Him because of her testimony. At that time women were not considered reliable witnesses, yet Jesus chose this woman as His witness. God also chose women as the first witnesses of Christ's resurrection (**Matthew 28:1-8)** and they were entrusted with Christ's post resurrection message to His disciples (**John 20:15-18**). The coming of the Spirit reinforced the role of women in evangelism. Women together with men were empowered to be witnesses to the ends of the earth. The establishment of the Philippian church involved women **(Acts 16:11-15)** and women were involved in spreading the gospel in Berea (**Acts 17:12**). Women were commissioned along with men to be the light of the world and were thus extensively involved in the ministry of evangelism (**Matthew 5 14-16**). The requirements for soul winning is a love for Christ and for people, willingness to be used by the Holy Spirit in sharing the gospel, creativity in saying a word about Christ and women are specially gifted for this, plus the ability to pray. In these end times Jesus is giving women the opportunity to fulfill the great Commission. **Acts 2:17, Joel 2:28** In the last days I will pour out my Spirit upon all men and women. Women can do this publicly or privately, visibly or invisibly, starting in their own homes, influencing their husbands, and discipling their own children. But the greatest challenge is out there to reach out to the hurting world, to have deep passion for the unsaved who are not related to us. It is not God's wish that any should perish. Doing this on your own may not be easy. As co ministers in the evangelism ministry, women will strategize and develop plans with the help of the Holy Spirit on how to witness and share Christ and bring in souls. Women have left their countries to go to other lands to minister, to evangelize. A church that does not extend itself and does not make effort to extend itself will remain static and soon burn out. It is the responsibility of women to launch out into the deep sea to catch women for Jesus. There are very many of our sisters out there who may perish if we do not go out to rescue them. In our neighborhoods, in our workplace we must impact, we must contact them, minister to them, all for the glory of our Lord. Amen.

The Women Teachers' Ministry: Colossians. 3:16 Let the word of Christ dwell in you richly in all wisdom, teaching and admonishing one another. **Proverbs 9:9** says Give instruction to a wise woman and she will yet be wiser: teach a just woman and she will increase in learning. **2 Corinthians 1:21-22-** God has anointed us, by putting His seal on us and giving us His Spirit in our hearts as first instalment. **2 Timothy 2:2** -Preach the Word! be ready in and out of season, convince, rebuke, exhort with all longsuffering and teaching. What do we make of Paul's letter **1Timothy 2:12** "I do not permit a woman to teach". I think he was referring to the usurpation of authority, and women who were being led by false teachings and passing it on to other people. Teaching is a spiritual gift that God's Spirit gives to both men and women. It is a divine gift of being able to understand, clearly explain and apply the Word of God to the lives of listeners. Explaining God's word is an important responsibility because false teachers or even ignorant teachers can do more harm to God's people. All believers are to teach one another and to share with the community what they have learned. In **1 Corinthians 14:26,** Priscilla together with her husband Aquilla instructed a Christian brother Apollo in matters of theology. In **Acts 18:26.** Apostle Paul obviously recognized Priscilla's ministry and obviously loved and respected her as well as other female co-laborers. Paul admonished Timothy to respect Lois, and Eunice, his mother and grandmother for instructing him in the faith (**2 Timothy 1:2-5**) Although Paul was a great advocate for women to exercise spiritual gifts. He taught that this needed to be exercised in a manner that honors the Word of God. New Testament women were encouraged to exercise teaching ministries, they are to provide instruction from God's word and to nurture and challenge the life of the church. I read some-where that evangelists are compared with **Midwives** who deliver babies, they bring in people in to the Christian faith. But these new Christians also need **Pediatricians** to nurture them to growth and maturity. If these are not nurtured in the Church, there will be a nursery of several infant Christians who have not grown and who will never grow. They will permanently be baby Christians. That is why the work of women teachers is very important, to nurture women and others to growth through the Word of God after they have been delivered into the Family of God. Amen.

The Women Serving and Hospitality Ministry: Being a minister is also about serving. Serving is about offering ourselves to do something, to volunteer and to help in anyways that we can in the house of God. Jesus in **John 12:26** says whoever wants to serve me must follow me and my father will honor anyone who serves me Hospitality is a God given trait that allows a person to care for other people by providing fellowship, food or shelter. It is an unselfish desire to meet the needs of others. We learn of Lydia in **Acts 16:14-15** who was exceptionally hospitable to the early Christians. Even though she was a new believer she was ready and eager to share her home with the Apostles. A server is one who shows mercy, she is tender, sensitive, and has concerns for those who are hurting. It is the divine enablement to minister cheerfully and appropriately to people who are suffering, assisting the needy, and the homeless and generally offering valuable services cheerfully. Service and Hospitality a ministry that women are naturally fitted for, by virtue of their nurturing nature. There is never a shortage of work of mercy for women to do in the Body of Christ. Hospitality is the practice of welcoming, sheltering, and feeding with no thought of personal gain. It is more than supplying meals. It is sharing what we have and who we are with whoever God sends our way. It includes setting aside time for fellowship and being flexible. The resources available for serving and hospitality ministry are time, food, money, energy, creativity and love. (**Matthew 25: 34-40**, **Titus 24, 1John4:11).** We all know the story of Dorcas: **Acts 9:39** All the widows stood by him weeping, showing the tunics and garments which Dorcas had made while she was with them. Dorcas was a server. She was in the hospitality ministry. All the women with the gift of giving, of helping, encouragement, hospitality, mercy are in this ministry. A giver shares material assistance, has joy in giving, keeps specific needs provided for. It is the divinely given ability to contribute money and resources in a generous cheerful manner. The same is the helper who has joy in doing practical and necessary tasks for others and also support the Body of Christ. Included in this ministry is the help and care of the elderly. It is also about ministering to those who are in very critical stage like having just lost a loved one. These are much more in line with Jesus injunction to love. "Since you do these for others you do it for me" is what Jesus said. There are specific rewards attached to these. The natural serving and hospitality ministers are women. Amen.

The Minister's Wives Ministry: 1Timothy 3:11-Wives of Bishops and Deacons must be reverent, not slanderers, temperate faithful in all things. A minister's wife I would call an "elect lady" (**2 John 1:**1). Traditionally, it is believed that a good marriage furthers a man's ministry. There is usually no mention of the man's contribution to when the woman is a minister. The wife is expected to have some babies who must be well behaved because they live in a parsonage. Usually the wife does not work, that is she has no other career of her own, except to glow in the husband's/minister's/pastor's glory. The family is usually supported by the church. Her life is to serve the husband. and the husband is to serve the church, and God. Occasionally, she has some few responsibilities thrown her way like organizing the bazaar with other women or the jumble sale, or activities to raise funds for the church. Word of caution here, in this setting most ministers' wives like Sarah submit to their husbands to the point of calling them Lord. Then one wonders who is really the Lord in the lives of some of these Minister's wives? Jesus said He who loves his father and mother and certainly husband or wife more than Him has no right to the kingdom of heaven. Jesus the author and finisher of our faith, He alone is Lord. It seems that some minister's wives focus is not squarely on The Most Potentate, King of Kings, Lord of Lord. I once heard a Minister's wife say "I went into ministry for the sole purpose of helping my husband". And I wondered if there would be crowns for serving husbands who are pastors on Judgement Day. The reward is for serving the Lord. The minister's wife should be quite visible. She could preach if she so desires and has the ability. She should head some group like the women or ladies' groups if she is so disposed or talented enough and have the same religious training as the husband, has a lot of anointing. Women are at times also ordained as ministers in their own right, spirit filled and working intensely for the Lord. The demands of women who marry ministers are quite high. They are expected to model the highest spiritual standards. A high level of commitment is needed and expected to balance marriage, home, family, with exemplary devotion to and dedication and zealous compassion for the cause of Christ. Minister's wives have responsibility to come together to review their positions in the Church. Being a minister's wife is not a special privilege but a special responsibility. A Minister's wives ministry will be a forum for strengthening women who are minister's wives, encouraging each other and spending time together in prayer, fasting, fellowship, study and generally helping each other by the power of the Holy Spirit to grow more in the Lord and mentoring young minister's wives. A minister's wife is a minister in her own right and should be recognized as such. Amen.

The Ministry of the Prophetess: 1 Cor 14:1says "Pursue love and desire spiritual gifts but especially that you may prophesy". vs.3.He who prophesies speaks edification, exhortation and comfort to men and women. The Bible abounds with many examples of women who ministered prophetically. The prophetess Miriam led the women to celebrate the Lord's triumph over Egypt after the crossing of the Red Sea. Deborah was a prophetess who functioned as a judge. The prophetess Hulda was consulted on behalf of the King Josiah who tore His clothes when he heard about the Word of God**. 2 Kings 22:14-20.** Anna was a New Testament prophetess who served God for 84 years with fasting, and prayers night and day. She thanked God and spoke about Jesus to all those who looked for redemption (**Luke 2:36-38**). The four daughters of Philip were prophetesses. The gift of prophecy is regarded as valuable and a necessary gift for the Church and an area of effective ministry for women. Paul encourages women to cover their heads while praying and prophesying. The gift of prophesy is a gift of supernatural utterance. It is God given ability to proclaim, His truth, with power and clarity in a timely and culturally sensitive fashion for correction, for repentance and for edification. The ministry is to give a divine message as directed by the Spirit of God. Prophetesses and Prophets are to confront both personal and corporate sins with the message of God's displeasure at evil and to bring people to repentance. This ministry requires women to look with objectivity, and discernment at political and religious institutions, and at the social structures It requires boldness and courage to speak critically on behalf of God in order to denounce injustice and oppression. These women would need to seek the Lord, would wait for the Lord. These women would know how to keep still to hear from the Lord. These women would be the servants of God who stand by night in the House of The Lord, who come to bless the Lord. This ministry will be the mouth of God to bring forth His messages. This ministry needs several hours of communion with God and learning to be in His Presence all the time. This ministry is placed high as a valuable gift for the church and as an area of effective ministry for women.

Finally, Are you a Woman Minister? Will you be a Woman Minister? We have read who exactly is a Woman Minister. We have seen what happens when the Woman is a Minister. We have seen what it takes to be a Woman Minister. The next step is what is your resolve as a woman to establish yourself in a ministry, to operate within a ministry. **1 Peter 4:9** says "As one has received a gift, minister it to one another as good stewards of the manifold grace of God". **1Timothy. 4:6** says "if you minister to the brethren in these things you will be a minister of Jesus Christ." **1Timothy 4:16** says 'take heed to yourself and to the doctrine. Continue in them for in doing this you will save both yourself and those who hear you'. **1Peter 2:5 says** "you also as living stones are being built up as a spiritual house, a holy priesthood, to up spiritual sacrifices acceptable to God through Jesus Christ". **2 Timothy 2:20** says but in a great house there not only vessels of gold and silver but also of wood and clay some for honor some for dishonor". **vs 21** says a vessel of honor is sanctified and useful for the Master prepared for every good work. As Women in the Body of Christ we will have to account for how many souls we have nurtured into spiritual growth within the kingdom. Each woman will account for her salvation. What is our decision today? Are we ready to do the Master's will? Are we ready to be the Lord's Ministers? Are we ready to be Jesus hands extended in various ways? Are we ready to impact our world for God? There is no faith without responsibility. If you are already operating in a Ministry. Thank God for you. Continue serving the Lord. If not resolve to start one or join one today. Tell yourself: I am a Woman Minister, I will impact the world for God. Amen.

Thank God for Jesus

Thank God for Jesus. 1 John 3:16 reminds us that Jesus is the ultimate embodiment of God's love was shared with us. Praise be to God for this Great Divine Gift. Jesus in turn loves us. Jesus love is the love that forgives our sins and iniquities. Jesus love is the love that gives spiritual healing to our souls, physical healing to our bodies, mental healing to our mind. Jesus love is the love tells us that it is well with us. Jesus love tells us of mansions that have been prepared for us. Jesus love is the love that helps us to live joyfully in Him. May Jesus continue to open our eyes to see Him as He is, to know Him as He should be known and to appreciate Him for His great love for us. Amen.

Thank God for Jesus.

Final Prayer I have chosen the prayer below for you with this book in your hand.

Aaronic Blessings: Numbers 6:24-26

The Lord Bless you and Keep you,
The Lord make His face to shine upon you and be gracious unto you;
The Lord lift His countenance upon you and give you peace. Amen.

Coda

This Book of Reflections is my contribution to Outreach Ministry, to people of ALL ages and ALL leanings. Everyone will surely find something appealing in the Book as the topics are quite varied. The Book is not only suitable for individual personal reading, small groups will benefit from reading the reflections together, followed by discussions. When you have read these Reflections, kindly send me the Author, a text or an email, and tell me which is your favorite Reflection and why. I have indicated mine. I want to know yours. Blessings

Email **ayesufu44@gmail, 17809164638**

CPSIA information can be obtained
at www.ICGtesting.com
Printed in the USA
LVHW041909121119
637167LV00002B/2

9 781532 084584